INDIGENOUS POETICS

INDIGENOUS POETICS

Edited by Inés Hernández-Ávila and Molly McGlennen

MICHIGAN STATE UNIVERSITY PRESS | *East Lansing*

Michigan State University Press
East Lansing, Michigan 48823-5245

Printed and bound in the United States of America.

Library of Congress Cataloging-in-Publication Data
Names: Hernández-Avila, Inés, editor. | McGlennen, Molly, editor.
Title: Indigenous poetics / edited by Inés Hernández-Ávila and Molly McGlennen.
Other titles: American Indian studies series.
Description: East Lansing : Michigan State University Press, [2025] | Series: American
Indian studies series | Includes bibliographical references.
Identifiers: LCCN 2024022627 | ISBN 9781611865264 (cloth) | ISBN 9781611865271 (paperback)
| ISBN 9781609177782 | ISBN 9781628955422
Subjects: LCSH: American poetry—Indian authors—History and criticism. | Indians of North America—
Poetry—History and criticism. | Indians of North America—Intellectual life—21st century.
Classification: LCC PS153.I52 I57 2025 | DDC 810.9897—dc23/eng/20240607
LC record available at https://lccn.loc.gov/2024022627

Cover design by Erin Kirk
Cover art is *even where the ancestors live*, by l frank manriquez

---

Visit Michigan State University Press at *www.msupress.org*

to the spirit of poetry

to the spirit N. Scott Momaday, who joined the
ancestors during this collection's final stages

to the generations of Indigenous poets, known and unknown, who live(d) a life of poetics
through their creativity, stories, languages, oratory, and song

Contents

Foreword

Esther Belin

My relationship with Indigenous poetics began as a child. My mother often held me close, funneling the lyric rhythms of Diné bizaad into my ear. The sounds of my language calmed me, transported me to Diné bikéyah. I would translate the soundscape of Diné bizaad, and immediately my homeland became vivid. I still find comfort in listening to the soundscape of Diné bizaad. And now after many years of developing an ear for sound (and silence), I equally enjoy hearing the poetics inherent within Indigenous languages.

Using language brings us home because the sounds and images come from our homelands, our land(ocean)scapes. From her essay "The Resonance of Poetry," Molly McGlennen asks, "Where does poetry start?"—a question explored within each essay gathered in this collection, all of which affirm the various methods Indigenous poetics contextualizes Indigenous language. Each writer deepens the clarity as to how poetics becomes the vehicle to the ways we use language—the way we create kinship through language. Indigenous language borrows sound from the land—including silence, form, and thought. It is from a land(ocean)-based context that language poeticizes, echoing sounds of home.

It is also upon the return to those soundscapes that the foreign status of Indigenous sound dissolves—and the release relaxes our throats and softens our tongues to our Creator-given languages. No longer will Indigenous sound contort into settler sounds and letters that subjects us to colonial epistemic violence and undermines Indigenous ontology. Throughout the book, Indigenous language—its sound, its meter—emerges as ancient oceanic swells wetting the page, mutually intense is the thirst of The People—those of us who remain—lingually joined to those first generations of relatives whose tongues were mutilated, severed from our language at the onset of colonization. This collection celebrates the sturdiness of Indigenous epistemology. The reckoning of genocidal conscience emerges as these Indigenous scholars and storytellers name and define nested sinkholes, historical containers used to mute the literary contributions from Native American authors. This emergence of storying spaces serves a catalytic role in dismantling settler narratives.

I like to say that the children who attended the earliest Indian boarding schools were the first generation of creative writers. I am indebted to those little ancestors. During the cultural assimilation process, they infused Indigeneity into a system designed to extract and destroy. A significant body of creative writing examples come from boarding school poetry often found in government archives because these schools were managed by the U.S. Bureau of Indian Affairs. Poetry was used as a method to teach Native American students how to master the grammar and syntax of the English language. Not only did those students grasp those concepts but they also coded their own tribal poetics into their creative works. I acknowledge those early creative writers as my inspiration to re-grammar Indigenous sound and order into my poetics while using the English alphabet.

This book is a testament to the fire stoking within Native American poetics. The time (trust) is here. We have reached a plateau—even within colonial structures—we find ways to contribute while (re)building our own spaces. We are on this side of recovery—these stories—these writers have written through the genocidal tactics and shrapnel still present. They position Indigenous poetics as a method to reconcile language as a ceremonial act—a spatial temporal way of being. They speak poetics with such vitality that we cannot help but embrace a poetic identity that is imagistic—situational—trans-reciprocal—an airway resuscitating our languages.

It is only a matter of time until more tribes join the Osage and Cherokee nations in creating their own tribal orthography––their own syllabary. We eagerly await those futuristic paradigms, with schema inherent to each tribal worldview. During this time of cognitive code-mixing, we await another oceanic tug, dissolving the implicit cognitive parameters of colonization—wrestling against exposure to settler narratives.

Reading this book is a practice of decolonization—so keep reading—keep making your way back—with story—with poetry.

Preface

First, we want to pay our respects to the original peoples of the lands where we live and work. Inés is writing from Patwin land, and Molly is writing from Munsee Lenape land. We also pay our respects to the original peoples of the lands from which our contributors are writing.

Our work as co-editors for this collection is a mark of our personal histories coinciding over time in distinct but familiar felt ways. We (Inés and Molly, respectively) met in 2000 as major professor and PhD student in the Native American Studies graduate program at the University of California, Davis, and ever since then we have been colleagues. I, Inés, am now retiring from academia (but not from writing and creating), and Molly is a full professor at Vassar, recently named the Tatlock Endowed Chair in Multidisciplinary Studies, embarking on a new adventure in her professional career. I am also embarking on a life outside of the institution—a liberatory move I have been anticipating with jubilation.

We are both poets who have "lived in academia" for some time. What does that mean? It means that neither of us has had the privilege of working and living a poet's life unconnected to academia, to the life of the institution. At the same time, in academia, we have both been devoted to building Native American Studies, and especially the field of creative writing within the broader interdiscipline.

Our collection is, in many ways, a statement on the interdiscipline of Native American Studies, and how poetry plays a role in its growth. As co-editors, the story of our meeting and twenty-three-year relationship is directly tied to poetry. When I (Molly) applied to the UC Davis NAS PhD program (where Inés, as department chair, had led the process of creating the graduate program), I did so as a poet, freshly minted with an MFA in creative writing. Once in the program, I was told that I was accepted *as a poet*. This was instructive: creative thought, and poetry specifically, plays a methodological role in the field of NAS and illuminates how our field stays attentive to what constitutes "data," "evidence," "the archive," and "primary source material" in the construction of knowledge. One could say that creativity (in all forms) illuminates an anti-disciplinarity trend working against western disciplinary methods, which reinforce imperial legacies. Creativity, and poetry specifically, foregrounds our ways of forging a (re)creation of disciplinarity on our own terms. It is a process already emerging in the field, as NAS is ever-dynamic in resisting western paradigms. Art making/poetry/creative thinking is what can move us forward intentionally.

We recall the very first *Native American and Indigenous Studies Association* meeting in Oklahoma in 2007, before NAISA was an official organization, when the conference was simply called "What's Next for Native American and Indigenous Studies." We remember when one hundred or more people gathered in a hall to discuss the future of the potential organization, what name the organization would take, and what it would prioritize. Among the who's-who of Native scholars, activists, writers and community people, we vividly remember the brilliant Oneida poet Roberta Hill standing up to make a comment that, up to that point, had been missing from the conversation. She spoke eloquently about how we must insist that our gatherings make space for creativity in ways that are not gratuitous or peripheral, but rather—foundational. She asked, "Where are the sessions on creativity, on poetry?" Both of us (Molly, a newly minted Native American Studies PhD, and Inés, a professor of Native American Studies and a member of the conference's steering committee) remarked on the importance and resonance of that moment. Later at the conference, Craig Womack (Creek-Cherokee) emceed an open mic that was truly "open" to anyone to come up on stage and read their work.

In the world of academia, as Roberta's question reveals, creative writing has been known to take a hit as the area that is "oh, . . . creative," as in artsy, and therefore, presumably not as relevant as the "serious" scholarship—theoretical framings, innovative methodologies, and radical pedagogies—being produced in Native American and Indigenous Studies. Poetry, in particular, seems to be un-considered as intellectual production. However, Roberta's question interrogates why the making of meaning is not always recognized in both critical and creative realms. Each has the potential to theorize difficult problems that are before us. Nevertheless, things are beginning to change, as we point out in our introduction. And the world of Indigenous literatures is becoming more and more robust by the day.

The contributors in this collection responded to an open call for submissions inviting Native American poets in the United States to engage our proposed questions on the theme of poetry as an instrument of inquiry. We also chose to include two previously published pieces, "On Overcoming the Anxiety of Making Creative Work" (interview), by Layli Long Soldier ,and "The Memory Field: Musings on the Diné Perspective of Time, Memory, and Land" (essay), by Jake Skeets. We reached out personally to several poets whose voices we thought would, like all of the contributors in our collection, enhance the conversation. We intended, from the beginning, for the call to be broad.

We want our collection to create a space for the poets to articulate how creative thought and writing "do the work," albeit differently, in paradigmatic-, methodological-, and disciplinary-changing ways. We hope that as you read across the chapters you will see the way each contributor writes—in the words of one contributor, Craig Santos Perez—"*from* our poetic landscapes," as well as the way each speaks to one another through the poetic connective tissue that holds our Nations together across the hemisphere.

On a personal note, as co-editors, we are delighted to say that our working process was one of true collaboration. We listened to each other, thought with each other, and wrote with each other.

Acknowledgments

We—Inés and Molly—the co-editors of this collection, remembering that we live in kinship with the earth, waters, and all of our more-than human relations, acknowledge and give thanks to the lands where we live and work, the lands where the Michigan State University Press press sits, and the lands from which the contributors are writing. We also pay our respects to the original homelands of each of us in this collection.

Mii gwech and qe'ciyéwyew to our contributors for their creative brilliance and generous spirit. We continue to learn from and be guided by their poetry. In each of their essays, their voices manifest an Indigenous poetics that, collectively, we offer in this collection—poets writing about their own practice, vision, and creative impulse. It was and has been thrilling for us to see how key poets responded and gave shape to our initial vision, taking the questions we offered in the call, giving them life, and, collectively, creating a compelling resonance.

We want to extend our thanks to Jill Doerfler, Liz Deegan, Anastasia Wraight, and the Michigan State University Press staff for their support, guidance, and patience throughout the stages of publication. Thank you to Erika Berlin for her sharp indexing skills. A big mii gwech and qe'ciyéwyew to Gordon Henry Jr., who originally saw the value in our proposal and need for such a collection of poets writing on poetry.

We want to recognize and thank the readers for their supportive comments and suggestions on the manuscript draft. We appreciate very much the time and care they took in providing feedback, ultimately helping to shape the collection in meaningful ways.

Mii gwech and qe'ciyéwyew to Tongvetam/Ajachmem and Rarámuri artist, writer, and tribal activist L. Frank Manriquez, who through her artwork and activism reminds each of us of our connection as human beings. For our cover, we selected Manriquez's work titled "Even Where the Ancestors Live." Like many of Manriquez's works, the cover piece creates an air of whimsy, of play, but in reality it is a "serious" whimsy/play. Coyote is standing at the top of the chaos, contemplating the situation, but at the same time ready. Ready to engage, ready for ritual, ready to bring about transformation. Manriquez says, "My art's function is to address invisibility and a way to start a conversation," which is much like what we are doing here in this book. We have brought Native poets who are theorists of Indigenous poetics into the foreground to lead a conversation.

I (Molly) want to thank all of my family back home in Minnesota for encouraging me to follow the poet's path, even when that was not a clearly marked trail. Over and over again, poetry has allowed me to figure out all of the ways I can find my way home. Heartfelt thanks to Winston, Ellia, and Marcelo whose love and support keep me learning, laughing, and inspired. Mii gwech to my long-time inspiration, mentor, teacher, friend, and co-editor, Inés, for being a true collaborative partner in creating this collection.

I (Inés) want to thank Molly for making the work on this manuscript joyful. She is my first PhD student and for some time now a favored colleague. I'm enormously proud of her accomplishments, as a poet, a scholar, and an editor. We truly worked together through every aspect of this collection seamlessly. I'm so grateful to poetry. And I'm grateful, always, to my human family (my sons and their families), to Juan, my husband, and to the wonderful more-than-human relations who live with us. Qe'ciyéwyew.

Introduction

I believe every poem is ritual: there is a naming, a beginning, a knot or question, then possibly revelation, and then closure, which can be opening, setting the reader, speaker, or singer out and back on a journey. I can hear the tribal speaker in his voice, in whatever mode of performance. And when I trust my voice to go where it needs to be, to find home, it returns to where it belongs, back to the source of its longing.

—Joy Harjo, Poet Warrior

As poets ourselves, our curiosity is piqued by seeking why Native American writers are drawn to, take up, and embrace the genre of poetry specifically. Though style and form are important to the study of poetry, literary analysis is not what we are interested in performing in this book. What intrigues us is how the creative process, as a practice, has its own capacities, through the "ritual" of creation, to name the "knot or question," and to travel toward "revelation, and then closure, which can be opening." Like Harjo, we trust our voices and the voices of our contributors. We have journeyed with them, and together we are expressing home, in a way our poetic homes, where we see ourselves belonging. What does poetic process uniquely allow us to do? And does our poetic practice express its own type of Indigenous hermeneutics?

We acknowledge, first, that the field of Native American poetry is far too much for any one book to take on. The sheer volume of poetry written by American Indians, First Nations, Native American, and Indigenous writers across the Americas is immense. American Indian poets, for example, have been publishing their work, in both Indigenous languages and English, since the early 1700s, as Robert Dale Parker's important book *Changing is Not Vanishing* shows us. Since 1969, Native American poetry has proliferated immensely, with Indigenous poets being some of the most recognizable names in contemporary American poetry today: Joy Harjo (Muscogee Creek), Natalie Diaz (Mojave), Sherwin Bitsui (Diné), and so many others.

In addition to the great span of writers over three centuries of writing, Native American Studies scholars have argued in recent decades that Native American poetry, as a literary genre, registers well beyond the written form, official publication, and the use of settler languages—sometimes even interrogating the nature of *genre* itself.[1] Broadly, much of Native American literary scholarship purports that Indigenous poetry originates from time immemorial on this continent, and includes the songs, stories, rituals, and ceremonies, orally spoken or sung into the world, in communal forums, across the hundreds of Native Nations in what is now known as the United States.[2] Scholars trace the continuum of the tribally specific poetic practices right through and despite settler invasion, even as colonialism has affected Native poetics in varied ways.[3]

To many of us, what seems ever constant over time is how Native peoples have employed poetic practice, whether in written or oral form, in ways that have been tied to the *survivance* of Indigeneity. Native poets take hold of poetic expression as one would a tool: they have something in mind they want to materialize, and that materialization illuminates the terms Native writers set for themselves. For this collection, we are interested in how Native poets describe what happens when they take up the tool, where they are able to go with it, and what they are able to figure out along the way.

Hemisphere

While we, as co-editors, made a decision to focus on Native American poets in the United States for this collection, we do want to acknowledge the flourishing of Indigenous literatures in all genres in this hemisphere known as the Americas. In Mexico, for example, there is the national association called Escritores en Lenguas Indígenas, "Writers in Indigenous Languages," founded in 1996, which promotes language revitalization through creative writing in Indigenous languages. Mexico as a nation-state annually awards the Premio Nezahualcoyotl, for a literary work written in an Indigenous language (and translated into Spanish). Nezahualcoyotl, "Hungry" or "Fasting Coyote," is the name of an internationally known Nahuatl poet, philosopher, ruler of Texcoco (1402–1472). In Chiapas, as a result of the San Andrés Accords signed by the Zapatistas and the Mexican federal government, CELALI, Centro Estatal de Lenguas, Arte, y Literatura Indígenas (State Center for Indigenous Languages, Art, and Literature) was established in 1997. CELALI represents statewide networking through the development of cultural centers in twenty-nine Indigenous communities, where young people, K–12, take part in a variety of workshops, including art, literature, theater, dance, music, computer literacy, and more. Indigenous writers also go into their communities to teach creative writing in the language of the people and in Spanish translation. In Chile, Colombia, Guatemala, Venezuela, Peru, Bolivia, throughout the hemisphere, la palabra florida, the "flowering word," an intimately favored reference to the literary arts, is strong and thriving.

In Canada, the arts are flourishing as well. The En'owkin Centre has long been known as an valuable space for furthering the sustenance of Indigenous communities in many ways. Richard Van Camp (Dogrib) recalls his time there, where he was nourished in the rigor of writing: "The En'owkin Centre is really where I found my voice as a writer and as a storyteller. When I was [there] in '91 and '92 they worked me really hard. You had to do a short story a week, a narrative piece a week, an essay, a children's story a week, you had to write poetry every week, so when I went to the University of Victoria after graduating from En'owkin, I was not prepared for having to write something once every two or three weeks."[4] First Nations peoples have their own panorama of powerful poets, including the late inimitable and prolific Lee Maracle (Stolo), one of the founders of En'owkin, Jeannette Armstrong (Okanogan), Rita Joe (Mi'kmaq), Billy-Ray Belcourt (Cree), Marilyn Dumont (Cree/Metis), Louise Halfe (Cree), and scores of others.

In the United States, there are certain exhilarating moments that mark this current period of the state of Native American literature, in particular poetry. Joy Harjo's three terms as Poet Laureate of the United States (2019–2022); the emergence of IN-NA-PO (Indigenous Nations Poets), founded by Kim Blaeser (Anishinaabe) in 2020, "recognizing the role of poetry in sustaining tribal sovereign nations and Native languages";[5] Natalie Diaz's (Mojave) being awarded the Pulitzer Prize in poetry in fall 2021 as well as the MacArthur Genius Award in 2018; the publication of the *The Diné Reader*; and the continuing vibrant presence of Institute of American Indian Arts (IAIA) for Native artists. Harjo's amazing three terms as U.S. Poet Laureate has created much more of a presence for Native writers on the national scene. The emergence of IN-NA-PO and its initiative "Language Back" are markers of our coming-of-age. And, it took forty-two years, from the time of N. Scott Momaday's Pulitzer Prize for *House Made of Dawn* in 1969, for two Native women writers to win Pulitzer Prizes in 2021, Natalie Diaz, for poetry, and Louise Erdrich (Anishinaabe), for fiction (Erdrich herself is a wonderful poet). *The Diné Reader* deserves mention as a forerunner of what will hopefully be more collections that represent our distinct Nations, where our languages are used, where the generations are represented, where there is diversity within unity, where the idea of literature is determined from a tribally specific perspective. IAIA continues to nurture and produce Indigenous artists who work in wonderfully provocative ways. A major project in October 2022 was their cosponsored *Words of the People* conference, organized by Chelsea Tayrien Hicks (Osage), whose quote, "Those who are writing in their Indigenous languages and providing translations are leaders in Indigenous poetry," is on the main conference website. In the United States, Native American poetry is enjoying a much-deserved celebration, and rightly so, for all the poets who paved the way and for all those emerging in these propitious times.

While our poetry is as diverse as any other poetry in its exploration of themes and use of forms, Native poetry presents a particular stake in engaging its own sovereign (albeit tribally polyphonic) voice. Ernestine Hayes (Tlingit) writes eloquently about how the work of Native writers foils the inevitability and dominance of story-making crafted by Euro-Americans and the ways those stories (be they history, fiction, or otherwise) continually affirm a common narrative that legitimizes and bolsters a singular American mythology. "But," she states, "Indigenous artists tell different stories and advance different values. Indigenous artists are the storytellers of their generations. Indigenous artists are the history keepers of their generations. Indigenous artists are their generations' witnesses. As much as any fairy tale, those stories remain alive and carry their testimony into the millennia."[6] Hayes is not the only Native writer to convey this argument; from Vine Deloria (Dakota) to Leslie Marmon Silko (Laguna) to Craig Womack, many have noted the double-edgeness of Native creative expression as having both beauty and utility—the telling (or displaying) and the material effects (cultural resonance). We submit, however, that poetry involves a *particular type* of creative engagement with that doubleness, especially when we look to the poets themselves to express poetry's potential in uniquely Indigenous ways.

In the very act of creating, we are refusing genocide, and any other type of imposition that would silence or diminish us. It is a visioning process. We are acknowledging grief. Historical, cosmic grief. But also not staying there. The impulse to transform the grief is an impulse born from love for our peoples, histories, cultures, and Nations—in profoundly diverse ways. We recognize Peter Blue Cloud (Mohawk), Chrystos (Menominee), Wendy Rose (Miwok/Hopi), Paula Gunn Allen (Laguna), Gerald Vizenor (Anishinaabe), John Trudell (Dakota), and Linda Hogan (Choctaw) as just *some* of the early writers who showed us poets how transformative the creative process can be and how affecting it can be in our lives. Whether through irony and humor, righteous anger, activist parlance, collaboration and solidarity, poets such as these invert the colonial gaze and open Indigenous worlds. Indeed, we are rich in poetry.

Over the decades of both the practice and study of poetry, we have noticed the ways in which the poetry written by Native Americans evinces particular ways of knowing and being—and particular forms of memory. Our attention to poetics as creative-writers-and-scholars has allowed us the opportunity to meditate on the proposition that engaging Indigenous poetry is a type of methodology, replete with a system of methods taken up by creative writers who "channel collective creativity in order to produce solutions to Indigenous problems."[7]

We asked our contributors to the collection to ruminate and write on this same proposition. Is there such a thing as an Indigenous poetics, and if so, what does it take into consideration? According to the poets themselves, what is essential to it, or original about it? In an interview with *Poets.org*, Lummi citizen and Washington State Poet Laureate Rena Priest stated: "Everywhere I go, I see that people are eager to have a safe place in which to share who they are. Because poetry provides this space and allows people to connect in ways that go beyond the mundane, transcending time and space to reach into the deeply personal while honoring individuality and respecting alternate beliefs and perspectives, it is an ideal tool for bringing people together."[8]

Poetry collections and volumes such as ours do bring people together—first, by creating community in the pages of the volume, then by the sharing of the work, by hearing the poets read and/or perform their work, completing that eternal return to the power of the oral tradition, which by its very name suggests the need to listen closely, to read deeply, to contemplate what the poet has offered. At times, poetry sounds like it emerges from the oral tradition, but even when the poem does not explicitly "sound" that tradition, a transformation happens when it is spoken aloud because those sounds are vibrating with other voices across space and time. As Harjo has said, "When I write, those old voices inspire me, and surprise me with what they know. Maybe that's how most wisdom works. Sometimes it can be corralled into print, in languages in books, but it lives more abundantly when spoken and welcomes a place to live on earth."9

To be sure, there are key critical/creative writers who have long lent themselves to excavating the meanings and impulses behind poetry written by Native peoples. For the moment of this collection, we recognize N. Scott Momaday, Simon Ortiz (Acoma), Joy Harjo, and Kimberly Blaeser as four principal poet-scholars who have laid the foundation to most of the important conversations about what Native writers "set out to do" when they take up the pen. We see the corpora of their work as essential to our questions and instructive to our ruminations about the ways in which Native poets specifically engage the practice of poetry to make and unmake meaning on their own Indigenous terms.

From Momaday, we are especially drawn into the ways he uses poetry to foil the acts of western ethnography and anthropology. We learn from him about how imagination, informed by memory, can be linked closely with poetic expression and experience, wherein the "memory field" (a term from Diné poet Jake Skeets) is connected to land and spirit, ancestry and story. As a powerful orator, Momaday said what he thought, and in such a way that lent itself to understanding something more deeply about the role of poetry because of his focus on "the word." In a similar vein, Ortiz reinforces the experience baked into poetry, offering throughout his oeuvre powerful statements of poetics. We learn from Ortiz about the role of listening/sound in writing, especially in the way listening preempts speaking, and therefore writing. We carry with us toward the design of this collection Ortiz's poetic teachings on the ways song/poetry enacts the world and its making, a communal experience enriched by protocol. According to Janice Gould (Konkow Maidu), Ortiz's essay "Song/Poetry and Language" is "a critique of that kind of literary criticism that seeks to dissect a work, break it down until it has no life left."[10] Contrary to western critique, Native poetry takes into account *life* and is necessarily attentive to historical and ancestral teachings as it imagines Indigenous futures. Harjo's work is crucially important in understanding this common thread in the poetry written by Native peoples. She has also been a trailblazer when it comes to distinguishing what Native poets are attentive to in the creative act: Indigenous worlds filled with sacred teachings. Finally, Blaeser teaches us that creative writers embark upon a journey when attending to language. Ancestral memory is not only tied to place/land, but also recalled through the physical/spiritual act of journeying. Wherever the motion and energy are derived from in a poem, "the poet aligns [his/her/their] journey with the older one," as if the poem itself is the "ritualistic preparation for sacred encounter" with oral traditions.[11]

We also acknowledge Ortiz's *Speaking for the Generations: Native Writers on Writing* and Janice Gould and Dean Rader's *Speak to Me Words: Essays on Contemporary American Indian Poetry* as two foundational anthologies that foreground the importance of Native American writers interpreting and expounding upon the milieu of Indigenous creativity and for regarding the origins and emanations of Native poetry specifically.

Speaking for the Generations is a significant collection of essays by none other than Acoma poet, Simon Ortiz, editor and the visioner of this volume, with contributors Leslie Silko, Gloria Bird (Spokane), Esther Belin (Diné), A. A. Hedge Coke (mixed heritage), Daniel David Moses (Six Nations), Elizabeth Woody (Warm Springs, Wasco, Yakama, Diné), Jeanette Armstrong (Okanagan), and Victor Montejo (Jakaltec Mayan). Ortiz titles his introduction "Wah-nuthyuh dyy neetah tyahstih: Now it is my turn to speak," and he tells the readers that they must listen as the contributors say collectively, "Now it is our turn to speak." *Speaking for the Generations* speaks for "the sake of the land and the people," which is a constant refrain in Ortiz's distinguished trajectory as a poet and as a winner of the 1993 Lifetime Achievement Award by the Native Writers Circle of the Americas—the second writer to receive the award after Momaday. Ortiz guides us in his introduction, using his language to mark its significance and centrality; indicating his awareness of "the Indigenous Americas"; honoring our creation stories and our "reciprocal relationship" with each other and all of Creation. To pay attention to this reciprocity is an ethical responsibility for Native peoples. He writes, "Listen. They are speaking." We would like to ask our readers to do the same for our contributors.

Ortiz's volume, attentive to the hemisphere (with contributors from the United States, Canada, Guatemala), demonstrates the nuanced complexity of the writers' lives. The collection is grounded in the present, with an eye to the past and a heart facing the future. In her essay, Leslie Silko reminds us that humans are part of the landscape, suggesting that the more we know the landscape, the more we know ourselves. In Gloria Bird's essay, "Breaking the Silence: Writing as Witness," a favorite of UCD's NAS graduate students, she notes her conversation with the esteemed Dakota scholar Liz Cook-Lynn, who says that the personal story is not what "we tell." Bird responds by writing of the importance of witness and testimony in her poetry, through her personal story, as an act of decolonization. She says, in an often-quoted passage, "I feel a need to ask the reader to focus less on the perceived pain that has been handed down through the generations and more on . . . the decolonization of the mind that comes with identifying the source of the pain in order to be free of its power over us." Bird, like all the contributors to this volume, works in multi-genres. Liz Woody's chapter, "Voices of the Land: Giving the Good Word," focuses on how "the embodiment of our ancestors" reveals an intricate complexity of hers and her peoples' lives and lands. Woody shares her mother's comment to her with us, "Remember, your capacity to hear is through your words. We need to hear them, too." Woody, like the rest of her co-contributors, illuminates how poets can act as "irreplaceable carriers of [their] own story."[12]

The quintessence of *Speak to Me Words* lies in how its editors, Gould and Rader, pay such intricate attention to the way in which genre factors into Native American poetry writing and analysis—in both explicit *and* ambivalent terms. Throughout their introduction, Gould and Rader keep scratching at the uniqueness of Native American poetry—for what it does and can do. Gould importantly states at one point in their dialogic opening remarks "that one function of American Indian poetry has been to 'resist cultural erasure,' to question the dominant narrative, and to remember our histories clearly as a way to resist both amnesia and nostalgia."[13] We continue to marvel at Gould's and Rader's ability to clearly see the links between poetry writing and decolonizing efforts, for their prescience in the field of Native American literature and deep historical acknowledgment of those who have come before us, including in their anthology important contributors such as Carter Revard (Osage), Janet McAdams (Alabama Creek), and Marilou Awiakta (Cherokee).

Yet, Gould and Rader seem to insist that we be wary of too-definitively carving strict boundaries around something called Native American poetry, so that we do not misguidedly obfuscate the ways in which Native poets are influenced by a plurality of writers, styles, forms, and even languages. In fact, Gould asserts in the introduction: "As I see it, Native American poets are part and parcel of the American poetry scene, whether non-Indians know it or not."[14] After all, there are a growing number of us poets with experience being trained by an array of writers in MFA programs and workshops across the spectrum of poetic schools of thought and practice. We certainly agree with Gould and Rader—but would add here for the purposes of our book that we are less interested in how to differentiate or align the field of Native American poetry than in how the poets themselves describe the stakes of their artistic callings and efforts.

Poets laying out the stakes of their writing reminds us of important works of Native American poetry such as Ortiz's *From Sand Creek*, wherein the collection, Ortiz takes head on "the problem with history" and the legacy of colonial amnesia. The poet explicitly sets out not only to resurrect the truth buried by the conqueror, but also to pay attention to the ethical responsibility of reclaiming a history that has excluded Native peoples on purpose. Ortiz writes in his preface, "Indians had been 'conquered,' so it didn't really matter anymore. We had been made to disappear. We were invisible. We had vanished. Therefore we had no history. And it was almost like we deserved to have no history. *That was the feeling.*"[15] The poet Ortiz suggests to his reader that in order to dismantle the violent and "polarizing historical schema" that relies on "victors and victims," we must look to poetry as our way to insist on enjoining history-telling with human integrity. Poetry—we hear Ortiz telling us—is the means by which Native poets carry with them a deep consciousness of history as they dream of revolutionary acts and radical articulations of love for our Nations and their futures. Poetry brings us to the realm in which *our feelings* (our human integrity, our spirit, our subconscious, our embodiment, our relatives, our ancestors, our homelands) factor into and even lead the creative act.[16]

We join our voices with previous publications that have gathered Native writers in their pages. We acknowledge the way Indigenous editors of these volumes have acted and act as curators of poetic thought, often calling together poems that speak to particular aesthetics and issues when presented in concert with other voices. We acknowledge the following early publications: *The Remembered Earth: Contemporary Native American Literature*, edited by Geary Hobson (1981); *Songs from this Earth on Turtle's Back: Contemporary American Indian Poetry*, edited by Joseph Bruchac (1983); *Survival This Way: Interviews with American Indian Poets*, edited by Joseph Bruchac (1987); *I Tell You Now: Autobiographical Essays by Native Writers*, edited by Brian Swann and Arnold Krupat (1989); *Reinventing the Enemy's Language: Contemporary Native Women's Writings of North America*, edited by Joy Harjo and Gloria Bird (1998); *A Gathering of Spirit: A Collection by North American Indian Women*, edited by Beth Brant (1989); *Through the Eye of the Deer: An Anthology of Native American Women Writers*, edited by Carolyn Dunn and Carol Comfort (1999); *Here First: Autobiographical Essays by Native American Writers*, edited by Arnold Krupat and Brian Swann (2000); *Sister Nations: Native American Women Writers on Community*, edited by Heid E. Erdrich and Laura Tohe (2002); *Sing: Poetry from the Indigenous Americas*, edited by Allison Hedge Coke (2011); and *New Poets of Native Nations*, edited by Heid E. Erdrich (2018). With these literary gathering spaces in our historical purview, we envision our collection centering Native poets' reflection on and interrogation of poetry as an Indigenous method of inquiry, knowledge production, and healing.

Translation

It is becoming clear to us that there is a need for Native American/Indigenous scholars and artists to think about translation, especially if and when they are working with their own languages. In fact, the field of translation studies could complement NAS disciplinarily. Some Native American poets are employing their languages in their works, or writing completely in their languages. If they translate (they may choose not to), they have to face what it means to translate from their own language to a colonizer's language. Even when Native poets write monolingually, there could be a time in the future when their works could be translated into any number of languages, French, Italian, German, Spanish, and more—perhaps into other Indigenous languages—an incredibly exciting possibility. Suddenly, the transition of the work to another language surfaces as a matter of importance. In Mexico and parts south, the issue of translation is one that Indigenous poets grapple with, when their original works are in their "lenguas maternas," "mother languages." Manuel Bolom Pale, Maya Tsotsil poet/scholar, has a piece written for PEN International in which he discusses the problematics of even his own translations into Spanish of the poems he first wrote in Tsotstil.[17] Mikel Ruíz, Maya Tsotsil, fiction writer, poet, scholar, writes about another Maya Tsotsil poet, Ruperta Bautista Vázquez and her refusal to make her poetry in Tsotsil conform to the rules of Spanish, which in a way, reminds us of Audra Simpson's (Mohawk) concept of "ethnographic refusal."[18]

In the United States, two of the poets known for writing in their own Indigenous languages as well as in English are Luci Tapahonso, Diné, first Poet Laureate of the Navajo Nation, and Ofelia Zepeda, T'ohono O'odham, winner of the MacArthur Genius Award. There is something incredibly soothing about hearing poetry, and reading poetry, in Indigenous languages, something healing, something comforting to the heart, mind, body, spirit. In Tapahonso's poetry, tenderness is palpable: a tenderness toward the subjects of her poems, be they human, or more-than-human, be they of this world or the dream world—and even, we would say, a tenderness toward writing itself, toward language, toward words. It was a brilliant move for Luci to provide a CD of her reading her poetry to accompany *A Radiant Curve*. The CD fuses the written word with a beautiful and decidedly Diné inflection, whether the poet is reading in English or in Diné. Likewise, we recognize Ofelia Zepeda as an important language speaker-poet who uses poetry to retain, revitalize, and teach about O'odham, her first language. She, like Tapahonso, often resists the need to translate, including poems completely composed in the O'odham language, that—in her words—"could be meant for the small but growing number of O'odham speakers who are becoming literate." She writes in her introduction to *Ocean Power*, "here, then, is [*sic*] little bit of O'odham literature for them to read,"[19] showing how, in this moment, the poet acts as teacher and gift bearer.

Several of the poets in this collection tend to matters of language and the writing of poetry in their original languages: Beth Piatote, Michael Wasson, Shaina Nez, ku'ualoha ho'omanawanui, and Inés.

For over twenty years, we have thought together about how poetry as a creative process is uniquely positioned to enable its practitioners to excavate meaning from difficult problems and questions; to provide a distinct and creative hermeneutics in relationship with the interdiscipline of Native American Studies; to illuminate the links and intimacies between Indigenous poetics and Native American Studies approaches to real-life issues; to demarcate "epistemologies of difference" regarding broader decolonial projects; and finally, to reveal how poetry has and can be implemented in language revitalization and translation efforts.

For all of the contributors, it seems undeniable that poetry teaches. As practicing poets we are led by "teachers" who guide our creative impulses (be they ancestors, the natural world, the spirit world), and as readers of poetry, we are taught by the very expression of the work itself. In fact, we argue that *the poetic process engages a methodology of acknowledgment.* In Joy Harjo's *Poet Warrior*, in the section, "Teachers," she states "Every poem has ancestors." These ancestors pertain uniquely to the life of each poet, each poem. It is as if to say, every poem is an opening to the storied world of the poet, a world that fuses past, present, and future, a world that places us at the poet's center, in a given moment of the creation of the poem. This is an intimate relationship.

In Harjo's powerful "Ancestor Poets" master-class lecture, she explains how poets have ancestor-teachers in their work that, beyond influence, become relatives through the process of creating. This is clearly recognizable in the recent and important *When the Light of the World Was Subdued, Our Songs Came Through: A Norton Anthology of Native Nations Poetry*, edited by Harjo, LeAnne Howe, and Jennifer Foerster. The anthology is sectioned by geographical area with a prominent poet introducing each. Heid E. Erdrich, who prefaces the Plains and Mountains section, leans into the words of John Trudell to illuminate the relationality of "earth power" in Native poetry: "When John Trudell recalls being under police control and told to squat, he points out the mistake his captors made: 'The placed me with my power'—the earth. Such power allows the speaker to move across time, even while restrained: 'I was their captive / But my heart was racing / Through the generations.' The ability to hold and express a distinct sense of time is how these poets remain, in Momaday's words, 'in good relation' to those who came before and those still yet to come."[20] In similar fashion, CMarie Fuhrman and Dean Rader's *Native Voices: Indigenous American Poetry, Craft and Conversations* is uniquely designed around not only a sample of each contributor's poetry but also a short essay on his/her/their poetic influences. Fuhrman and Rader make the point that a hallmark of Native poetry is the networking of influence and conversations it places us all in: "Indigenous poetry is not just a *field of subject matter*, but a way of being in the world."[21]

No matter the form of engagement, poetry forges a means to understand ourselves, our communities, lands, and worlds in deeper ways. And just as the scholar is guided by the principles of her/their/his disciplinary field of study in order to make meaning of difficult ideas and problems, so too is the poet—her/their/his imaginative spirit affording an ability to adapt and think creatively toward richer awareness. If we want to know something more deeply and more intimately, poetry helps us do that. In ancient Mesoamerica, there was an understanding of poetry as the path to truth, a truth that emerges from a profound dialogue in one's heart with spirit.[22] In Native/Indigenous ceremonial traditions, the songs are poetry's way of opening worlds for the renewal of our peoples.

Given the growing appeal to embrace a nonbinary world, and that doing so opens up exciting new ways of approaching life, we suggest that poetry, by its very nature, also manifests a nonbinary presence, fusing as it does the creative with the critical. Other art forms do this as well. It is as if Native poets know that there is no left brain versus right brain division. Poets are not bound to paradigms or agendas. While poets seriously attend to form, line, stanza, and meter, poets can also be free to contemplate and stretch beyond reason and logic. To be a poet is to be open and attentive to language in all forms: the language(s) of mind, heart, spirit, body, senses, relations, kinships, yearnings, vision, and dreams are translated through the poetic process.

Embedded and embodied in Native poetry is a deep consciousness of Indigenous history. It is why a poem such as Long Soldier's "38" affects the way it does—as it rewrites "official" histories. It is why so much Native poetry is an act of dedication, Native poets regularly dedicating their work to one another, to our more-than-human relations, to historical moments, to sacred places. Sometimes Native poetry even acts as shorthand for each other, where explication is not needed for its readership—because so much is already understood and known between Indigenous peoples. And it is in these moments when we realize how our words mediate, over ever-expanding circles, toward our hearts and the places we call home.

In the chapters that follow, contributors illustrate just how varied poetic process, praxis, and expression can be as they lean into what the genre has allowed them to ultimately confront and deepen. As each chapter illuminates these variances across Native Nations and stages in life, the contributors teach us about the important utility of creative expression in their lives and, often, on behalf of all their relations. We acknowledge that Indigenous identity and citizenship are complex matters. For our collection, we are inclusive of Native poets who are citizens of their Native Nation or community as well as those who may not be enrolled but who demonstrate a familial connection or descent through lineage. As we introduce each contributor, we lead with a line pulled from his/her/their chapter, a creative entryway into each poet's own personal meditation on the meanings of Indigenous poetics.

"Poetry gestures beyond itself, beyond mere language." In "How Poetry Breaks Language Open, How the Broken Can Feed Us," Kimberly Blaeser explores how Native poetry reaches the unsayable, and ultimately performs as gesture. As a powerful first chapter to the collection, Blaeser drives home the ways in which poetry reinforces community as it creatively archives its cultural keepings and its natural beauty. Just as Ojibwe language is verb-based and in many ways defined by its spontaneity, adaptability, and sophistication, so too is the poetic process a means to creative solutions to questions. If poems are small acts of attention, according to Blaeser, poetry is ever enacting a way of being in the world.

"When the page transformed into an ocean, each word became an island. The visible part of the word is its textual body; the invisible part of the word is the submerged mountain of meaning." In "Song Maps and Moving Islands: On Writing Poetry from a Chamoru Perspective," Craig Santos Perez shares with us the intimacy of relation to "the archipelago of belonging" that is home. Throughout his essay, he situates us historically, spatially, culturally, and aesthetically. His multi-media approach to writing uses mapping, navigation, story, and visuals "to show that personal or familial narratives have an equivalent importance to official historical and political discourses." A central point of his essay is the elaboration of the word "from." Perez is from Guåhan, but he lives in diaspora. However, he writes, "Remember: our ancestors / taught us how to carry our culture in the canoes of our bodies."

"I turned to poetry out of necessity." Casandra López, in her chapter, "Rasquachismo: An Indigenous Approach to Poetry," writes, "poetry welcomed me when I most needed it." In a way, it seems that poetry knew to call her, to invite her, to remind her of the healing power of her word. Her teaching at a tribal college also positioned her to see things from the perspective of place, self-determination, and Indigenous knowledges. The tribal college acted as a relief from mainstream academia, allowing López, in her words, to "to center my pedagogy and my writing practices " in a "logically Indigenous" approach for herself. Like other contributors to this volume, López is inspired by other artists, and in relation to Chicanx artists, she is attracted to the Mexican (and, by extension, Chicanx) concept of Rasquachismo. In its most basic definition, rasquache (the word's roots are in the Nahuatl language) could mean "barrio"—neighborhood—as in, "You're from the barrio, make use of anything and everything you can." López says, "The people in my mostly Latinx and Black town are industrious. Creative. They are rasquache." Rasquache is improvisation, using your wits to solve a problem with unlikely and often seemingly inappropriate materials that somehow seem to work. It is not so unfathomable to consider connections between the barrio and the rez or urban NDN settings in relation to this concept of Rasquachismo.

"We use poetry as a pathway to ignite a flame for therapeutic healing." Natahnee Winder and Tanaya Winder's "Colliding Heartwork and Poetry: Writing about the Legacy of Colonial School Systems" is a creative exploration of the concept of colliding heartwork—"a self-reflective process that creates links to allow for empathic feelings to connect in a common shared experience." Through an exploration of their personal family history of boarding school experience, the sisters—as poets, as co-creators—relay how poetry can act as a mechanism to express compassionate reflection and revelation, and a way to "pay homage," prayers, and collective healing for the "Indigenous children who did not return" and for those who did. As the co-authors beautifully say, "Poetry allows us to time travel, to revisit the rubble to reshape its meaning into something new."

"In writing or creating or making something, there's this process of accessing and relying upon the unseen." Layli Long Soldier's interview with Brandon Stosuy, "On Overcoming the Anxiety of Making Creative Work," is about the energy and force of prayer, and about poetry and prayer, or the state of prayer, as a process, and the interplay between poetry and other art forms as mutually nourishing. She comments on how there must be trust in the process and the inspiration. A poet is vulnerable in this way—when he/she/they are open to the possibility of something happening that is not yet conceived of or understood. The openness can be in the form of a dream as she tells us, a dream that followed a prayer before bedtime. Her journal of language becomes her "palette of paint." As she says, "I'm always listening and collecting language."

"For me, a blank page becomes an altar where the memory field is teased into existence." In "The Memory Field: Musings on the Diné Perspective of Time, Memory, and Land," Jake Skeets calls for a "radical remembering" of land. Memory is part of our being as land is part of our being. Skeets has an effortless ability to theorize while at the same time telling story. His essay demonstrates how each poem has a memoried, grounded, story, and how each phrase of each line of the poem has such a story, and how within the poem there can be stories within the lines from distinct times, particular moments. As he writes, "Native people have already mastered time travel: they are able to conjure the deepest parts of humanhood through the act of memory. Radical remembering, then, has the potential to teach a way of being that isn't tied to a capitalist future but is instead reliant on the self's engagement with the natural world."

"Story is foundational to our personal hermeneutics and also a lens or praxis inherent in our work." In Rain Prud'homme-Cranford and Carolyn M. Dunn's chapter, "Shell Shaking Sisters and Chain Cries Blues: Creole Tidalectics and Echolocative Self-Reflexive Rhetorical Praxis," the thread of grief is woven throughout, but also the threads of presence and perseverance, story, the nuances of kinships, of bodies—human, land, water, and the energy, spirit, musicality, and performativity of all of these bodies interwoven. In their theorizing, they present a kinetic call-and-response, revealing poetic channels of communication, always dialogical, to call people in, to name, and to claim. The essay is a welcoming embrace of being of mixed heritage, claiming it as a source of transformative power, signaling an immense joy at the way(s) in which "praxis is never solitary," but rather in community.

"Poetry has the capacity to illuminate not only the power of words but the power of systems of thought." In "Poetry as Performance of Language," Beth Piatote places creation/life-generation at the center, as an entryway into her poetry and the thought-world of Indigenous languages, in particular Niimiipuutimtki. As the language is performative, being verb-based, thus living and ever adaptable, so too is the capacity for poetry and its performativity in the language. Piatote writes about the remarkable embedded pedagogy she has created in her poems, by the way she offers morphological analysis in the "feet" of the poem. The language itself becomes a teacher, such that Piatote writes of "apprenticing herself" to a poem written in the early twentieth century by a Nez Perce/Cayuse writer. Her work is about intimacy with, and immense devotion to, her original language.

"Because our world was born in poetry, ʻŌiwi ways of being and knowing are forever informed by it." Kuʻualoha hoʻomanawanui's chapter, "Our World Was Born from Poetry: Koʻihonua as ʻŌiwi Poetic Praxis," begins by foregrounding the ways Oiwi (Hawaiian) cultural worldview is born of poetry, through the songs, chants, and teachings. Hoʻomanawanui explores how poetry, then, informs all of life and life's efforts to know itself, from history writing, to political activism, to climate struggles. She reflects on how her own poetry process works to refute settler colonial incursions on how the story of Hawaii and Hawaiian people is told and how it stands as a form of protection from the destruction of Native lands and peoples.

"Poets have always theorized." In "After the Before Time: Mapping the Temporal in Poetry by Jennifer Foerster, Allison Adelle Hedge Coke, and Karenne Wood," Janet McAdams proposes the ways fellow Indigenous poets are instructive to one another and because of this network of creative Indigeneity, poets and poetry teach her how to theorize and make sense of the world on Indigenous terms. McAdams reveals in her chapter how Native poetry is instructive, as other poets can be companions in our poetic lives. Akin to Harjo's notion of "ancestor poets," McAdams looks to three southeastern poets (Foerster, Hedge Coke, and Wood) for instruction to understand the ways we "unsettle naturalized 'settler-time'" and refigure Indigenous spatial-temporal logics onto our lands, lives, and Nations.

"Poetry is an act of human agency and encapsulates what it means to be human." Shaina A. Nez explores the influence of Diné poetics in her chapter "Diné Brevity as Indigenous Theory." In important ways, Nez mines the theoretical frameworks of *Hózhó* and *Saʼąh Naagháí Bikʼeh Hózhǫ́ǫ* as the world-building guideposts for her poetry, the "connections that return us to our lands, our communities, and ourselves," she says. As a newer poet on the scene, Nez stresses the importance of mentorship in creative writing and the ways in which poetry allows the freedom to choose, with intention, how to "think of the page as more than a canvas." As a chapter that is also about the Diné language, Nez's contribution is in conversation with other chapters in this collection when poets reflect on how hearing poetry aloud in our languages provides necessary connections.

"In poetry resides the place where I can teeter across multiple cable wires and not fear falling." In "Snowmaking: A Native Poetics of Winter, Mountains, and Bathing," Cj Jackson writes movingly about how poetry acts as a type of movement and performance toward Indigenous reciprocity. Through personal story, they illuminate how Native poetry is a form of sovereign investment, and it is also a form of risk. In their chapter, Jackson says, "*I am feeling something*, that is why I write. *I am holding on to too much*, that is also why I write." For them, poetry is the means by which all tensions, all conflicts, are gently held in balance.

"Engaging poetry is always a petition for sentience, for understanding the signs." Molly McGlennen's chapter "The Resonance of Poetry" relays the story of how poetry came to her and helped her make sense of lineage, belonging, and connection. In arguing for the way in which poetry has the capacity to draw things up close for examination, it becomes the vehicle to make sense of the world through one's most authentic and most generous self and voice. As McGlennen says, "Engaging in the poetic process could be the way we tune our bodies to the vibration of sounds produced generations ago," and to be claimed in relational ways. Listening is central to this process. McGlennen illuminates through her family's story that a Native poetics can be a type of documentation that western maps, archives, and written communications purposely leave out or obscure.

"My love of literature would take me by the hand and lead me to poetry." In "Memory Strings: Formative Moments in My Life with Poetry," Inés Hernández-Ávila uses the Niimiipuu women's concept, *aayatom timíip qéemu*, "memory string," to frame her essay. Creating a memory string is a contemplative practice, and as such, the essay represents her own process of contemplation regarding her relationship with poetry throughout her life. Moving between cultures (Niimiipuu/Tejana), languages (English, Spanish, and Niimiipuutimtki), and geographies, she situates herself within family, community(ies), and social struggles. For her, poetry is an act of liberation.

"This hunger to hear is a poetics that my life is trying to locate." Michael Wasson's "The Sound of a Butterfly Opening and Closing Its Wings: Musings on Nez Perce Sound Poetics" offers the collection a powerful, yet contemplative, meditation on the confluence of Niimiipuu language, soundscapes, and consciousness. Wasson explains that sound and meaning commingle in Niimiipuu linguistic landscapes. He was taught growing up "to listen" and "heighten [his] senses" to move toward the poetry of one's animate surroundings—where the "colonizer's language can no longer occupy everything." Poetry is the way, he says, to remember the sounds and "remain in awe."

Notes

1. For a fuller discussion, see Dean Rader's essay, "The Epic Lyric: Genre and Contemporary American Indian Poetry," in *Speak to Me Words: Essays on Contemporary American Indian Poetry*, ed. Dean Rader and Janice Gould (Tucson: University of Arizona Press, 2003). 123–129.

2. Early anthologies examined the oral progenitors of Indigenous poetry: Brian Swann and Arnold Krupat's *Recovering the Word: Essays on Native American Literature* (Berkeley: University of California Press, 1987) and Larry Evers and Felipe Molina's *Yaqui Deer Songs: Maso Bwikam* (Tucson: University of Arizona Press, 1987).

3. For a fuller discussion, see Molly McGlennen's *Creative Alliances: The Transnational Designs of Indigenous Women's Poetry* (Norman: University of Oklahoma Press, 2014).

4. See "The En'owkin Centre," *Tribal College: Journal of American Indian Higher Education* 26, no. 3 (2015), https://tribalcollegejournal.org/enowkin-centre/.

5. See Poetry Foundation, "Meet Our Grantee Partner: In-Na-Po," *Foundation News* (blog), *Poetry Foundation*, Fall 2022, https://www.poetryfoundation.org/articles/161974/meet-our-grantee-partner-in-na-po.

6. Ernestine Hayes, "Contemporary Creative Writing and Ancient Oral Tradition," in *Shapes of Native Nonfiction: Collected Essays by Contemporary Writers*, ed. Elissa Washuta and Theresa Warburton (Seattle: University of Washington Press, 2019), 24.

7. Linda Tuhiwai Smith, *Decolonizing Methodologies: Research and Indigenous Peoples* (London: Zed Books, 1999), 158.

8. "Poets Laureate Fellows Interviews: Rana Priest," Academy of American Poets, April 25, 2023, https://poets.org/text/poets-laureate-fellows-interviews-rena-priest.

9. Joy Harjo, *Poet Warrior: A Memoir* (New York: W. W. Norton, 2021), 179.

10. Dean Rader and Janice Gould, "Introduction: Generations and Emanations," in Rader and Gould, *Speak to Me Words*, 13.

11. Kimberly Blaeser, "Sacred Journey Cycles: Pilgrimage as Re-Turning and Re-Telling in American Indigenous Literatures," *Religion and Literature* 35, nos. 2–3 (2003): 83–104. For more of Blaeser's longtime and longform study of Native American poets, see her one hundred–page essay "Cannons and Canonization: American Indian Poetries through Autonomy, Colonization, Nationalism, and Decolonization," in *The Columbia Guide to American Indian Literatures of the United States Since 1945*, ed. Eric Cheyfitz (New York:

Columbia University Press, 2006).

12. Elizabeth Woody, "Voices of the Land: Giving the Good Word," in *Speaking for the Generations: Native Writers on Writing*, ed. Simon Ortiz (Tucson: University of Arizona Press, 1998), 165, 162, 173.

13. Dean Rader and Janice Gould, "Introduction: Generations and Emanations," in Rader and Gould, *Speak to Me Words*, 10.

14. Rader and Gould, "Introduction," 9. We urge further reading from Gould's important essay within this collection entitled "Poems as Maps in American Indian Women's Writing," in which she stresses the importance of Native poetic cartography as the portal for Native knowledge: "The poetic map offers an imaginative means, based in beautiful, austere, or playful language, to find our way toward balance" (23).

15. Simon Ortiz, *From Sand Creek* (Tucson: University of Arizona Press, 1981), emphasis ours.

16. For more on the realm of emotion and affect as it intersects with writing, see Dian Million's "There Is a River in Me: Theory from Life," in *Theorizing Native Studies*, ed. Audra Simpson and Andrea Smith (Durham, NC: Duke University Press, 2014), 31–42. In her essay, Million says that Native stories are a "useful form of knowledge" and that "the stories, unlike data, contain the affective legacy of our experiences. They are a felt knowledge that accumulates and becomes a force that empowers stories that are otherwise separate to become a focus, a potential for movement" (31–32).

17. Manuel Bolom Pale, "Self-Translation as a Political Activity," *PEN/OPP*, November 26, 2019.

18. Mikel Ruiz, "El Repliegue Poético en La Obra de Ruperta Bautista," *Ojarasca Suplemento Mensual* 212 (December 2014). See also Audra Simpson's *Mohawk Interruptus: Political Life Across the Borders of Settler States* (Durham: Duke University Press, 2014), 95–114.

19. Ofelia Zepeda, *Ocean Power: Poems from the Desert*, vol. 32 (Tucson: University of Arizona Press, 1995), 4.

20. Heid E. Erdrich, in *When the Light of the World Was Subdued, Our Songs Came Through*, ed. Joy Harjo et al. (New York: Norton, 2020), 101–102.

21. C. Marie Fuhrman and Dean Rader, *Native Voices: Indigenous American Poetry, Craft and Conversations* (North Adams, MA: Tupelo Press, 2019), xxv.

22. See Miguel León-Portilla, *Aztec Thought and Culture: A Study of the Ancient Nahuatl Mind*, trans. Jack Emory Davis (Norman: University of Oklahoma Press, 1990).

How Poetry Breaks Language Open,
How the Broken Can Feed Us

Kimberly Blaeser

i.

Poetry leaves room for what is unsaid or unsayable. This possibility grows for Indigenous poets who live within, between, or beneath the shadows of two languages.

The dynamic of making poetry as an Indigenous writer involves a negotiation between the meanings, intentions, and philosophical or spiritual underpinnings of speaking—when speaking itself is a political act.

What we call "voice" in poetry emerges from the complicated colonized spaces we navigate.

> Inhabited, we whisper and sort
> tongue hungers.[1]

ii.

Voice may not be choice. Song may be gift, prayer, or even destiny. But, of course, claiming "traditional" relationships to poetry or performance (to place, story, ceremony, etc.) puts Indigenous poets in the vulnerable position of seeming to fulfill romantic stereotypes. Who are we then, but Tommy Pico's Kumeyaay persona struggling against the urge to "write a fucking nature poem"?

How do we negotiate the landmines of identity politics in the public sphere while also fulfilling the role of "singer" in our Native communities? Can we be both Indigenous "songmaker" and contemporary poet? Both seer and a literary scholar? In any of these endeavors, how do we keep from becoming a caricature?

Publishers, academics, and, yes, readers from tribal nations, harbor expectations for their Indigenous poets. We may write in defiance of these expectations. We may write to fulfill them. But we cannot write outside the knowledge of the power the expectations wield. We are always already aware of, and therefore, always responding to the literary templates of both tribal and settler colonial systems.

Our poetry arises in the midst of entangled dualities.

> To that book-sharp gaze—
> the one we call colonial,
> we have lost enough.
> Cold. Like an ox-eye
> warning of storm.
> Always fixed on me on you—
> we pursued measured
>
>
> appraised like a crumbling nation
> put up for quick sale—reduced.[2]

iii.

But, poetry by its very nature, exists to shatter the illusion of containment. Enacted, it defies alphabetized meanings—challenges the simplified references of language. Through metaphor, allusion, gesture, absence, cadence, and the wealth of other poetic devices, poetry undermines definitions, equivalencies, and the idea of singular truth.

I write across genres: fiction, scholarship, creative nonfiction—and poetry. I am often asked *why* poetry, asked about the power or possibility of the poetic act. As I move through my most ordinary days, I often find myself struck by an image, a cadence or turn of language, a quick flash of something seen or understood in a new way—rumors or secrets surrounding a troubling event, an intimacy with a plant or animal being, a revelation about an oft-told story. This flash of re-seeing is where poetry begins for me. That gap between the known and unknown, seen and unseen, becomes the space of revelation or transformation. I am drawn to this permeable territory, to possibility.

In my own aesthetic, I think about poetry as an act of attention, as a way of looking more deeply, seeing and then seeing behind or beneath the surface. The spare suggestive language of poetry also engages the reader in the process of discovery. Poetry gestures beyond itself, beyond mere language. It breaks open the idea of language as definition, turns it into trace.

> our pockets empty of words for measure:
> how eloquent this lapping—
> against singularity.[3]

iv.

In the tradition of both haiku and Anishinaabeg dream songs, the concise lyric invites us all—writer, reader, listener—into the experience, the making of or search for meaning. R. H. Blyth says of haiku: "A haiku is not a poem, it is not literature; it is a hand beckoning, a door half-opened, a mirror wiped clean. It is a way of returning to nature."[4] Similarly, Anishinaabe writer Gerald Vizenor claims: "The reader creates a dreamscape from haiku."[5]

But the entrance Vizenor discovers has a particular cultural resonance—his "dreamscape" is akin to that invoked through Anishinaabe dream songs: "There is a visual dreamscape in haiku which is similar to the sense of natural human connections to the earth found in tribal music, dream songs."

For me, both haiku and dream songs are best understood as an aesthetic, not a form. They hearken not after language, but after experience—seek a deeper encounter with the world. Perhaps in the phrase "dream song," dream is not adjective, but a verb. Does the emphasis belong on action, as in the Anishinaabemowin language itself? Maybe the singer "dreams" an-other way of knowing or being. Does poetry invite the same action? Vizenor says, "The printed words in haiku are rendered; nothing remains but dreams, oral traditions, the light around our hands, petals, the rain."[6]

> learn to wait for poems this way
>
> fill words with small sure lights
> and follow them home[7]

V.

If language dissolves, with what does poetry leave us? With question—and continuum.

Poet Wislawa Szymborska said, "Poets if they are genuine, must keep repeating, 'I don't know.'"[8] For me, art is all about question and gesture. Poets do not simply represent the world (although that, too, is part of it), but on our best days, we wonder. As the language of a poem touches ideas and considers the material universe, poetry invites us to look with new vision at our world to imagine and re-imagine a complex interwoven reality, to enter the motion or journey of making meaning.

Years ago, I was team-teaching an intro-level "Cultures and Communities" class with a former public defender. As we were strategizing the best way to prepare students for the writing of their first paper, she said, "I always tell my students that, like a good public defender, they should never ask a question for which they don't already know the answer." I, of course, was flabbergasted. "As a poet," I countered, "you never ask a question for which you do already know the answer—otherwise why bother!"

We take a journey when we write a poem. Suquamish poet Cedar Sigo comments on the precariousness of that undertaking: "People think poetry is like needlepoint. Like you are sitting quietly in the corner somewhere. They don't understand that there's risk in taking on a poem."[9] Indeed, in the poetic journey, we should not end in the place we started. We learn to let go of the control of logic, of intention; succumb to the momentum of the poem. Propelled by image, sonics, chance associations, form, the tributaries of diverging research—by all the forces of the poetic process, we travel to a territory we had not previously envisioned, we come to a new understanding of relationships, arrive at an unexpected interpretation of facts, find parallel moments in time—in short, allow ourselves to venture beyond the known. We embrace an uncertainty in writing—submit ourselves to answer a fathomless summons. We must make room for discovery, contradictions, and further questions.

If we are intrepid, we might allow the poem to end in ambiguity, rather than certainty. Indeed, we do well to remember that poems have already escaped us in the process of writing, because our subconscious or an-other force some call muse, I may call spirit, is always working beside us or through us.

> until, in that moment, I forget
> which side of vision
> is mere realty.[10]

vi.

In my own aesthetic (which arises to a significant degree from my cultural sensibilities as an *Anishinaabekwe*), fulfillment comes—in both reading and writing—when poetry reaches toward the unsayable or performs as gesture. In our known cyclical reality, we exist in motion not stasis. We spiral spiral and return. We do not arrive, but continue. Similarly, poetry can trace or become such a continuing process—resist stasis and "completion."

It does this partly through its work of condensation. Like a Chinese painting using precise suggestive lines, concisely constructed language exercises a conscious restraint, leaves space for the unsaid—even for the not-yet-arrived ideas of poet and reader. In this way, the language remains alive, does not close down possibility.

Absence naturally plays a role in the most potent poetic phrasing. Gaps leave room for, even invite, participation in the poem's realization. Readers may imagine or add the unstated ideas, relationships, revelations. But poets prime a reader's potential for discovery in other ways as well. Notably, poetic invitation comes through cunning juxtaposition and what I like to think of as the inevitable combustion of language. Poetry is relational (not mainly, or at least not merely, grammatical). Words and phrases bump against one another in a surprising way the reader may notice. Rubbed together like tinder, they create a spark. Friction yields fire and fire equals new light.

Other dynamic tools of poetic gesture—line breaks and the architecture of the page—often require a reader to build sense beyond the stated. By its manipulation of lineation, a poem can break before meaning, break perhaps on the edge of explanation. It can build by cadence or rhythm, create under-standing not through language, but through music. Similarly, concrete poetry multiplies variables used in deciphering the poetic "truth." Through the endless possibilities that arise from punctuation, placement, and the strategic use of space, poets tap these resources to pull the reader in to decoding the layout, "reading" the unstated relationships of the poem.

Words join breath-marks, fall into silence. Language stutters and searches. Poems build by an inquiry etched in text, in form, in absences.[11]

<pre>
How delicate—
            dark
material of dream.
What we become
in space:

    An etch-
        ing.
    Stilled
    vector—
        two   dimensions
        of
holy.

    A cut-out
        hunger.
Sweet shadow-filled
                    trace—
how we bargain
against
    lurid possession.
</pre>

Silhouette

our edges

in

L

E

T

T

E

R

S

.

.

.12

vii.

Potential impacts of the opening of language intensify when we code-switch, move between, or employ multiple languages. They intensify with the innate allusion and embedded history at work in Indigenous language use. Each word from an Indigenous tradition becomes an act of resistance, an emblem of resilience.

In her book *The Droning Shaman*, Nora Marks Dauenhauer speaks of "Trapped voices, / frozen / under sea ice of English."[13] In my earliest years, I grew up in my Native grandparent's household. For them, Anishinaabemowin was a first language, while for my mother (whose first language was English), it was receding under a "sea of English." The language dynamic from that time and the repression of Indigenous languages in the boarding school era (experienced by my grandparents and older aunts and uncles) all find reflection in my work. Indeed, the Ojibway language that is visible in my poems is like the peak of a land mass that rises to the surface in a lake, while underwater mountains—the sources and influences—remain submerged. Given the history of assimilation policies that included linguicide, reclaiming Anishinaabemowin in and through poetry becomes an act of resistance. For me, it is also a gesture of *zaagidiwin*—of love for those who carried the language through the years of trauma.

Truths are embedded in the structure of the language and embodied in everyday phrases. For instance, Anishinaabe teachings and the language understand many elements or beings as animate, recognize their personhood. Meanings also multiply when their ripples of allusion extend to stories or word origins. Nookomis is both grandmother and grandmother moon, reinforcing the idea that the moon is our relative. The Anishinaabe word for heart, *ode,'* is embedded in many other words—clan, *indoodem*; strawberry or the "heart berry," *ode'imin*; drum, *dewe'igan* (or more easily seen in s/he has a drum, *odewe'igani*). Layers and poetic reverberations of words are wedded to everyday living and to teachings—about the drum, about strawberries as one of the foods at moon ceremonies, about clans as the heartbeat of our nation.

Indigenous languages live differently inside us and on the tongue. I code-switch, live "between languages—in the shadow of old losses," making a pathway for recovery.[14] In my writing—I unlock language memories, treasure and repeat the implanted cadence and the voices who carried it, reclaim and relearn Anishinaabemowin by using it. This work brings both rewards and frustrations. In the poem "Speaking, Like Old Desire," I ask, "how can you conjugate after forty" and "Will we make spirit houses for buried languages? / Or sing healing songs—*nanaandawi'iwe—nagamonan*."[15] My mistakes, too, I braid into the community mosaic. Through Indigenous language use we enact sovereignty, we claim continuance.

> Vowel sounds from a land
> language not yet lost:
> *Mooningwanekaaning-minis.*
> My tongue an island, too
> swimming where *Migis* rises.
> This ache tiny but growing—
>
> the place I keep it.[16]

viii.

Indeed, the very largesse of poetic language fulfills the foundational metaphoric reality of many Indigenous literary traditions. It also coincides well with spiritual teachings that require apprenticeship, reflects an ontology of relatedness. When, in my own everyday, I notice the reverberations of the small—the intricate claws of a newborn mouse, the complex geometry of "common" loon feather, the refractive reality of *nibi*/water—I reach for both the image and the unsayable quality of these interactions with the universe. Diné poet Jake Skeets claims, "We exist in physical spaces that are beyond language. I think it's time we begin to language these spaces into our understanding of reality."[17]

Sometimes everyday likeness overtakes our senses—the tree bark that becomes owl, the owl that vanishes into bark. We watch fog form then disperse into bird, hear wind lift into wolf howl, stick come alive as walking stick. What happens when we move beyond English or beyond language itself to recognize "otherness" as "sameness"? Is camouflage blending or becoming?

Poetry, by employing ambiguity, mimicry, or mirroring, awakens us to nature's correspondences and transformations, feeds imagination, feeds understanding. Rocks that mimic grasshoppers and fly away. A log that suddenly swims. Red breast—bird in prairie or flower blooming? Each shape becoming and unbecoming another. Similarities may signal relatedness. We begin to understand our own kinship with all beings of this planet.

The knowledge or beliefs regarding which beings speak to and with us, what voices and languages exist, are heard and attended to, may differ from community to community or from place to place. My Anishinaabe family modeled listening (and thus hearing) beyond the human. As Nora Marks Dauenhauer instructs us: "Listen for sounds./They are as important/as voices."[18]

Without or beyond language, we know—not by reason, but by instinct—that this is sacred. We taste our own smallness. How do you say "human insignificance" in writing and mean "belonging?" There is a space in poetry for this ambiguity, for this complexity of feeling.

And sometimes in our water dreams	*Nangodinong enji-nibii-bawaajiganan*
we pitiful land-dwellers	*gidimagozijig aakiing endaaying*
in longing	*bakadenodang*
recall, and singing	*dash nagamoying*
make spirits ready	*jiibenaakeying*
to follow:	*noosone'igeying*
bakobii.	*bakobiiying.*[19]

ix.

As Okanagan poet Jeannette Armstrong reminds us, "All indigenous people's languages are generated by a precise geography and arise from it."[20] My known universe for most of my life has been the rich water country of Northern Minnesota—the White Earth reservation and the Boundary Waters Canoe Area Wilderness (BWCAW) region. I feel blessed to have grown up among uncountable lakes and waterways and now to have the opportunity to make a home part of each year in a water-access-only cabin adjacent to the BWCAW.

The who and what we encounter on a daily basis alters us at a deep level, I'd like to suggest at a cellular level. It inevitably impacts all aspects of our lives and being, including artistic aesthetic.

> Mornings I paddle out to sit in the marsh with my coffee, tucking myself in the shade of a tree near where I once watched the rapid head of a black-backed woodpecker. Discovering nooks where river otters might pop up like jack-in-the-boxes—head up—head down, head up—head down. There, I live in a world where I become small again in the immensity of the ecosystem. One evening while paddling, I look up to find a bull moose, antlers still velveted with spring. Night after night, the depth of the stars swallow me. Loons call. Occasionally we hear wolves, their howl shivering along the marrow of our bones. Something, some way of being, sweeps clean the kingdom of I. We become rhythm of repeating waves, the slow spiral of hawks, fog dancing on morning lake.[21]

The rhythms and infinity of this natural world inspire my work—in every way. They inform subject, perspective, aesthetic, ethic, and method. If we understand language as patterns of communication—signs, sounds, gestures, marks—embedding in place literally teaches us new language. The circling of hawks. Sky colors. Footprints. Vocalization of animal beings. The complex layers of communication woven in any place expands our own literacy and that new literacy spills into our creative work whether in recognizable ways such as image and metaphor or in less traceable ways including language order or rhythms.

> *primordial genealogy:*
> *(makwa indodem, the climb of corn plants,*
> *bee buffalo raccoon branch lightning—*

each mothed starred and furred
holy the hooved the leafed the four-winged kin.)

How we story: water // bodies
crow and messenger shadows, *Memegwesiwug.*
Each feast, spirit plate, offering of *aseema*
a follow—how lines of pencil smoke lift like music,
scent and conjure *mino-bimaadiziwin.*[22]

X.

Just as the natural world permeates my poetry so, too, does my experience as an Anishinaabe woman from White Earth Nation. My childhood, family, community, and tribe—our stories, songs and games, community experiences, tribal teachings, Anishinaabe language, humor, seasonal activities, the character of places, creatures, plants, and much more simply make up who I am. I always say we become the stories we tell, the people and places of our past. Ultimately, they are at the most basic level the lens through which we view any experience.

Sometimes these elements of culture appear in obvious ways in Indigenous poetry—place names, voices, history, etc., but other times only the perspective of tribal culture informs the poetry. I believe, for example, behind anything I write lives an understanding of reciprocity, an acquaintance with injustice, a belief in animacy. In some instances, the subject of a poem may consciously be attending to Indigenous issues, sometimes the stance of a poem may find its grounding in Anishinaabe reality without my ever thinking about it.

For example, a recent documentary poem of mine, "1850. Sandy Lake, Minnesota," focuses on the Ojibway Trail of Tears. The poem is filled with detail and language identifiably linked to Anishinaabe culture and history. On the other hand, the title poem to my first collection, "Trailing You," includes the story of an unnamed individual falling through the lake ice, trying to pull themselves out, and ultimately pushing their gun ahead of them "all the way to shore." Little in the piece seems specifically tied to Anishinaabe culture. Likely the ways in which the latter poem might be *Anishinaabe* may even be invisible to most readers. Nevertheless, its stance is cultural. For me, the Seven Grandfather's Teachings of the Anishinaabeg inform the poem as do tribal stories of water monsters and ice woman. We write from our understandings; mine find grounding in Anishinaabe ways.

Like language, form in my poetry often arises from differing or dual cultural origins. I trace the origin of the picto-poem form I created to the influence of Anishinaabe pictographs and dream songs as well as to that of Native ledger art. But, of course, form often expresses an underlying aesthetic, cannot be separated from cultural influences. My recent writing includes slight lyric poems, each entitled "The Way We Love Something Small." I realize they are not a series, but a method, aesthetic, or tradition—perhaps even part of a school of poetry. They share a philosophical or ontological understanding or intention, one that has a through-line to Anishinaabe song poems and to haiku form, especially in the Zen tradition. Filled with pause and silence, they become the equivalent of generations of my ancestors gesturing with their lips, generations modeling deep attentiveness, and the praise song of holding silence.

When I tire of explaining—

time a warm and tended fire
a compass wheelbarrow a flour-sifter
cream can winnowing basket—

a tune we hum
     wordless as sun, as lace, as shadow.[23]

XI.

In these many ways, the play of language in poetry, which incorporates the existence of all meanings simultaneously, deepens our understanding. For Indigenous writers and readers of poetry, it also enacts an essential repair—a reassertion of the transparent filaments of kinship. English logic succumbs to poetry, even more so to multilingual poetry. When we crack open the dictionary surface, the occupations of language, we liberate it. The broken, once open, can feed us.

Poetry, in envisioning the shattered in our midst, in naming both absence and presence, shifts our conversation with the world. For Indigenous poets, often that conversation unmasks buried truths, looks squarely at trauma, and confronts contemporary injustice or instances of what Vizenor calls "manifest manners." The idea of "speaking truth to power" is a long-standing way of explaining the role of activist poetics. Audre Lorde claimed: "Poetry is not a luxury. . . . It forms the quality of the light within which we predicate our hopes and dreams toward survival and change, first made into language, then into idea, then into more tangible action."[24]

Although some will argue in favor of "art for art's sake," I think of poetry as both "affective" and "effective"—beautiful as language and simultaneously doing something in the world. We need poetry precisely because it is an act of attention and becomes an agent of change. Seeing differently is the first step toward acting differently

Through many scenarios involving repression, censorship, and genocide, poetry has served as a survivance tool. The words and voices of poets across generations have risen—to resist, carry story, teach resilience, and generate compassion. Indigenous arts have always been utilitarian as well as beautiful. We wear our beautiful beaded *makizinan*. We use our *wiigwaas* baskets for collecting berries. Our arts are alive and they support us in our flourishing: stories, songs, traditional arts, and poetry help us navigate the postmodern, hyper-technical world; to navigate the challenges of climate change, Missing and Murdered Indigenous Women, identity politics, and threats to sovereignty. In all of the circumstances of our lives, art has a role to play. Paul Chaat Smith playfully asserts: "Artists are deeply respected in the Native World. We ask of them just two things: (1) make fabulous art, and (2) lead the revolution."[25]

Because of the massive political and environmental challenges of the times in which we live, poetic attention will ultimately fall on contemporary issues. In my own reality, art and activism do not reside in different chambers of my brain or *ode*.' The "eco" in my writing, for example, often engages with place-specific struggles such as mining threats to my known cosmology of *nibi*, while also focusing on the larger scale physical and spiritual impact of environmental actions.

Sometimes the poems become part of political action. I originally wrote "Tribal Mound, Earth Sutra" for a gathering at the Milwaukee lakefront which was held in resistance to an effort to pass a state law that would have endangered effigy mounds. Recently, in response to threats to the BWCAW from potential copper mining, I became a plaintiff in a lawsuit filed against the United States by a group called Northeastern Minnesotans for Wilderness. The declaration I wrote actually includes passages extracted from creative works, because my "creative" works arise out of the same ethic of reciprocity, kinship, and sustainability as my "activist" work. Ideally, both our laws and our art embody the foundational beliefs to which we adhere.

> the rattle of a new revolution
> these fingers
> drumming on keys.[26]

xii.

Art can "lead the revolution" only if it first engages or touches a reader/listener. Poetic energies vary and we engage them strategically—purposefully in different circumstances. As it employs image and engages the senses, can the intimate language of poetry present a situation in enough vivid detail to offer an individual a new way of seeing? Only if it makes space for the reader in the process of making meaning. Poetry works by image and absence. Impactful poetic art is ultimately gesture. It leaves space for the reader/listener in what is not said, what should not or cannot be said. In this way, it offers an invitation. As Laguna writer Leslie Silko reminds us, "Storytelling always includes the listeners. In fact, a great deal of the story is believed to be inside the listeners."[27] If the reader imaginatively leaps in to make meaning of the parts, perhaps then they change by a degree their understanding.

Each being lives their own enmeshed reality. As artists we can open our known to those willing to make its acquaintance. We may embody or enact foundational ideas of reciprocity, relatedness, and a belief in the animate world. Those who accept the entrance may continue on the journey, may accept a new role of relative or protector. Thus, by invitation to experience experience, writing may feed eco-understanding. Because, ultimately, feeling related and responsible breeds more honorable behavior; perhaps bringing readers/listeners to an intimate experience of the alive beauty of *nibi* or *aki* will awaken their own dedication for care of the universe.

Dare I ask—is it enough? How can we sing the planet in all its intimate beauty in the midst of its destruction? Is writing place, water, relatedness, responsibility—writing our ancient belonging, now inevitably elegy? As poets and songmakers working in the Anthropocene, how shall we spend ourselves for repair?

When we write the wonders of earth, sky, air, animal relatives, and spirits, do we honor or seek consolation?

Can contemporary Indigenous poems continue to work in traditional ways? Does the act of speech or do words themselves harbor power? Kiowa writer N. Scott Momaday has claimed:

> Words are intrinsically powerful. They are magical. By means of words one can bring about physical change in the universe. By means of words can one quiet the raging weather, bring forth the harvest, ward off evil, rid the body of sickness and pain, subdue an enemy, capture the heart of a lover, live in the proper way, and venture beyond death.[28]

Similarly, Muscogee Creek Joy Harjo, past U.S. Poet Laureate, asserts the power of poetry when she claims, "My role as a poet is as a healer. Poetry is a healing force."[29]

> Now from our tongues a salve—an animal saliva called language.
> *Mikwendaman*—retelling we wake, seek repair.[30]

XIII.

How we as Indigenous writers situate ourselves and our practice of poetry varies—not just across tribes and individuals, but within each of our histories. The questions that attend the practice of poetry arise from many circumstances. Some questions seem eternal, others surface in particular moments or places and recede. Likewise varied are the ranges of success we experience in awakening poetry's power. For whom do we write and who will read or hear our words? Indeed, the very measurement of success is not uniform—do we long for publication, community engagement, prizes, the poem itself?

Most rewarding for me are moments when what I send out into the world finds a home, keeps growing, or comes back in some way—a poem put to use in a classroom or exhibit, or hearing my work performed by others who have made it their own. Poetry especially is meant to live in the spoken. In April 2022, I had a particularly fulfilling poetry moment while celebrating the first mentoring retreat for In-Na-Po, Indigenous Nations Poets, a nonprofit organization I founded. During the faculty's closing reading at the Library of Congress in DC, I performed my poem "On the Dignity of Gestures." Dedicated to Nathan Phillips, the poem is built of both praise and instruction as it presents concise images of human and natural care-taking. Two lines allude to the dignity Phillips showed in 2019 when MAGA youth confronted him while he was drumming and singing on the National Mall: "Do not become beast in the fray. Remember the Indigenous hands that drummed on, the man who stood calm."[31] Hours after the reading, as we were leaving Joy Harjo's dance party (the last wonderful and crazy activity of the retreat), several In-Na-Po Fellows told me Nathan Phillips was at the gathering. When I met him, someone from his youth group asked me to read the poem for him. We stood side by side, the lighted capital behind us, and I had the honor of giving this elder the gift of my poem. What poetry magic brought us together in that place and time? Diné writer Luci Tapahonso would remark at dinner later that night, "The spirits were all over that."

I do my work in solitude in order to build community. Sometimes poems find their way. I feel humbled and blessed when they do.

> *Inky leaf shadows on snow,*
> *each animal track a hollow:*
> *trace of bird feet, double oval of deer,*
> *the glyphs we make—*
>
> *the ones we follow.*[32]

xiv.

Whether we are reader, listener, singer, or writer, poetry is a teacher. In Anishinaabemowin, the word *gikinawaabi* means we learn by watching. Poetry enacts this way of being in the world—teaches us to watch, to pay attention. When we look closely, the world reveals itself. But the world reveals itself partly because we open ourselves—search for meaning, knowledge, beauty. That path we take partly through the trace of language.

Speaking or writing, we offer gratitude for the traces planted before us, the pathways that lead us closer to balance. But I often wonder if *gizhe-manidoo* provides us with such gifts so that we might solve each mystery, or rather that we might live it?

Nibwaakaawin. Perhaps wisdom is not a putting on, but a taking off. When our artist words and images become transparent, we become another's lens.

> This is to hunger (*bakade*)
> this is to break (*biigoshkaad*),
>
> to speak is to eat
> *wiikwandiwin,* feast food
>
> our jagged stuttering a giveaway—
> *maada'oonidiwag* (this is to share).[33]

XV.

If, as many theorists have suggested, language is ultimately destiny, then to be good Indigenous relatives or good ancestors to those who will follow, shouldn't we devote ourselves to reclaiming autonomy over our own language and story? As early as the 1970s, Gerald Vizenor recognized the struggle we face as Indigenous peoples as bound up in what he called the "Word Wars." He created language to name the linguistic strategies of empire, describe the "terminal creeds" and "literature of dominance."

Essentially, the colonizer constructed an image and reality for the "pagan savages" "discovered" in these Americas in the manner of the Orientalists, an image easily exploited in service of manifest destiny. Through totalitarian language, we are thus seen and educated to see ourselves in caricature as "Indian." The colonization of Indigeneity belongs to a larger philosophical stance that endorses capitalism and popular cultural consumption of all things Indian—even, as the Missing and Murdered Indigenous Women crisis has demonstrated, consumption of our very bodies.

If we and our nations have been defined and captured, erased in language, language, too, has become one tool of reclamation and resilience. Indigenous poets are rewriting history, retelling our stories, writing over falsehoods, and replacing the confining colonial languages. Liberating tones of tribal languages and voices carry ancient teachings, re-member our own semiotic systems—systems that reinforce notions of kinship and reciprocity. As Joy Harjo and Gloria Bird claim in their 1997 anthology, we are "reinventing the enemy's language." Indeed, the current "land back" movement aligns with an important contemporary "language back" movement—a claim of literary sovereignty powerfully embodied in poetry.

Because poetry by its nature disrupts static meanings, songs and poems in particular unsettle the settlers' language, break open colonial constructions, challenge and reimagine the dictionary destiny we were once assigned. Language, once broken, stands opens, becomes malleable on our liberated tongues—one poem at a time.

> *Waabigwaniikaag,* an abundance we make
> of the broken—when burst becomes seed.[34]

Notes

1. Kimberly Blaeser, "Akawe, a prelude," *Ancient Light* (Tucson: University of Arizona Press, 2024), 3.

2. Kimberly Blaeser, "When we have lost enough," *Poets' Republic* 10 (Winter 2021–2022): 43.

3. Kimberly Blaeser, "Alaskan poems you didn't write," in *Through This Door: Wisconsin in Poems,* ed. Margaret Rozga and Angela Trudell Vasquez (Madison: Art Night Books, 2020), 90.

4. R. H. Blyth, *Haiku,* vol. 1: *Eastern Culture* (Tokyo: Hokuseido Press, 1965), 243.

5. Gerald Vizenor, *Matsushima: Pine Islands* (Minneapolis: Nodin, 1984).

6. Vizenor, *Matsushima.*

7. Kimberly Blaeser, "zen for traveling bards," in *Absentee Indians and Other Poems* (East Lansing: Michigan State University Press, 2002), 41.

8. Wislawa Szymborska, "I Don't Know," *New Republic,* December 30, 1996, https://newrepublic.com/article/100368/i-dont-know.

9. Cedar Sigo and Ben Purkert, "Back Draft: Cedar Sigo," *Guernica,* September 28, 2018, https://www.ghuernicamag.com/back-draft-cedar-sigo/.

10. Kimberly Blaeser, "Refractions," in *Apprenticed to Justice* (Cambridge: Salt Publishing, 2007), 96.

11. Kimberly Blaeser, "Akawe, a prelude," in *Ancient Light*, 3.

12. Blaeser, "Of Poetry and the Making of Lines," in *Ancient Light*, 93.

13. Nora Marks Dauenhauer, "Listening for Native Voices," in *The Droning Shaman* (Haines, AL: Black Current Press, 1988), 28.

14. Kimberly Blaeser, "Akawe, a prelude," in *Ancient Light*, 3.

15. Kimberly Blaeser. "Speaking, Like Old Desire," in *Copper Yearning* (Duluth, MN: Holy Cow! Press, 2019), 75.

16. Blaeser, "The Way We Love Something Small: Vowel Sounds from a Land," in *Ancient Light*, 28.

17. Jake Skeets, "A Brave New World," *Indigenous Nations Poets*, June 30, 2021, https://www.indigenousnationspoets.org/a-brave-new-world-by-jake-skeets.

18. Dauenhauer, *The Droning Shaman*, 28.

19. Blaeser, "Dreams of Water Bodies," in *Copper Yearning*, 7.

20. Jeannette Armstrong, "Land Speaking," in *Introduction to Indigenous Literary Criticism in Canada*, ed. Heather Macfarlane and Armand Garnet Ruffo (Peterborough, ON: Broadview Press, 2015), 148.

21. Kimberly Blaeser, "*Ishkode:* Of Fires," in *Paideuma: Modern and Contemporary Poetry and Poetics* 52 (2025).

22. Kimberly Blaeser, "Tracing, Kinship Lines," *About Place Journal*, ed. Allison Hedge Coke, May 2022, https://aboutplacejournal.org/article/tracing-kinship-lines/.

23. Kimberly Blaeser, "The Way We Love Something Small: Sun through Lace Spills Delicate," in *Ancient Light*, 64.

24. Audre Lorde, "Poetry Is Not a Luxury," in *By Herself: Women Reclaim Poetry*, ed. Molly McQuade (Minneapolis: Graywolf, 2000), 365.

25. Paul Chaat Smith, "Famous Long Ago," in *Shapeshifting: Transformations in Native American Art* (New Haven, CT: Yale University Press, 2012), 215.

26. Blaeser, "Apprenticed to Justice," in *Apprenticed to Justice*, 104.

27. Leslie Marmon Silko, "Language and Literature from a Pueblo Indian Perspective," in *Yellow Woman and a Beauty of the Spirit* (New York: Simon and Schuster, 1996), 50.

28. N. Scott Momaday, *The Man Made of Words* (New York: St. Martin's Press, 1997), 15–16.

29. Joy Harjo, "Joy Harjo Is the First Native American U.S. Poet Laureate," *Washington Post*, June 19, 2019.

30. Kimberly Blaeser, "Akawe, a prelude," in *Ancient Light*, 3.

31. Kimberly Blaeser, "On the Dignity of Gestures," *Résister en dansant/Ikwe-niimi: Dancing Resistance* (Nyons, FR: Éditions des Lisières, 2020) 34.

32. Kimberly Blaeser, "The Way We Love Something Small: Inky Leaf Shadows on Snow," in

Ancient Light, 97.

33. Kimberly Blaeser, "Songs Like Bread: Wiikwandiwin," in *Ancient Light*, 37.

34. Kimberly Blaeser, "Mazinigwaaso: Florets," in "Indigenous Ecopoetry," ed. Beatrice Szymkowiak, *Under a Warm Green Linden* 14 (Winter 2022–2023), https://www. greenlindenpress.com/issue14.

Bibliography

Armstrong, Jeannette. "Land Speaking." In *Introduction to Indigenous Literary Criticism in Canada*, edited by Heather Macfarlane and Armand Garnet Ruffo, 145–159. Peterborough, ON: Broadview Press, 2016.

Blaeser, Kimberly M. *Absentee Indians and Other Poems*. East Lansing: Michigan State University Press, 2002.

———. "Alaskan poems you didn't write." In *Through This Door: Wisconsin in Poems*, edited by Margaret Rozga and Angela Trudell Vasquez, 90. Madison: Art Night Books, 2020.

———. *Ancient Light*. Tucson: University of Arizona Press, 2024.

———. *Apprenticed to Justice*. Cambridge, UK: Salt Publishing, 2007.

———. *Copper Yearning*. Duluth, MN: Holy Cow! Press, 2019.

———. "*Mazinigwaaso*: Florets." "Indigenous Ecopoetry," edited by Beatrice Szymkowiak, *Under a Warm Green Linden* 14 (Winter 2022–2023). https://www.greenlindenpress.com/issue14.

———. *Résister en dansant/Ikwe-niimi: Dancing Resistance*. Nyons, FR: Éditions des Lisières, 2020.

———. "Tracing, Kinship Lines." *About Place Journal*, edited by Allison Hedge Coke. 2022. https://aboutplacejournal.org/article/tracing-kinship-lines/.

———. "When we have lost enough." In *Poets' Republic* 10 (Winter 2021–2022).

Blyth, R. H. *Haiku*. Vol 1: *Eastern Culture*. Tokyo: Hokuseido Press, 1965.

Chaat Smith, Paul. "Famous Long Ago." In *Shapeshifting: Transformations in Native American Art*, edited by Karen Kramer Russell, 213–221. New Haven, CT: Yale University Press, 2012.

Harjo, Joy. "Joy Harjo Is the First Native American U.S. Poet Laureate." *Washington Post*, June 19, 2019.

Lorde, Audre. "Poetry Is Not a Luxury." In *By Herself: Women Reclaim Poetry*, edited by Molly McQuade, 364–367. Minneapolis: Graywolf, 2000.

Marks Dauenhauer, Nora. *The Droning Shaman*. Haines: Black Current Press, 1988.

Momaday, N. Scott. *The Man Made of Words*. New York: St. Martin's Press, 1997.

Sigo, Cedar, and Ben Purkert. "Back Draft: Cedar Sigo," *Guernica*, September 28, 2018.

Marmon Silko, Leslie. "Language and Literature from a Pueblo Indian Perspective." In *Yellow Woman and a Beauty of the Spirit*, 48–59. New York: Simon and Schuster, 1996.

Skeets, Jake. "A Brave New World," Indigenous Nations Poets, June 30, 2021. https://www.indigenousnationspoets.org/a-brave-new-world-by-jake-skeets.

Szymborska, Wislawa. "I Don't Know." *New Republic*, December 29, 1996. https://newrepublic.com/article/100368/i-dont-know.

Vizenor, Gerald. *Matsushima: Pine Islands*. Minneapolis: Nodin, 1984.

Song Maps and Moving Islands

On Writing Poetry from a Chamoru Perspective

Craig Santos Perez

I am an Indigenous Chamoru (Chamorro) born and raised on Guåhan (Guam), an island in the northwestern Pacific Ocean. In my small village of Mongmong (a name that translates as "the sound of a heartbeat"), electricity outages were common. At dinner time, my relatives would arrive to our house as if drawn by the magical smoke from my dad's barbecue grill. During those powerless nights, we sat in a circle eating and talking story outside. Actually, I never talked. I only listened as my elders' words carved the silence into a canoe that carried stories across the oceanic waves of time and space.

Canoes and seafaring are essential components of Pacific Islander cultures. Our navigational practices involved calculating distance traveled and position at sea by triangulating a reference island with the islands of departure and destination, as well as with other landmarks, wave signatures, and constellations. The islands are imagined as "moving" across a prescribed course while the canoe is conceived as remaining still. Another important seafaring technique involved memorizing the presence and migrations of marine life and birds Indigenous to given islands. So if you see a specific bird, then you know its island is nearby. The island is thus imagined as expanding (and contracting as the bird moves out of sight).

Before navigators embarked on a journey, they learned and recited chants that charted the islands, stars, and animals that they expected to encounter along their path. These chants are known as "song maps," and they were passed down for generations.

weave

words into

a mast

carve

lines into

a hull

ask

the reader

to hold

the poem

to be

the outrigger

(*from* "ars pasifika")

Guåhan was "discovered" by Ferdinand Magellan on his circumnavigation of the globe in 1521. This inaugurated the colonization of my homeland by Spain, which lasted for centuries as Guåhan became an important stopping point along the Spanish galleon trade route. Spain's imperial rule lasted until the Spanish-American War of 1898, after which Guåhan became an unincorporated territory of the United States—a colonial relationship that persists to this day. Guåhan is important to the American empire as a strategic military location. Currently, U.S. military bases occupy nearly 30 percent of Guåhan's landmass. Indeed, my homeland is often referred to as an "Unsinkable Aircraft Carrier" and "The Tip of America's Military Spear in Asia."

Over the past century, the military has dredged our coral reefs, poisoned fishing grounds, killed marine life, contaminated soil and drinking water, clearcut jungles, destroyed habitats, endangered Native species, and evicted my people from our ancestral lands. Guam was once a place of biodiversity; now, nearly a hundred Superfund and dumpsites plague our island.

I remember, during those nights without electricity, listening to my elders' voices, a story was always told about a relative who recently died from cancer, or a relative recently diagnosed with cancer. Toxins are buried in our bodies like unexploded ordnances. The only sound that ever interrupted our stories was the sonic blast of fighter jets flying overhead.

———————

My family migrated to California in 1995, when I was fifteen years old. Since the 1960s, my people have migrated to the "mainland" in search of work, school, and health care. Today, more of us live off-island than on-island.

On the first day of my new high school, a teacher asked where I was from. After I answered, he responded: "I've never heard of Guam. Prove it exists." As I approached the world map on the wall, it transformed into a mirror: my body, like the Pacific Ocean, was split in two and splayed to the margins.

"I'm from this invisible island," I said and pointed to an empty space where I knew my homeland to be. The students laughed. Guåhan is so small it often does not appear on maps.

"Are you a U.S. citizen?" he interrogated. "Yes," I said and explained that we learn American English, attend American schools, eat American food, listen to American music, watch American movies and television, play American sports, study American history, enlist in the American military, die in American wars, and dream American dreams.

"You speak English well," he proclaimed, "with *almost* no accent."

And isn't this what it means to be from an unincorporated territory: to be *foreign in a domestic sense*. To be *invisible*.

> Some of us will be able to return home for holidays, weddings,
> and funerals; others won't be able to afford the expensive plane
> ticket to the Western Pacific. Years and even decades might pass

> between trips, and each visit will feel too short. We'll lose contact
> with family and friends, and the island will continue to change
> until it becomes unfamiliar to us. And isn't that, too, what it means
> to be a diasporic Chamoru: to feel foreign in your own homeland.
>
> Even after 25 years away, there are still times I feel adrift, without
> itinerary or destination. When I wonder: What if we stayed? What if
> we return? When the undertow of these questions begins pulling
> you out to sea, remember: migration flows through our blood
> like the aerial roots of the banyan tree. Remember: our ancestors
> taught us how to carry our culture in the canoes of our bodies.
> Remember: our people, scattered like stars, form new constellations
> when we gather. Remember: home is not simply a house,
> village, or island; home is an archipelago of belonging.
> (*from* "Off-Island Chamorus")

Throughout high school and college, literature helped me navigate life on the "mainland" and form a deeper understanding of American history and politics. I was drawn to books by Native American and ethnic minority writers because I could relate to their stories of struggle, survival, and hope. To me, written narratives were an extension of the oral tradition I grew up around. The act of reading felt like listening to invisible storytellers silently whispering their tales.

Despite the fact that Pacific Islanders are one of the fastest-growing populations within the United States, I never saw myself in the curriculum. In the American literary imaginary, the Pacific is an empty space devoid of literature. This absence motivated me to write my own stories, and I eventually pursued an MFA at the University of San Francisco. I graduated in 2006 with a manuscript of poems about Chamorro identity, culture, and diaspora as well as about the political history of Guåhan.

That same year, the Department of Defense announced a plan for a massive military buildup on Guåhan. Valiant Shield, a military training exercise, was first held that year on Guåhan and in the surrounding waters. These actions were part of the U.S. geopolitical strategy, "The Pacific Pivot," to increase its military presence and power in the region.

The threat of the Pacific Pivot compelled me to join a California-based Chamorro activism group called *Famoksaiyan*, a word in our language that translates as "the place or time of nurturing" or "the time to paddle forward and move ahead." We organized events across the state to raise awareness about Guåhan and the devastating impacts of militarism. I performed my poetry at many of these events as a creative way to address the issues.

In 2008, a delegation of *Famoksaiyan* members traveled to the United Nations in New York City for the meeting of the Special Committee on Decolonization, which advocates for the remaining non-self-governing territories. When we began our testimonies, the U.S. representative walked out of the room. This, too, is what it means to write from a territory: *to speak our truth even when those who need to listen refuse to hear you.*

My MFA manuscript was published as my first book in 2008. It was titled *from unincorporated territory [hacha]*. As I note in the preface of the book, *from* indicates a particular time or place as a starting point; *from* refers to a specific location as the first of two limits; *from* imagines a cause, an agent, an instrument, a source, or an origin; *from* marks separation, removal, or exclusion; *from* differentiates borders.

I remember the question my teacher asked me: "Where are you from?" I continued in my preface: "On some maps, Guam doesn't exist; I point to an empty space in the Pacific and say, 'I'm from here.' On some maps, Guam is a small, unnamed island; I say, 'I'm from this unnamed place.' On some maps, Guam is named 'Guam, USA.' I say, 'I'm from a territory of the United States.'"

From also indicates an excerpt or a passage quoted from a source. My own passage and migration *from* Guam to California often feels like living an excerpted existence; while my body lives here, my heart still lives in my homeland. Poetry is a way for me to bring together these excerpted spaces via the transient, processional, and migratory cartographies of the page. Each of my poems, and each of my books, and seemingly every breath I take, carries the *from* and bears its weight and incompleteness. Each book is a navigation of being *from*.

I was also influenced by Native American writer Simon Ortiz's book *from Sand Creek*. The first sentence of the preface to Ortiz's book has also haunted me as a writer: "How to deal with history." His question is haunted by my own: *How to heal from history?*

As I continued to navigate the art of poetry, I began to imagine the blank page as an excerpt of the ocean. The ocean is storied and heavy with history, myth, rumor, genealogy, loss, war, money, death, life, and even plastic. The ocean is not "aqua nullius." The page, then, is never truly blank. The page consists of submerged volcanoes of story and unfathomable depths of meaning.

When the page transformed into an ocean, each word became an island. The visible part of the word is its textual body; the invisible part of the word is the submerged mountain of meaning. Words emerging from the silence are islands forming. No word is just an island, every word is part of a sentence, an archipelago. The space between is defined by referential waves and currents.

Oceanic stories are vessels for cultural beliefs, values, customs, histories, genealogies, politics, and memories. Stories weave generations and geographies. Stories protest and mourn the ravages of colonialism, articulate and promote cultural revitalization, and imagine and express decolonization.

I also imagine an individual book as an island with a unique linguistic geography and ecology as well as a unique poetic landscape and seascape. The book-island is inhabited by the living and the dead, the human and the non-human, multiple voices and silences. The book-island vibrates with the complexity of the present moment and the depths of history and genealogy, culture and politics, scars and bone and blood. A book series is an archipelago, a birthing and formation of book-islands. Like an archipelago, the books in an ongoing series are related and woven to the other islands, yet unique and different.

Because Guåhan is part of an archipelago, the geography inspired the form of my *from unincorporated territory* book series. Additionally, the unfolding nature of memory, learning, listening, sharing, and storytelling informed the serial nature of the work. To me, the complexity of the story of Guåhan and the Chamoru people inspired the ongoing serial form.

The first book of the series, *from unincorporated territory* [*hacha*] (2008), focused on my grandfather's life and experience on Guåhan when the island was occupied during World War II. The second book, *from unincorporated territory* [*saina*] (2010), focused on my grandmother's experience during that same period. The third book, *from unincorporated territory [guma']* (2014), echoes and enlarges the earlier books through the themes of family, militarization, cultural identity, migration, and colonialism. Furthermore, [*guma'*] focuses on my own return to my home island after living away in California for fifteen years. I explore how the island has changed and how my idea of home has changed. I also meditate upon the memories that I have carried with me as well as all that I have forgotten and left behind.

The titles are meant to mark and name different books in the same series. Just as an archipelago has a name, such as the Marianas Archipelago, each island of the archipelago has its own unique name. The names can be translated as [one], [elder], and [home]. My first book was given the name [*hacha*] to mark it as the first book, first island, first voice. While one might expect the second book to be named "second," I chose the name [elder] to resist that linearity and instead highlight genealogy, or the past. The third book, which means "house" or "home," was an attempt to weave together time and space (the house or book as spatial and temporal). The fourth book, *from unincorporated territory [lukao]* (2017), includes themes of birth, creation, parenthood, money, climate colonialism, militarization, migration, and extinction. The Chamoru name of the book, [*lukao*], means procession.

I use diagrams, maps, illustrations, collage visual poetry as a way to foreground the relationship between storytelling, mapping, and navigation. One prevalent typographical presence throughout my work is the tilde (~). Besides resembling an ocean current and containing the word "tide" in its body, the tilde has many intriguing uses. In languages, the tilde is used to indicate a change of pronunciation. I use many different kinds of discourse in my work (historical, political, personal, etc.) and the tilde is meant to indicate a shift in the discursive poetic frame. In mathematics, the tilde is used to show equivalence (i.e., x~y). Throughout my work, I want to show that personal or familial narratives have an equivalent importance to official historical and political discourses.

Cartographic representations of the Pacific Ocean developed in Europe at the end of the fifteenth century, when the Americas were incorporated into maps: the Pacific became a wide empty space separating Asia and America. In European world maps, Europe is placed at the center and "Oceania" is divided into two opposite halves on the margins. As imperialism progressed, every new voyage incorporated new data into new maps.

The invisibility of Guåhan on many maps—whether actual maps or the maps of history—has always haunted me. One hope for my poetry is to enact an emerging map of "Guåhan" both as a place and as a signifier. The maps in my books function in two ways: first, they center Guåhan, a locating signifier often omitted from many maps. Second, the maps are meant to provide a counterpoint to the actual stories that are told throughout the book. While maps can locate, chart, and represent (and through this representation tell an abstracted story), they never show us the human voices of a place. I place this abstract, aerial view of Guåhan alongside the more embodied and rooted portraits of place and people.

Last, I imagine reading as a kind of wayfinding. Pacific navigational techniques are often understood as a "visual literacy," in the sense that a navigator has to be able to "read" the natural world (stars, ocean efflorescence, wave currents, and fish and bird migrations) in order to make safe landfall. Reading poetry is a way to navigate the complex oceanic and archipelagic geography of poetry.

In 2010, the Guam Humanities Council invited me to be a keynote speaker in a series of "community conversations" about the legacy of U.S. militarism. This trip was my first time returning home after living in California for fifteen years, and it coincided with the publication of my second book.

While home, I was featured on the local television news channel, the major radio station, and the daily newspaper. I visited and performed my poetry at several of the public high schools as well as at the only community college and university. After each performance, facilitators from the council engaged the audience in conversations about the military. Poetry became a bridge to discuss politics. This profound experience solidified my belief in the power of the humanities to create space for civic reflection and engagement.

After my visit, the Guam Legislature passed a resolution that recognized me as "an accomplished poet who has been a phenomenal ambassador for our island, eloquently conveying through [my] words, the beauty and love that is the Chamoru culture."

The idea of being a poetic ambassador for my homeland took on new meaning when I received an opportunity to represent Guåhan at Poetry Parnassus in London during the 2012 Olympics. This "Cultural Olympiad" was a week-long festival held in London and organized by renowned poet Simon Armitage. The festival featured one poet from each of the two hundred countries competing in the Olympics. Besides performing my poems, I participated on two panels organized by PEN International: "Environmentalism and Eco-Poetry" and "Minority Languages, Marginalized Voices." I felt proud to represent Guåhan on this international stage, and I felt empowered to stand side-by-side with poets from around the world advocating for justice, freedom of expression, and human rights.

I read aloud from my new book
to an English class at one of Guam's
public high schools. Afterwards, I

notice a student crying. "What's wrong?"
I ask. She says, "I've never seen our culture
in a book before. I just thought we weren't

worthy of literature." How many young
islanders have dived into the depths
of a book, only to find bleached coral

and emptiness? We were taught
that missionaries were the first readers
in the Pacific because they could decipher

the strange signs of the Bible. We were taught
that missionaries were the first authors
in the Pacific because they possessed

the authority of written words. Today,
studies show that islander students
read and write below grade level.

"It's natural," experts claim. "Your ancestors
were an illiterate, oral people." *Do not
believe their claims.* Our ancestors deciphered

signs in nature, interpreted star formations
and sun positions, cloud and wind patterns,
wave currents and ocean efflorescence.

That's why master navigator Papa Mau
once said: "if you can *read* the ocean
you will never be lost." Now let me tell you

about *Pacific written traditions*, how our ancestors
tattooed their skin with scripts of intricately
inked genealogy; how they carved epics

into hard wood with a sharpened point,
their hands, and the pressure and responsibility
of memory; and how they stenciled

petroglyphic lyrics on cave walls with clay,
fire, and smoke. So the next time someone
tells you our people were illiterate, teach them

about our visual literacies, our skill
to read the intertextual sacredness
of all things. And always remember:

if we can write the ocean, we will never be silenced.
(*from* "The Pacific Written Tradition")

———————————

I have since moved to Hawai'i and accepted a position in the English department at the University of Hawai'i, Mānoa, where I teach creative writing and
Pacific literature. Even though I grew up not seeing any Pacific Islanders in
the curriculum, I am grateful that I have the opportunity to not only show my
Pacific Islander students that we have a rich literary tradition, but also educate
students from other cultures about the Pacific through our literature.

Pacific Islander poetry is a vessel that carries tragic stories of imperialism and colonialism. Poems address issues related to social injustice, economic dispossession, militarization, nuclearism, plantationism, disease, tourism, urbanization, racism, homophobia, and environmental degradation. Conversely, poetry is a vessel for stories about Pacific Islander survival and strength, stories about resistance and protest, stories about struggles for decolonization, environmental justice, and sovereignty.

My own work has been deeply influenced by this the tradition of Pacific oral storytelling, chant, and song as well as contemporary written Pacific literature. My beliefs that poetry has the power to raise political awareness, inspire environmental injustice, cultivate empathy, protest oppression, empower communities, and advocate for peace is rooted in the literary genealogy of Pacific literature.

I believe that our stories prove that our lives matter. We are worthy of literature. We deserve to be seen and heard. Like many other Native writers, I write to honor my ancestors and homeland, heal from history, empower my people, and advocate for decolonization.

Grounded in Chamoru culture, I imagine that my poems are "song maps." I imagine the reader is in a canoe, navigating these moving islands, expanding and contracting, inhaling and exhaling.

Rasquachismo

An Indigenous Approach to Poetry

Casandra López

Writing about poetry intimidates me. I am even more intimidated when I have to write academically. After twenty years of schooling and ten years of teaching composition, my insecurities can be easily brought to the surface when faced with criticism of my grammar. It is work to push past the memory of a graduate professor asking me if English was my first language. He was trying to make sense of my misuse of tense. But the tense changes made sense in a world where time can be present and past. It is easy for me to recall how my tongue would stumble over certain words and how a group of students made fun of my mispronunciations during one of my first years teaching college. Even though I question whether I have anything worthy to say about poetry, I know poetry welcomed me when I most needed it. Poetry didn't care about proper grammar and has given me so much pleasure.

I spent the last five years teaching at Northwest Indian College (NWIC), the only tribal college in Washington State. There, I felt like I could be the closest to myself. And even though I was away from home and I rarely interacted with another California Indian, it was where I felt the distance between my home communities and my academic life was the closest. I finally felt comfortable sharing some of my academic challenges with my students. I was upfront about words that turned my tongue in circles. My experience at this tribal college, emphasizing placed-based education, Indigenous self-determination, and knowledge, encouraged me to examine my teaching pedagogy and writing.

For the most part, graduate school taught me how to teach creative writing and composition from a Western perspective. While I was appreciative to have this opportunity to learn about craft, many of my teachers had been taught with a standard literary pedagogy that they then passed on to their students. While this was more true in my education regarding prose than poetry, by the end of my MFA, I felt that I had become schooled so that I didn't always trust my instincts. I also realized that breaking the cycle of centering Western perspectives would take work. At NWIC, the emphasis was on grounding teaching in tribally specific worldviews. I knew I needed to find a way to center my pedagogy and my writing practices in a way that was logically Indigenous to myself.

I often find myself inspired by the practice of other artists and creatives. I can sometimes have a narrow vision of my work and practice, so learning from artists of various mediums can be the crack in the window I need to let in the light; the opening I need to grow creatively. I came across the theory of Rasquachismo while reading about Chicanx artists. The Chicano scholar Tomás Ybarra-Fausto defines this concept as underdog sensibility and positions it as a form of resistance. Rasquache has Nahuatl origins and often has negative connotations when describing something or someone with bad taste, poor, or unrefined. But the Chicanx and Mexican art movement has been working to reclaim this term, working to see and honor the creativity and resilience within the culture, expressions, and aesthetics. In 2019, *Smithsonian Magazine* published the article "Why the Chicano Underdog Aesthetic 'Rasquachismo' Is Finally Having Its Day." The article features the Chicano actor and avid art collector Cheech Marin, who discusses how in the past, "When Chicano artists in L.A. wanted to show their art, they were told by the-powers-that-be at museums that Chicanos don't make fine art. They make agitprop folk art." In reference to rasquache, Marin says, "You have to make art or something resembling art in your life with baser objects. It's not art made of gold, it's made of tin, dirt or mud."[1] It is this "make do" attitude that results in the creativity that Marin and others are trying to elevate.

While reading about Rasquachismo, I immediately understood it from my lived experience. I was reminded of my hometown of San Bernardino. For many years, I felt shame about my hometown of San Bernardino because of the prevalence of poverty and violence. Even people from my community talk negatively about it.

When I was a teen, I dreamed of escaping. And I did. I went to college across the country and almost immediately missed home. I see it with new eyes when I return home and every time after that. I noticed the trash in the streets and broken windows as well as the bright flowers tied to chain-link fences. I could now appreciate the hustle and convenience of paleteros and eloteros on most street corners; or, how on the dusty and undeveloped fields in town sprout little markets of individual sellers: someone selling plants, another selling used goods, and various food vendors. The people in my mostly Latinx and Black town are industrious. Creative. They are rasquache.

Because Rasquachismo makes internal sense to me, because it is rooted in my daily experience, I am not intimidated by it as I would be by abstract theories. With Rasquachismo, I can weave praxis and theory together to create something bold. I can create something rooted in my cultures and communities while being inventive. What I find both challenging and promising about Rasquachismo is that it was not conceived or practiced in a controlled way. In Tomás Ybarra-Fausto's article "Rasquachismo: A Chicano Sensibility," he argues that Rasquachismo should be "considered first as an attitude and a sensibility, and secondarily as a set of formal art qualities." He also contends that "Rasquachismo is a visceral response to lived reality, not an intellectual cognition."[2] These ideas are what make rasquache feel most connected to my process and work.

I turned to poetry out of necessity. I had written only a handful of poems before I'd witnessed my brother's murder. In the first few years after my brother's death, poetry seemed the best way to express my emotions. When I first started to write poetry, I didn't know much about the conventions of poetry, and so many of my first poems were cliché and unconcerned with form. But I continued writing because I wanted to become a better poet and it was the only medium that felt like a conduit for speaking to my brother.

> I wrote to Brother, and I wrote to an ugly spirit I named Bullet.
>
> I wrote in defiance of silence; I wrote against those who said grief has an
> end date.
>
> I wrote to grief.
>
> I wrote as Witness before I even knew Poetry could witness.
>
> I wrote to remember my joy and to understand my anger.

Brother Bullet is primarily a narrative book meant to communicate grief straightforwardly. I had no intention of being formally inventive. The book has more in common with what is considered "low art" than "high art" because I wanted my work to be accessible. Accessible poetry and art may be looked down upon, but I have found so much value in developing a type of kinship with readers of my book who may not usually read poetry but are drawn to *Brother Bullet* because of the topics. When I was working on revisions, a part of me wanted to revise the project into something more experimental, something that might be considered more "artistic" and would create more distance between my grief and my words. But I decided my revision should not radically change my book or intention. I felt like there was an audience who could appreciate my direct narrative approach. I try to keep this in mind when providing feedback to others—that it is possible to polish work to a point that the work feels more intellectual than visceral. It is up to the writer to determine where they want their work to be on this continuum. I can use a writer's intention to guide my feedback as a teacher, as some of my best poetry mentors have done for me. I was fortunate to have Dana Levin and Luci Tapahonso as two of my first poetry teachers who facilitated my development as a poet while encouraging me to develop my own voice.

As an undergrad, I studied apparel design, but before that, I learned the basics of sewing from my mother. She learned from her mother. When I was very young, my mother would take me to the sweatshop where she and my Grandmother worked when she didn't have someone to watch me. The sweatshop is first memory and second womb. The room is rumble, buzz, and clank. Bodies in motion, their backs bend, thighs press and release the machines to start and stop them; hands slide forward, guiding fabric through industrial needles.

Someone is always push-brooming through a chorus of women's voices flowing and forming in clusters of languages. I'm supposed to be quiet—invisible. But I do not need reminders.

In high school, my mother would sew about half of my clothes. Back then, fabric was affordable, and several local fabric stores were in the neighborhood. The money she could have spent on my new school clothes would go further if she made a good portion of them. It was both a practical and creative outlet. When we would go to the fabric store, she would gravitate to bright colors and bold patterns. Mother thought my fabric choices could have been more exciting and more fun. She saw fashion as an opportunity for play, humor, and personality. I now recognize this style as a part of rasquache. In Stacy I. Macías's essay "(Ad)Dressing Chicana/Latina Femininities," she explores how "Chicanas/Latinas produce and channel racialized rasquache raunch aesthetics by dressing, making up and embellishing and encoding the body as explicitly non-white as unbound by contemporary trends and time."[3] But in high school, I saw fashion as a means of fitting in. I wanted to be muted. Perhaps, I worried that bright colors would be a sign of bad taste or someone would notice that my clothes were homemade. These days, I'm not afraid of colorful fabrics or bold patterns. I am drawn to them. I care less about what others think. After so many years of trying to downplay my body's excessiveness and eccentricities, I feel welcomed by the style.

I come full circle in many ways, returning to myself in my writing and fashion. Going to school for fashion is a lot like going to school for creative writing. I learned essential craft elements like flat pattern making, draping patterns, sewing, and other necessary skills. We were often given assignments with set parameters and critiqued by our classmates. And at the end of all this, I had learned many skills but was no longer passionate about apparel design. Creating is a lot of work, no matter the medium, but there should also be joy. These days, I try to honor my original sense of storytelling and expression as a way back to the pleasure of creating in various mediums.

Recently, I had conversations with friends of color from my MFA. We shared a similar sentiment about the difficulties and lengthy process of breaking free from what we had been taught in graduate school to develop our own aesthetics and styles. It seems possible now that we are older and farther along in our writing journeys to use the craft we learned in our MFAs, so we can take what is useful to us and challenge what prohibited us from being explicitly ourselves.

I have been experimenting with using visual images in my poetry process when I feel uninspired or want to challenge myself to approach a topic differently. I am intrigued by creating my own maps or annotations to maps and creating other visual documents that speak to my histories and experiences. My desire to create something more than words has meant pushing myself into discomfort. I am self-conscious of my lack of experience, skills, and knowledge of digital arts. And I don't always even trust myself enough to know to distinguish whether what I create is amateurish or whether it is a part of my vision. But I do it anyway. I try again and again until I have pieces that are almost how I imagined them.

Embodying rasquache in my work challenges me not to take myself so seriously. It gives me permission to play and fail. It gives me permission to use what I have available. It challenges me to see the rough edges, the loose hem, or the visible edge as its own aesthetic.

Years ago, at a poetry event in Los Angeles, one of the readers made a stereotypical Native American gesture which I found offensive. My voice cracked, but I tried to discuss the issue with the non-Native poet and was told I was wrong for being offended. I left unsatisfied, and to be ignored in my homelands made me angry. My poetic response is partially in the Tongva language, even though my knowledge is minimal. I used my traditional language to center and ground myself in my history, culture, and family. I wanted to ground myself in what we have as opposed to what has been taken or what we lack. In the poem, I write,

Che'eenaxre	We are singing—
Yaraarkomokreme' 'eyoohiinkmo honuukvetmo	We remember our ancestors;
Yaraarkomokre'e 'eyoo'ooxono.	We remember our land.

My tongue will stumble over these words, and I tell myself not to be ashamed. These words are the results of my people choosing to remember and choosing to fight for reclamation. I want to honor their work and love here, even if I need to speak with an embarrassed tongue. Like my parents and ancestors, I can create from all I have. When I work with children or those learning English in poetry workshops, I often notice a willingness to play that can often result in exciting and creative work. If we fear failure, then it might limit our creativity. And often, our "failures" are not really failures but lessons we can build from.

As someone who is also California Indian (Tongva/Luiseño/Cahuilla), I find that the act of reclamation is vital in my creative work and life. It is far too common for Indigenous peoples and their stories to be erased. But due to the violent history of colonization, which has impacted both sides of my family, what I have to reclaim is fragmented.

While working on new projects, I learned that some of my female relatives and ancestors didn't always have autonomy over their bodies. I also learned about other ancestors who had to make difficult choices for survival's sake. Sometimes this involved aligning with settlers or hiding their Indigenous identity. I experienced profound anger and sadness during the research process. It is not that I didn't know some of this history. But again, I had only had fragments that I was now putting in context to the history of colonization. I was now immersed in violence that I could directly see had negatively impacted my communities in so many ways.

There was the California mission system, the unratified treaties, and land dispossession. I needed to acknowledge these complicated feelings but didn't want them to paralyze me. My research involved reading many primary historical sources, which tend to be written from settlers' perspectives, which often silence Indigenous voices. The further I went into my research, the more Indigenous scholars and narratives I read, including family members whose perspectives pushed against these settler narratives and worked to fill in the gaps. Chicana artist Amalia Mesa-Bains argues that

> In rasquachismo, the irreverent and spontaneous are employed to make the most from the least. . . . Aesthetic expression comes from discards, fragments, even recycled everyday materials such as tires, broken plates, plastic containers, which are recombined with elaborate and bold display in yard shrines (capillas), domestic decor (altares), and even embellishment of the car. In its broadest sense, it is a combination of resistant and resilient attitudes devised to allow the Chicano to survive and persevere with a sense of dignity.[4]

I easily recognized that what Mesa-Bains described is embodied in my family and communities. My father is always saving mechanical parts in case he needs them someday. It is not uncommon for him to pull something out of the trash that could be reused or fixed or was accidentally thrown away. My mother embodies rasquache in her own way. She is skilled at composing a tasty meal with random ingredients. And in my current work, I am inspired by the fragments of the Tongva language, family stories, and photos that are accessible to me.

I want my creative work and lived experience to be one of reclamation. I want to center our perspectives and stories. This is work. This is a process. I worry about mis-stepping. I try to come from a humble place. *I take one step at a time.*

In mainstream society, we are often encouraged to "get over" our trauma and grief quickly. But grief and our responses to trauma are not linear, nor do they have expiration dates. A Rasquachismo aesthetic encourages me not to turn away from difficult subjects, and not to be ashamed of my wounds that are still healing. In *Brother Bullet*, I wrote:

> After Bullet night
> I promise to never turn away from the rib of the left behind,
> the long scope of loss.

This is a promise I have made to myself and my writing. Although Rasquachismo is rooted in Chicanx and Mexican culture, expressions of it can be seen within other cultures where there is a need for innovation. Rasquachismo is ever-evolving and customizable, making it a useful approach for art and poetry, especially Indigenous poetry. Drawing from the traditions of Rasquachismo has strengthened my vision of my work. It is also incredibly meaningful that I can draw from and apply culturally relevant Indigenous epistemologies to my creative work, which I consider my calling and that are in conversation with the communities I love.

Notes

1. Haleema Shah, "Why the Chicano Underdog Aesthetic 'Rasquachismo' Is Finally Having Its Day," *Smithsonian Magazine*, February 14, 2019, www.smithsonianmag.com/smithsonian-institution/why-chicano-underdog-aesthetic-rasquachismo-having-its-day-180971490/.

2. Tomás Ybarra-Frausto, "Rasquachismo: A Chicano Sensibility," in *Chicano Art: Resistance and Affirmation, 1965–1985*, ed. Richard Griswold del Castillo et al. (Los Angeles: Wright

Art Gallery of the University of California at Los Angeles, 1991), 155–179.

3. Stacy I. Macías, "(Ad)Dressing Chicana/Latina Femininities: Consumption, Labor, and the Cultural Politics of Style in Latin Fashion," in *Mexicana Fashions: Politics, Self-Adornment, and Identity Construction*, ed. Aida Hurtado and Norma Cantu (Austin: University of Texas Press, 2020).

4. Amalia Mesa-Bains, "'Domesticana': The Sensibility of Chicana Rasquache," in *Chicana Feminisms: A Critical Reader*, ed. Aida Hurtado et al. (Durham, NC: Duke University Press, 2003), 208–315.

Bibliography

Macías, Stacy I. "(Ad)Dressing Chicana/Latina Femininities: Consumption, Labor, and the Cultural Politics of Style in Latin Fashion." In *Mexicana Fashions: Politics, Self-Adornment, and Identity Construction*, edited by Aida Hurtado and Norma Cantu. Austin: University of Texas Press, 2020.

Mesa-Bains, Amalia. "'Domesticana': The Sensibility of Chicana Rasquache." In *Chicana Feminisms: A Critical Reader*, edited by Aida Hurtado et al., 208–315. Durham, NC: Duke University Press, 2003.

Shah, Haleema. "Why the Chicano Underdog Aesthetic 'Rasquachismo' Is Finally Having Its Day." *Smithsonian Magazine*, February 14, 2019, www.smithsonianmag.com/smithsonian-institution/why-chicano-underdog-aesthetic-rasquachismo-having-its-day-180971490/.

Ybarra-Frausto, Tomás. "Rasquachismo: A Chicano Sensibility." In *Chicano Art: Resistance and Affirmation, 1965–1985*, edited by Richard Griswold del Castillo et al., 155–179. Los Angeles: Wright Art Gallery of the University of California at Los Angeles, 1991.

Colliding Heartwork and Poetry

Writing about the Legacy of Colonial School Systems

Natahnee Winder and Tanaya Winder

Máykh, we are nana namminu (sisters) writing this chapter. To honor Indigenous protocol, we first acknowledge the Indigenous Nations' ancestral and traditional lands where we reside and work. The majority of this chapter is written on our traditional homelands of the Piinu Nucchi (Southern Ute Tribe) where we grew up. The part of this chapter was developed and drafted on the traditional, ancestral, and unceded lands of the Kʷikʷəλ̓əm (Kwikwetlem), Səl̓ilw̓ətaʔɬ (Tsleil-Waututh), Sḵwx̱wú7mesh Úxwumixw (Squamish), and Xʷməθkʷəy̓əm (Musqueam). The rest of the chapter was crafted on the traditional homelands of the Tuf Shur Tia (Pueblo of Sandia). Next, we will introduce ourselves.

Our mother's side of the family is Cui Ui Ticutta (Pyramid Lake Paiute) and Bḥya' Baa' Niwine (Duckwater Shoshone). On our father's side, we are Diné (Navajo), Piinu Nucchi (Southern Ute), and Tuuttaipo (Black). We were raised on the Piinu Nucchi reservation with a strong Nuuch(i) (Ute) identity and continue to participate in ceremonies throughout the year. During the summers, we visited and stayed with our maternal grandparents in Pyramid Lake until it was time to return to school. We are both enrolled members of the

Bhya' Baa' Niwine. Natahnee Winder is an assistant professor at Simon Fraser University with the Department of Indigenous Studies and the School of Public Policy. Tanaya Winder works for NDN Collective and is a poet, writer, artist, and educator. We are both alumni of the University of Colorado Boulder's Upward Bound program and University of New Mexico in Albuquerque.

In this chapter, we share our relationship with poetry and the gift of storytelling as nana namminu who are weaving together our family connections to the residential school system in the settler state of the United States. We are on a journey to create a canvas of creative works to honor their truths and describe how our hearts collide to initiate the healing process both individually and collectively. As Indigenous women warriors, we have a passion to honor and give back to Indigenous communities through our heartwork contributions as a healing mechanism for processing the traumas from and aftermath of the intergenerational impacts of the Native American Boarding School and the Indian Residential School systems in the United States and Canada. The term *residential school* will be used to refer to the assimilating institutions that the two settler states of Canada and United States forced Indigenous children to attend. This healing heartwork occurs by sharing how we use poetry as a pathway to ignite a flame for therapeutic healing, one where we trust the direction the fire burns and smoke leads as the fire grows to create a continuity of dialogue about intergenerational impacts. This chapter was developed applying a recorded storytelling approach between two sisters, Natahnee Winder and Tanaya Winder, in the spring of 2022. Our methodological approach to this chapter used storytelling, which consisted of excerpts from our recorded narrative of how we were introduced to and developed our poetry craft, a brief overview of colonizing school systems in the settler states of Canada and the United States, applying Colliding Heartwork and poetry, and how we use poetry for healing and processing the residential schools, which features our collaborative work.

Colliding Heartwork and Poetry

Colliding Heartwork stemmed from the research findings of Indigenous university students' personal experiences with the impacts of the residential schools in the settler states of Canada and the United States. Colliding Heartwork is "the emotional work [that] allows for healing and learning" about the assimilationist

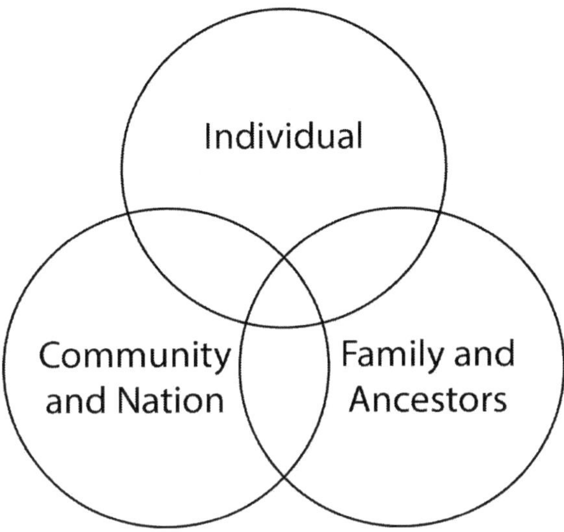

The Individual Collective Self

policies and colonial educational systems where individuals become "completely vulnerable to the emotional side" of learning.[1] Colliding Heartwork is applied to poetry because it is a self-reflective process that creates links to allow for empathic feelings to connect in shared experiences. Colliding Heartwork is where three aspects of a person's collective self or identities—individual, community and nation, and family and ancestors—intersect.

These three interpersonal connections are an individual's collective self. Although we did not attend these institutions, we have been impacted. When writing about the ongoing consequences and resiliency of Indigenous Peoples and family members who attended these institutions, we can write from the perspective of ourselves, our community and other Indigenous Nations, and finally, family and ancestors. Therefore, when we employ Colliding Heartwork as poetry, it is "an exposition of empathy towards traumatic events or histories" and represents the passions of Indigenous Peoples who uphold their communities, which "bridges our hearts to reflect, and to come to a common understanding of where diverse Indigenous histories and lived experiences intersect."[2]

We applied the framework of Colliding Heartwork and writing poetry to pay homage to our Indigenous relations and other Indigenous communities by offering prayers for their individual and collective healing and to honor the Indigenous children who did not return. Poems are a method of storytelling and, as such, these stories "tell the truths of [Indigenous] presence in the world today, in days past, and in days to come."[3] Poems helped us to make sense of the world and of our lived experiences as well as connecting us to other Indigenous relations. We immersed ourselves in feeling the ongoing impacts of settler colonialism. In working through traumatic events, we allowed ourselves to be comfortable with being uncomfortable. It is a strength to embrace the beauty of being vulnerable, where we can reach a climactic focal point. This is where our unique emotions and feelings become meshed, hence, where our hearts collide. There are five phases of Colliding Heartwork: (1) Preparing Our Hearts, (2) Opening Our Hearts, (3) Developing Empathy of Our Hearts, (4) Renewing Connections to Our Hearts, and (5) Colliding Hearts. Phase 1: Preparing Our Hearts is where we have relationships with others and how we prepare ourselves to initiate writing poetry about the impacts of the residential school system in order to begin the healing process. As nana namminu, we both have different journeys to becoming poets, which will be explained in the first phase of Colliding Heartwork. We rekindled the fond memories about our introduction to poetry and our learning processes to write poems during our youth. Preparing Our Hearts to write about the impacts these colonial institutions had on ourselves, family, community, and Indigenous Nations was stringing the first bead and selecting the colors (memories) to identify our connections, build rapport as poets, and find our commonalities.

Preparing Our Hearts: Learning about Poetry

NATAHNEE: Where did I learn about poetry? I remember first being introduced to creative writing in elementary school and learning to write haiku poems. My next memory is writing an original story in Dr. Black's class in the fifth grade. I wrote a story about swimming in Pyramid Lake and how it was an adventure to get there. I don't think that is really poetry, but it is similar. For me, poetry is the ability to craft a story. Later, I was immersed in poetry writing for a creative writing course during the Upward Bound program as a rising high school sophomore. Creative writing was my favorite class because I learned so much about myself. I channeled my feelings about being homesick, missing family, and friends into my poems. I felt it helped to connect with myself and gain more of an understanding and compassion for my identity as not being a fluent speaker of Ute or Shoshone. I loved Upward Bound and the lifelong friendships that I made. I also realized how fortunate my peers were because they could speak their languages fluently.

TANAYA: I have a similar introduction to poetry. I remember being in fifth grade writing limericks about leprechauns. Then, years later in the same Upward Bound program, I had my world rocked in that creative writing class. Our instructor showed us a scene from a movie called *Slam*. The pivotal scene we were shown started with the main character performing a poem in the prison yard; his poem immediately captured everyone's attention, stopping a fight from emerging. I thought how powerful poetry can be to incite reflection, change, and movement. That experience planted the seed for me wanting to become a poet. Later, I went on to study creative writing at Stanford and ultimately received my MFA in creative writing from the University of New Mexico. But I never knew that poetry was a form of medicine. I never thought it would help me heal the soul wounds I needed to process.

NATAHNEE: I am not a poet by training. I feel that writing poetry is a powerful outlet to release my emotional distress, pain, and frustrations, especially from letting go of the aftermath of traumatic situations. When there is no release or a door to let go of one's hurt, it starts to build up in your body and mind. I write poetry as a way to heal and make connections—empathize with other individuals—to inform, educate, and let them know I am here to help carry the load of that pain so healing can occur.

After sharing how we were introduced to poetry and creative writing, our conversation shifted to feelings about learning of the burial site of the 215 children at the former Kamloops Indian Residential School and talking about the ongoing remnants of the residential schools in the lives of Indigenous Peoples across Turtle Island. We talked about how the two settler states, Canada and the United States, have similar trajectories, histories, and policies to assimilate, civilize, and erase Indigenous Peoples. As descendants of Survivors, we "hold our stories close to the heart," because acts of truth-telling "shape us, uplift us, hurt us," because these stories are continuously passed down among family and community members.[4] We identified these colonial patterns of assimilationist agendas. Through our conversation, we established a healthy and safe space to reflect and share how these two countries' policies and practices are linked to each other and have similar outcomes. As stated by Brenda Child, these colonial institutions are comparable since they were "created out of a colonial desire for Indigenous assimilation and lands."[5] These colonial institutions were also entrenched in how "ethnocentrism drove assimilationist English-only education" for Indigenous students.[6] In addition, there were a variety of different outcomes from accounts of traumatic experiences, academic and economic disparities, and attacks on Indigenous languages, and cultures that were rooted in assimilationist policies.[7] Colliding Heartwork is a process of unpacking the emotions and feelings of a single (or several) event, situation, memory, or story impacting Indigenous Peoples. Poetry allows for the peeling back of emotional layers in one's heart, to create a process for opening, melting, connecting, and reconnecting. This process allows participants to weave together heartwork fibers for difficult conversations to take shape through constant reflection to learn, unlearn, relearn, and process the impacts of residential school for both Indigenous and non-Indigenous Peoples.

Opening Our Hearts: Our Initial Reaction to the Unmarked Graves of Indigenous Children

There exists a narrative that Indigenous Peoples need to move on from the past harms of assimilation policies. Yet the impacts of the colonizing education are like osmosis and creep into our lives when we least expect it. For instance, the Tk'emlúps te Secwépemc Nation announced the finding the remains of 215 children in unmarked graves on May 27, 2021, at the former Kamloops Indian Residential School in British Columbia, Canada. The findings sent shock waves and expressions of heartbreak throughout Indigenous communities, the Canadian national consciousness, to Prime Minister Justin Trudeau, universities, news networks, Canadians, and more. The findings increased international awareness of the Indian Residential Schools; but for many Indigenous Peoples, news of the children's remains substantiated what they already knew had happened at these colonial institutions. Tk'emlúps te Secwépemc Kukpi7 (Chief) Rosanne Casimir stated that the identification of the children confirmed "an unthinkable loss that was spoken about but never documented by the Kamloops Indian Residential School."[8] This announcement created a wave of immense sadness and heavy hearts that swept through Indigenous communities in Canada, the United States, and other Indigenous Nations and individuals across the globe. In addition, Interior Secretary Deb Haaland, Laguna Pueblo, expressed deep sorrow for the loss of Indigenous children at the residential schools in Canada; she also launched an in-depth investigation into the burial and unmarked graves at the Native American Boarding Schools.[9]

Indigenous Peoples have long been aware of children going missing and not returning to their communities after being sent to federally mandated institutions that have sought to erase our Indigeneity. While the settler states of Canada and the United States grapple with the unearthing of Indigenous children at these institutions, Indigenous Peoples are reminded of our own ancestors and family members who attended these schools. We think about the unimaginable grief and pain of the families and communities of the missing Indigenous children. We empathize and mourn with them, too. Since May 2021, over one thousand unmarked graves at residential school sites have been identified across Canada in British Columbia and Saskatchewan.[10] According to the Truth and Reconciliation Commission of Canada, a minimum of 139 residential schools may have one cemetery and possibly more, which makes it difficult to identify the number of children who died at these institutions and how many are buried.[11] The U.S. Interior Department's report *Federal Indian Boarding School Initiative* was released on May 11, 2022, and identified an estimated fifty-three schools with marked or unmarked burial sites where more than five hundred children died.[12] Many Indigenous children did not return to their families and homes. As descendants of Survivors, we honor the lives of Indigenous children who never had a chance to revisit their families and homes. We honor them by using poetry to bring awareness, share, empower, and demonstrate the resiliency in their stories so that they are not forgotten, because their memories live in our hearts. Poetry allows us to time travel, to revisit the rubble and reshape its meaning into something new, something tangible and healed. Poetry breathes life into our family members' testimonies, and we share them in the hope of resonating empathy for others to care about the impacts these institutions continue to have on Indigenous Peoples.

TANAYA: It almost feels surreal when you hear about things like Kamloops. Like we all know, these things happened to our people but it's hard to believe that so much pain and trauma was caused by this evil in the world, and that evil came from a place of hate from people who didn't believe we were worthy living, of being humans with our own culture, language, and ways of being. It's heartbreaking knowing so many babies and young innocent sacred beings were taken and never got to return to their home and loved ones. Whenever I hear about residential schools, I think of Grandma. She survived so much and came through the other side still so positive, hopeful, and full of love. That makes me think how powerful and strong our people are because we never lost our love; that's the strongest part of our spirits.

NATAHNEE: I cried when I heard about the children at Kamloops. We're taught that children are gifts from the Creator. I felt heartbroken that children were not cared for and seen as a blessing to the school officials. I also thought about our relatives who attended these institutions and what would have happened if they hadn't survived. My heart went out to the families of the children and to their communities. I think of Grandma, too. She was resilient and cherished family bonds.

The forced removal of Indigenous children by the settler governments of Canada and the United States has been described as soul wounds that can open scars, and have been referred to as intergenerational trauma and historical unresolved grief.[13] Indigenous Peoples have experienced numerous historical trauma events also referred to as soul wounds—from colonization, ongoing settler colonialism, residential schools, loss of land, and so on.[14] Indigenous Peoples experience historical unresolved grief accompanied by the trauma they experience.[15] As practicing poets, we use writing as a mechanism for processing the ruptures from trauma both with the students and community populations we work with and teach and in our journeys to healing soul wounds.[16] We journey into the third phase of Colliding Heartwork, Developing Empathy of Our Hearts, which involves being a listener and active participant, being a facilitator (storyteller), and embracing emotions and feelings.

Developing Empathy of Our Hearts: Our Connections to Residential Schools

We have many relatives who attended these colonizing institutions on both our maternal and paternal sides: great-grandmothers, grandmothers, great-grandfathers, grandfathers, great-uncles, great aunties, and cousins. Some of our relatives attended these institutions—such as Bacone, Haskell, Southern Ute, Stewart, and Teller—for most of their lives; others went for a few years. Our family history is complex when it comes to the residential schools. For instance, there were relatives that later became matrons. Even though our great grandparents and maternal grandmother were fluent speakers of their traditional language, they did not pass it onto their children and grandchildren.[17] While we are not fluent speakers, we are blessed that our family was resilient enough to pass down important teachings and ceremonial songs. As a family, we continue to participate in our traditional ceremonies and gatherings, and are relearning our language.

How do we utilize the stories from our relatives to shape our poetry? We became active listeners and participants in the healing process from these institutions to facilitate their stories through telling, retelling, sharing, and honoring their lived and living truths. This intimate exchange of stories woven with collective emotions and feelings about shared family experiences creates an inherent space that gives rise to an empathetic learning environment in which we can open our hearts to understand and relate to our family members. These blood memories of felt experiences form knowledge about familial history, culture, and spirit, and are connected for lifelong Indigenous learning, which represents "a significant, contemporary, paradigmatically-challenging point of explanation" to Indigenous existence. These memories help with our healing because they are "the significance [that form the] deep connections with our ancestors" by using personal narratives.[18] We embraced our collective empathic learning by following up our conversation about how we applied researching colonizing schools and weaving it into our poetry writing.

TANAYA: I was never good at research. It still makes me feel impostor syndrome when I'm asked to research or do academic work. But this history is important to learn more about and requires those deep dives into our past because, like you said earlier, you can only outrun your trauma for so long, eventually it catches up with you. So how do you heal it? Researching, writing, and re-membering (putting yourself and the truth back together) is one way to begin healing.

NATAHNEE: There are so many ways to research residential schools. I examine the residential school literature, family stories, and the media to write about the impacts of these colonizing institutions on Indigenous communities and families. I write to assist with healing and to educate others.

The poem below is an erasure poem. It's a form of blackout poetry, where you take an original text and make something new by blacking out certain words. It's a process, a give and take between the words you choose to black out (or erase) and those you choose to keep (stay). The process brings about new meaning and demonstrates being in relationship with each other as poets and sisters doing griefwork, heartwork, and healing by taking a poem Tanaya wrote in response to our grandma's and relatives' residential school experiences and having my sister Natahnee do the erasure. The poem, "Extraction," below is what we came up with, using this shared emphatic journey of opening our hearts:

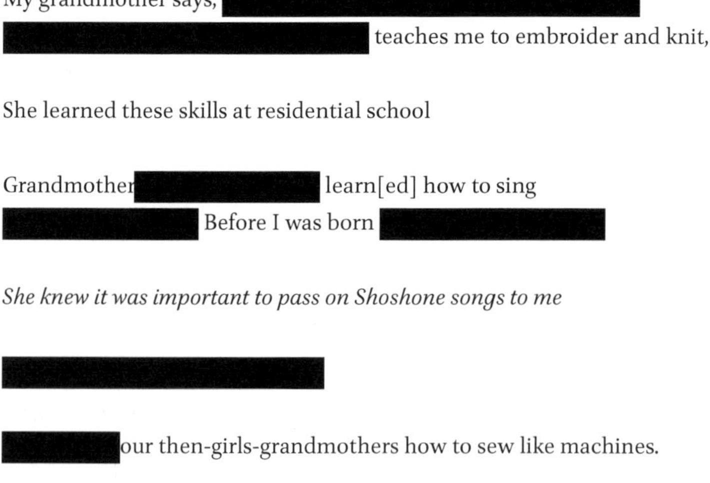

██████████████████████████

at residential school, which was passed on to my mother then to me

███████████████████

███████████████grandmother patiently teaches me words,
████████ she says. Mugua-vi means heart████████████████
███

My granddaughters you are my heart; Grandmother, you'll always be in our hearts

██████████████████████████████
████████████████████we knew how to keep breathing.

Grandmother waits for us in the Spirit World, we catch glimpse of her as we stare up at the milky way

I want to say████████████████████

I am grateful you held onto our traditions, and you didn't let the residential school fully assimilate you

█████████████████████████████████There is no word
for undo but many ways to say return. ███████████████

Grandmother, there are many Indigenous children being found at the burial sites

our fathers ██████████ and our mothers ███████████████

████████████████████████ were taken long ago.

Now, they are finally returning to their proper resting place
We are still searching ███████████ until we find every body

███████████ For as long as I can remember, we've been stolen:
from reservation to Industrial boarding schools and today

Grandmother, my heart hurts for our ancestors especially for our people who
try to run from the pain and consequences left by the residential school scars
████████████████████████████
I could find no word for this.

Intergenerational trauma, soul wounds, blood memories flood my mind and
spirit

███ yáakwi is to sink or disappear.

Are these the reasons my peers try to numb the pain?

███████████ When did we █████████████████
█ sew ████████ old scars, ██████████████

Why do we sometimes let settler colonialism win, Grandmother?

█████████████████████ when it comes to letting go
█████████████████ but my mouth wants to tell the story

Of how you survived this colonial institution to give birth so we could carry on
your legacy of resiliency,

███ the songs you still sing softly.

Colliding Heartwork involves being a storyteller of family history like
residential school experiences. The poet has an ethical responsibility to transmit

the emotions and feelings onto the page to share a loved one's story in a good way. We belong to our Indigenous Nations just as we belong to our families and communities. With this belonging comes accountability; we only share what family members give us permission to tell and share. Storytellers are Indigenous knowledge holders and keepers of lived and living testimonies.

Renewing Connections to Our Hearts: Applying Poetry as Healing

Poetry can heal the mind, body, and spirit. In *Why Indigenous Literatures Matter*, Daniel Heath Justice reminds us that stories speak to the greatness of where Indigenous Peoples came from and who we are meant to be and, more importantly, that Indigenous Peoples are not derived from colonial narratives of deficiency.[19] "We Grew Up Hearing Stories" is about the healing process as sisters and how we weave together our individual collective selves using Colliding Heartwork to renew our connections to our family history. Poetry opens the door for us to speak to our family members and ancestors who are in the spirit world and blends a therapeutic approach to make sense of the intergenerational impacts of colonial institutions in our lives. Poetry is more than stories, it is an ancestral connection that continues to grow, and every time each word is read or spoken, it gives life to its meaning.

> I.
> Tsaangu yeitataba**í** yi
> Haá. Tsaan dai neesungaahka
> Ishe hagade em má <u>ai</u>?
> Ishen nea hainji
>
> II.
> Tühpö'ni, Tühpö'ni, Tühpö'ni
> Indian Agents arrive.
> Muan fights to stop the door from opening,
> not wanting our Gagú pakahkwachan
> to [residential] school where rooms were filled with
> unspoken words, silenced prayers.

We grew up hearing the stories
of our grandmother's survival, Gagú told us
when she was taken they put her and her siblings in a police car
She wasn't sure there would be tekkappeh5
so she grabbed hershey kisses she'd saved,
hid the chocolate in her suitcase,
just in case they needed to eat.

Memories melt like seasons, the years
Grandmother lived away from her homelands, a survivor.
We ask, *"what happened, Gagú?"*
"They took us," she whispers.

Some children did not come back.
[Residential] school was a door you walked through
and became forever changed. You were there "to learn"
how to be white, how to be "American," and read
dusty chalkboards etched with foreign words.
Colonial history books showcase Newe1 and Nuucic with short hair
kneeling at their beds whispering Catholic prayers
to a God they didn't believe in.

III.
We gather shooting hoops,
our sneakers pounding cement,
against a backdrop of abandoned. A bricked building,
with grandiose shattered windows and graffiti filled walls.
What stories are hidden inside those
unspoken words and silenced prayers?

Piischiu grew up hearing the tüniyay
Where we could pönaati and kiyay and places we could not.
Some places hold shadows, a danger
not meant to be disturbed. Like the old [residential] school nearby,
Biá told us not to kiyay there,
"It's where people died." She learned this from her hutsí,

But, curious piischiu, went searching,
roaming the [residential] school grounds. Step by step
piischiu uncovered history: doors chained,
a sign with words in English: this place is off limits to kiyay
We could hear Biá's voice in the back of our minds—unspoken words,
silenced prayers.

IV.
We grew up hearing the stories
of our Gagú's survival. Gagú newe taikwa fluent
as a naipittsi who never forgot how to sing and pray.
She didn't pass on how to nuu'apagay,
but she passed on mapitsi'a and tsaan suankan
We grew up because of our grandma's survival.

As grown-ups, we tell the natekwinappeh,
of how Gagú' always remembered the newed<u>aig</u>wape
She would tell us, "newe taikwappeh."
So, we relearn our language like Gagú's recipe for bread,
something unwritten but remembered through body, movement,
and heart. We burn traditional medicines and sing songs with words
no longer unspoken, prayers no longer silenced.

We are strong, we are loud, we are resilient
because of Grandmother. Proud of who we are

Ute atsai sua'ah
Suwaay

In this poem, we renewed our connections with our ancestors, self and family, and community to generate a common understanding of these multifaceted experiences and how they accumulate in our hearts. We produced this reflective self to understand and relate to our grandma's experiences of colonial education as well as ours, those of other Indigenous communities and Nations as well as the experiences of our families and ancestors. All of these experiences manifested as a collective self that binds us together. These four phases of Colliding Heartwork culminated in the final phase, in which our hearts bridged through collective learning and processing to understand our personal connections, learning, and understanding of the residential school experiences.

Colliding Our Hearts: Collective Learning and Processing

Writing poems about the ongoing legacy of colonial education engages our familial experiences and helps us to understand our lives. Colliding Heartwork is an action and, when woven with poetry, forms a bond between the poet and lived experience, allowing them to move toward reconciliation, to acknowledge the trauma invoked through writing about communal, familial, and personal truths. In two poems, "Extraction" and "We Grew Up Hearing Stories," we applied the Colliding Heartwork framework to exhibit emotional responses in ourselves and readers, in an attempt to trigger an emotional response to the multiple losses and impacts that stemmed from Indigenous experiences at and with residential schools. As both Indigenous and non-Indigenous Peoples still need to learn, talk, and relearn about the atrocities of the residential school systems in the United States and Canada, poetry provides us—as educators, knowledge bearers, sisters, and relatives in relation with our home communities—a safe and culturally appropriate mechanism to forge an honest and transparent pathway for self and community healing. Our hearts collide so we can be empowered and use empathy to revitalize Indigenous languages, cultures, and traditions using poetry as a healing mechanism to strengthen Indigenous ties through collective understanding, learning, and unlearning about the ongoing effects of colonizing institutions. Breaking the silence means to talk and write about the aftermaths of these institutions, which helps us to heal others and ourselves. The power of feelings and emotions from using one's heart to prompt resiliency and a commitment to work with and for Indigenous communities without expecting something in return is rooted in heartwork.[20] Colliding Heartwork is another route to eliciting forgiveness within families, communities, and those who are healing from the intergenerational trauma of residential schools by using the power of collective feelings and emotions available through therapeutic poetry.

Notes

1. Natahnee Winder, "Post-Secondary Education (PSE) Indigenous Students' Perspectives: Sharing Our Voices on How We Fit into Residential School (RS) History of Canada and the United States Using Photovoice" (PhD diss., University of Western Ontario, 2020), 208.

2. Natahnee Nuay Winder, "Colliding Heartwork," in *Residential Schools and Indigenous Peoples: From Genocide via Education to the Possibilities for Processes of Truth, Restitution, Reconciliation, and Reclamation*, ed. Stephen James Minton (New York: Routledge, 2020), 159.

3. Daniel Heath Justice, *Why Indigenous Literatures Matter* (Waterloo: Wilfrid Laurier University Press, 2018), 2.

4. K. Tsianina Lomawaima, "Indian Boarding Schools, Before and After: A Personal Introduction," *Journal of American Indian Education* 57, no. 1 (Spring 2018): 12.

5. Brenda J. Child, "The Boarding School as Metaphor," *Journal of American Indian Education* 57, no. 1 (Spring 2018): 40.

6. Jon Reyhner, "American Indian Boarding Schools: What Went Wrong? What Is Going Right?," *Journal of American Indian Education* 57, no. 1 (Spring 2018): 70.

7. David Wallace Adams, *Education for Extinction: American Indians and the Boarding School Experience, 1875–1928* (Lawrence: University of Kansas Press, 1995); Angelina E. Castagno and Bryan McKinley Jones Brayboy, "Culturally Responsive Schooling for Indigenous Youth: A Review of the Literature," *Review of Educational Research* 78, no. 4 (December 2008): 941–993; John S. Milloy and Mary Jane Logan McCallum, *A National Crime: The Canadian Government and the Residential School System, 1879 to 1986* (Winnipeg: University of Manitoba Press, 2017).

8. Tk'emlúps te Secwépemc Nation, "Remains of Children of Kamloops Residential School Discovered," press release, May 27, 2021, https://tkemlups.ca/wp-content/uploads/05-May-27-2021-TteS-MEDIA-RELEASE.pdf.

9. James Hohmann, "Interior Secretary Deb Haaland on the Dark History of Indigenous Boarding Schools," *Washington Post*, podcast, June 25, 2021, https://www.washingtonpost.com/podcasts/please-go-on/interior-secretary-deb-haaland-on-the-dark-history-of-indigenous-boarding-schools.

10. Rhianna Schmunk, "How You Bring Them Home," *CBC News*, June 12, 2022, https://www.cbc.ca/newsinteractives/features/residential-school-remains-repatriation-rosebud-sioux-tribe-south-dakota.

11. Katherine L. Nichols, Eldon Yellowhorn, Deanna Reder, Emily Holland, Dongya Yang,

John Albanese, Darian Kennedy, Elton Taylor, and Hugo F. V. Cardoso, "Forensic Anthropology and Archaeology as Tools for Reconciliation in Investigation into Unmarked Graves at Indian Residential Schools," in *Royally Wronged: The Royal Society of Canada and Indigenous Peoples*, ed. Constance Blackhouse, Cynthia E. Milton, Margaret Kovach, and Adele Perry (Montreal: McGill-Queen's University Press, 2021), 203–229.

12. Bryan Newland, *Federal Indian Boarding School Initiative Investigative Report*, Washington, DC: U.S. Department of the Interior, May 2022.

13. Maria Yellow Horse Brave Heart and Lemyra DeBruyn, "The American Indian Holocaust: Healing Historical Unresolved Grief," *American Indian and Alaska Native Mental Health Research* 8, no. 2 (1998): 56–78; Winder, "Post-Secondary Education (PSE) Indigenous Students' Perspectives."

14. Eduardo Duran, Bonnie Duran, Maria Yellow Horse Brave Heart, and Susan Yellow Horse-Davis, "Healing the American Indian Soul Wound," in *International Handbook of Multigenerational Legacies of Trauma*, ed. Yael Danieli (Boston: Springer, 1998), 341.

15. Maria Yellow Horse Brave Heart, Josephine Chase, Jennifer Elkins, and Deborah Altschul, "Historical Trauma Among Indigenous Peoples of the Americas: Concepts, Research, and Clinical Considerations," *Journal of Psychoactive Drugs* 43, no. 4 (2011): 283.

16. We define *soul wound* as a "reaction to the multigenerational, collective, historical, and cumulative psychic wounding over time" that occurs over the lifespan of an individual's life and to their descendants." Duran, Heart, and Davis, *Healing the American Indian Soul Wound*, 341–342.

17. Winder, "Post-Secondary Education (PSE) Indigenous Students' Perspectives," 7.

18. Cora Weber-Pilwax, "It's in the Blood: Theory and Praxis of Lifelong Indigenous Education," *International Journal of Lifelong Education* 40, no. 4 (2021): 397, 396.

19. Justice, *Why Indigenous Literatures Matter*, 28, 4–5.

20. Robin Zape-tah-hol-ah Minthorn, "Being Brave in the Ivory Towers as 'Zape-Tah-Hol-Ah' (Sticks with Bow)," in *Counternarratives from Women of Color Academics: Bravery, Vulnerability, and Resistance*, ed. Manya Whitaker and Eric Anthony Grollman (New York: Routledge, 2019), 25–32; Tanaya Winder, "Heartwork," https://tanayawinder.com/heartwork/.

Bibliography

Adams, David Wallace. *Education for Extinction: American Indians and the Boarding School Experience, 1875–1928*. Lawrence: University Press of Kansas, 1995.

Castagno, Angelina E., and Bryan McKinley Jones Brayboy. "Culturally Responsive Schooling for Indigenous Youth: A Review of the Literature." *Review of Educational Research* 78, no. 4 (December 2008): 941–993. https://doi.org/10.3102/0034654308323036.

Child, Brenda J. "The Boarding School as Metaphor." *Journal of American Indian Education* 57, no. 1 (Spring 2018): 37–57. https://doi.org/10.1353/jaie.2018.a798599.

Duran, Eduardo, Bonnie Duran, Maria Yellow Horse Brave Heart, and Susan Yellow Horse-Davis. "Healing the American Indian Soul Wound." In *International Handbook of Multigenerational Legacies of Trauma*, edited by Yael Danieli, 341–354. Boston: Springer, 1998.

Hohmann, James. "Interior Secretary Deb Haaland on the Dark History of Indigenous Boarding Schools." *Washington Post*, podcast, June 25, 2021, https://www.washingtonpost.com/podcasts/please-go-on/interior-secretary-deb-haaland-on-the-dark-history-of-indigenous-boarding-schools/.

Justice, Daniel Heath. Why *Indigenous Literatures Matter*. Waterloo: Wilfrid Laurier University Press, 2018.

Lomawaima, K. Tsianina. "Indian Boarding Schools, Before and After: A Personal Introduction." *Journal of American Indian Education* 57, no. 1(Spring 20218): 11–21. https://doi.org/10.1353/jaie.2018.a798590.

Milloy, John S., and Mary Jane Logan McCallum. *A National Crime: The Canadian Government and the Residential School System, 1879 to 1986*. Winnipeg: University of Manitoba Press, 2017.

Minthorn, Robin Zape-tah-hol-ah. "Being Brave in the Ivory Towers as 'Zape-Tah-Hol-Ah' (Sticks with Bow)." In *Counternarratives from Women of Color Academics: Bravery, Vulnerability, and Resistance*, edited by Manya Whitaker and Eric Anthony Grollman, 25–32. New York: Routledge, 2019.

Newland, Bryan. *Federal Indian Boarding School Initiative Investigative Report*. Washington, DC: U.S. Department of the Interior, May 2022.

Nichols, Katherine L., Eldon Yellowhorn, Deanna Reder, Emily Holland, Dongya Yang, John Albanese, Darian Kennedy, Elton Taylor, and Hugo F. V. Cardoso. "Forensic Anthropology and Archaeology as Tools for Reconciliation in Investigation into Unmarked Graves at Indian Residential Schools." In *Royally Wronged: The Royal Society of Canada and Indigenous Peoples*, edited by Constance Blackhouse, Cynthia E. Milton, Margaret Kovach, and Adele Perry, 203–229. Montreal: McGill-Queen's University Press, 2021.

Reyhner, Jon. "American Indian Boarding Schools: What Went Wrong? What Is Going Right?" *Journal of American Indian Education* 57, no. 1 (Spring 2018): 58–78. https://doi.org/10.5749/jamerindieduc.57.1.0058.

Schmunk, Rhianna. "How You Bring Them Home." *CBC News*, June 12, 2022. https://www.cbc.

ca/newsinteractives/features/residential-school-remains-repatriation-rosebud-sioux-tribe-south-dakota.

Tk'emlúps te Secwépemc Nation. "Remains of Children of Kamloops Residential School Discovered." Press release, May 27, 2021. https://tkemlups.ca/wp-content/uploads/05-May-27-2021-TteS-MEDIA-RELEASE.pdf.

Weber-Pillwax, Cora. "It's in the Blood: Theory and Praxis of Lifelong Indigenous Education." *International Journal of Lifelong Education* 40, no. 4 (2021): 395–414. https://doi.org/10.1080/02601370.2021.1966528.

Winder, Natahnee. "Post-Secondary Education (PSE) Indigenous Students' Perspectives: Sharing Our Voices on How We Fit into Residential School (RS) History of Canada and the United States Using Photovoice." PhD diss., University of Western Ontario, 2020.

Winder, Natahnee Nuay. "Colliding Heartwork." In *Residential Schools and Indigenous Peoples: From Genocide via Education to the Possibilities for Processes of Truth, Restitution, Reconciliation, and Reclamation*, edited by Stephen James Minton, 141–162. London: Routledge, 2019. https://doi.org/10.4324/9780429463044-7.

Winder, Tanaya. "Heartwork." Tanaya Winder. https://tanayawinder.com/heartwork/.

Yellow Horse, Maria Brave Heart, Josephine Chase, Jennifer Elkins, and Deborah B. Altschul. "Historical Trauma Among Indigenous Peoples of the Americas: Concepts, Research, and Clinical Considerations." *Journal of Psychoactive Drugs* 43, no. 4 (2011): 282–290. https://doi.org/10.1080/02791072.2011.628913.

Yellow Horse, Maria Brave Heart, and Lemyra DeBruyn. "The American Indian Holocaust: Healing Historical Unresolved Grief." *American Indian and Alaska Native Mental Health Research* 8, no. 2 (1998): 56–78. https://doi.org/10.5820/aian.0802.1998.60.

On Overcoming the Anxiety
of Making Creative Work

Interview with Brandon Stosuy

Layli Long Soldier

How do you go about writing poems with prayer in mind?

When I talk about the poem as prayer, I mean it in the sense of process. I don't
know where to begin, but before I do share anything, I want to say it's a risk for
me to talk about things in this way, only because I don't want to sound like I'm
on some path forging new ground. This is ground that has already been covered.
I don't want to come off like a guru or something.

Prayer is something I've been thinking about recently . . . in many ways.
Prayer in its many version and applications. Maybe one of the things I've been
thinking about is some of my friends in Standing Rock, for example, and the
community there, how they insisted on prayer as being the primary tool for
resistance. That was central to everything they did. It really made me think
about that energy, that force, and what happens when we utilize it.

I have also just been thinking about prayer in terms of my own process,
which I think has always been there. I never really articulated it, so I don't know
where to begin. Maybe you can help me.

When you're writing a poem, do you have this idea of prayer in mind? Do you see the poem itself as some sort of "sacred text"?

Actually, no. I don't necessarily sit down and think, "Okay, this poem is going to be a prayer, or should be utilized that way," but I do think that when I begin writing. It's a part of my process. What I want to say is, maybe, being in a state of prayer as I write. I've heard this from other writers. When they sit down to write, sometimes they're terrified because we sit down, we know we've written poems before, but every time we sit down to write again, we don't know if we can do it again. We don't know if we can do it well.

There's a real vulnerability in that, a fear, and a threshold you have to cross. At least for me—I'll speak for myself—I have to acknowledge that trepidation, that anxiety in myself. I think it's at the very beginning point, in that vulnerability, where I have to begin to reach outward or rely on something else, not just of myself. That's what I mean when I say prayer is a part of my process.

Also, in writing or creating or making something, there's this process of accessing and relying upon the unseen. Again, I don't mean that in sort of this esoteric mystical way. I just mean even in ourselves, we are relying upon our minds and our imagination. Those are things we can't see. There's a sense of trust that we build within ourselves with the unseen. At the same time, I feel again, there's this thing outside of myself: I don't necessarily myself feel always capable of writing something "good," you know?

Whatever it is out there that's bigger than I am, that energy, can you help me out? Just help me out this evening as I sit down, and let's see what we can do. I'm willing to be helped.

How do you tap into that in the process when writing, of reaching out and finding that space?

There are a few things, even in the practical things I do. I'll mention just briefly the idea of ceremony. I don't mean ceremony that people just make up, but traditional ceremony. There are certain things that you do that are in place to put you in that state of prayer, physical things.

There are times of year for certain ceremonies, or what have you.

Just as a parallel, I'd even say for myself there are certain things I do. Maybe they're just cheesy. But, for example, my working hours are usually very late at night. Most of my poems have been written, I'd say between ten p.m. and four or five a.m. For me, there's something about the night that's very helpful. First of all, it provides a stretch of time, a block of time where there's not a lot of distraction. In order for me to think things through, I need that.

There's also something about nighttime in the sense that you're tired. When you get to that place of being tired, certain layers are stripped off and start to fall away. I find myself beginning to open up to things that I'm not necessarily going to be open to during the day, when I'm running around and taking care of practical things. That's part of my practice, to help me access that place.

Craft is a way, too. We need tools. We need things. Language is immaterial, but it's through certain devices or tools that we have in working with the language that I think, magically or miraculously, help me access that place as well.

Do you write at night when you have a manuscript in mind? Or is it something you do on a regular basis, no matter what?

It's like that all the time. I used to actually blame it on my daughter. I'd say, "Oh, it's because I have a child, so that's the only time I can find to write." But I had a residency awhile back, and I had time to myself without her. It was just my thing, about ten o'clock, I would crank up the coffee machine and set to work. Some of my peers would kind of scrunch their brows at me, like, "What are you doing?" But, yeah, it's something I do all the time, it doesn't always have to do with a project or a larger manuscript.

When you say that words are immaterial, what sort of more material things do you pull from to help you kind of harness the words?

Well, there are a few things. Sometimes I work with Lakota language in my poems, and that is always a beautiful source for me to turn to. I use Lakota dictionaries, but I also ask people how to say certain things. You know, I have conversations about our language with others. I think sometimes that even just one word can propel me into a thread that I might follow through on in a poem. I also think I'm always listening and collecting language, just English language.

Sometimes I'm pressed for time and I can't sit down and meditate for hours and hours. I will keep a running journal, for example, a little notebook of language that I encounter throughout the day—things I hear people say or little turns in phrase that are interesting. Then at the end of the day, I'll sit down and type those out. I see that like a palette of paint. I have a palette, or color scheme in mind. You know, as a painter, you might set out colors and think, "I'm going to work with this today." I'll do that with my journal: "This is what I have encountered today. Let's see what happens when I put them on the page. What are those connections and how can I work with them?"

You clearly have a specific process. Do you still find moments when you try to write and can't get past a creative block, even using your techniques?

For sure. I think that's why I also work in other mediums. Sometimes I have the urge to make something. Sometimes I want to make a poem but at that moment I can't for whatever reason, so I work with other materials. I like to do sculpture; my sculptures are usually more like objects. I also play music here and there, but I just do these things to kind of help me with writing . . . I use these other ways of making to help keep my wheels moving in one way or another, and eventually the language will come for writing. Sometimes I do get writer's block, but I have never really viewed it in that way. I still try to make things even if I don't have the language or words to put to it in at the moment.

I'll give you an example. I'm participating in an exhibit in Montreal, and I'm leaving on Friday. I'm going up to there, setting up some of my work. The exhibit is called *Drawing a Line from January to December*.

I was talking to another artist, Tanya Lukin Linklater—she's an Alutiiq artist from Alaska, and she invited me to participate. They were interested in me contributing text, but when we were brainstorming about what I might do for the show, all I could think of was making boxes at the time, which was really funny, like physically making boxes, which was not really what they were asking for. I said to her, "You know, I'm not sure what I'm going to do, but this is where I'm starting from. I want to do some boxes, but I'll certainly develop text to go with it as well."

In the end I did work on three boxes, which was my initial impulse. I have no idea why I just had to make these things, but in the end I made three 10-inch by 10-inch boxes out of balsa wood.

I was reading this poem by C. D. Wright in her book *One with Others*. There's this little line that she has that says, "There is sanctuary in the mind made of balsa and glue." It's so funny. I read that today.

After you made the boxes, did you end up writing the text to go with it?

Yes. This is what's crazy. I don't know how this all came together, but it all came together. It's a yearlong show. For all of the artists contributing work, there seemed to be a connection in our work that had to do with loss or grief. It made sense because winter is a time for thinking about some of those things, this idea of loss. I was meditating on that theme, on that subject.

In this last year, I've had a number of losses. I had a relationship end, a breakup that was very difficult. I also lost my grandma on my dad's side, and I lost one of my cousins in a very sad, tragic way. All these things happened sort of back to back in the last few months, and so it was something that was really on my mind.

I tried a whole bunch of different versions of text and different kinds of poems, and they didn't seem to feel right.

I ended up writing a poem about my grandmother. The thing a poem is, how does it go? "What a poem is about is not what the poem's about," right?

In any case, I had this dream. I said a prayer. I was praying, talking to my grandma one night before I went to bed. Then I had a dream—I woke up to this dream that same night. In that dream, I was teaching an art class. One of my students was selling sheets of balsa wood, of all things. They were $12 each. I said, "Oh, I want to buy some balsa wood from you. I want to buy some sheets. I need some balsa wood."

I reached into my pocket and I said, "I want two sheets." I reached into my pocket and I only had enough money for one. I had $16, not $12. I said, "Oh, I only have enough for one sheet." Then my student said, "No, you can keep them both, teacher." It was such a kind, generous act. I woke up and wrote down this dream. Then I wrote down the things I had been talking to my grandmother about.

Really, what I had been asking her was questions about love, about relationships. One of my main questions was, am I enough for someone? Of course, in a breakup, these are things we wonder . . . like, "What happened? What's wrong with me?" and so on. I was sitting there in bed crying to my grandma, "How come I can't find love? I'm not enough," all this.

I showed what I wrote to a friend, and he said, "My goodness, Layli, do you see what I see?" I was like, "What? What are you talking about?" He said, "You know, you asked if you're enough and then in your dream even though you only had enough money for one sheet, it was enough for your student. It was enough."

It was right there in black and white, in the text, this connection that even I had missed as the writer. I was like, "Oh my god, how did that work?"

Suddenly, it was this piece about my grandma and the boxes that I was so motivated to create, and I didn't know why. It all came together.

Note

From a conversation with Brandon Stosuy originally published on February 27, 2017, in *The Creative Independent*, https://thecreativeindependent.com/people/layli-long-soldier-on-poetry-as-prayer/.

The Memory Field

Musings on the Diné Perspective of Time, Memory, and Land

Jake Skeets

Memory is a touchy thing, and I mean that in the realest sense. The earliest memory I have is of my hand feeling the chin stubble of an older man. The room is evening-lit. My hand reaches out, and I graze the chin's prickly skin. The older man smiles. I can't see his entire face. I don't recognize the house we are in, but it feels like a small home. I see the color red, but I don't know what in the room is red. Maybe it's the man's jacket, made of a shiny fabric with a red band across the back and chest. I hear no sound, taste no thing, and I smell no distinct aroma. I can only feel the rugged chin and my hand gliding across it. Then, the smile of the man.

It won't be until after returning home from college that I learn the older man is actually my maternal grandfather. I was in the car with my family, and my mother was telling me the same story she has told me a thousand times: when I was an infant, my maternal grandmother would tie me to my high chair and spoon feed me. She also used to tie me to her chest and walk to the sheep corral to care for the goats.

This time, however, my mother told me a new story. She told me I used to reach out to my grandfather's chin, wanting to feel his stubble. I told her then that I remember an instance of doing that: my hand and his chin stubble. My mother nearly broke into tears. My maternal grandparents passed when I was still very young; I should have no recollection of them. Somehow, I remember that one moment between me and my grandfather.

In another early memory, I always see in the third person. I see myself coming out of my aunt's house. This moment tends to replay itself at random times. I can clearly make out the darkness of my eyes, my hair somehow a lighter brown than it is now, and my face scowling. I have a bowl cut, one of the many my father gave us when our hair grew too long during the summer. I stand there looking out toward my other aunt's house. I have on a blue T-shirt, and I remember having just eaten, because I feel full. I have this moment stained inside me: I'm looking outward and mad for some reason. I know it's late afternoon because the house casts a large shadow in the front yard that makes it cool enough to linger outside. I don't know much else about this moment, or why it's somehow repeated in the machinery of my mind. I also don't know why I see myself in the third person. Who is the *I* looking back at my former self? Is it my present self? Or was it my past self that etched that moment into my memory? I have repeatedly dissected this moment, trying to identify any real reason as to why it exists. The only thing that stands out to me from this memory is how dark my eyes are in the shade and the rough feeling of my aunt's house when I trace my finger along its outer wall.

Memory fields: pond by the windmill, lime-green skin, my cousin's fish tank, the sheep corral, dark soil, dark coffee.

One time, my brothers and I swam in a small pond by the windmill that came and went with the rain. Each monsoon, the pond would swell and buzz with a thousand tadpoles. The water was always cool. Suddenly, my youngest brother screeched in horror as he lifted his hand from the murk, clutching a green, lizard-like creature. It was long like a snake and had gill-like ears protruding from the side of its head. Its skin was lime-green and shockingly clean. It squirmed to be free of my brother's clenched fist. We ran from the water and onto the crusted surface dirt, careful not to excite the creature.

What had we caught? Was it a salamander, a newt, or a Loch Ness Monster pup sent here from across the world by harsh winds, dust storms, and ribboned rains? In my memory, that's what we asked. In my memory, we carefully extracted the creature from the pond and placed it into a glass pickle jar that we found in the rubble near the windmill until we got home. Once home, we filled the glass pickle jar with sink water so we could study the animal. Inside the jar, the animal magnified into a large beast as we watched its eyes dart back and forth. That night, we kept the beast at my house. The next day, my oldest cousin came by and picked the beast up to put it into his larger fish tank. I watched him fill the tank with tub water; a fine aquarium dust settled at the bottom. I remember sitting in his room while my cousins all played Nintendo and studying the beast as it danced in the tank, glowing and free. Its legs were dress-like: they flowed beneath its body, swirling around the tank in radiant glimmers. In a few days' time, the beast was dead. I never knew its name.

One time, my aunt came over in a panic. A huge storm passed through; I could see the black mud layered on my aunt's shoes as she barged into the house. Her face was wet and her eyeglasses were foggy. She explained that a lot of her goats were dead from a lightning strike. More of my aunts came over as the dark outside seemed darker than ever. I saw faint glimmers of lightning in the east as a cool wind calmed the storm down. My mom asked me to make coffee as everybody opened cookies and yeast bread to share. My aunts sat around the dining table sharing stories. Every now and then, they would transition back to discussing the task at hand: building a new sheep corral. After a few plans were made, they would venture off again into another time when this *thing* happened, or that *one time* that *one relative* did that *one thing* in town. They managed to travel through time without effort, in loud bursts of laughter and quiet sighs.

I remember putting a big pot of black coffee on the table. My aunt smiled and told me she liked my coffee best because of how strong I made it. Then, she dumped spoonfuls of powder creamer and sugar into her cup until the coffee turned beige. My aunt then gestured toward her cup, telling me with just body language to taste it. I picked up the cup and tasted the bittersweetness. I almost spit the coffee out and everyone laughed at my unwillingness to swallow it. I washed down the taste with some soda from the fridge and went to my room. I remember thinking about the sheep corral and the dead goats left there. I could smell the dark soil; the coffee tasted like it.

———

Memory is a physical construction. While memory is normally associated with the cognitive functions of the brain, I argue that memory's connection to time imposes its existence onto physical space as much as it does onto cognitive space. I am always fascinated by the idea that the starlight we see today is in fact old light cast out from a time existing simultaneously in the past, present, and future. The star's light began in its present, a past to us when we see it in our present, which is the star's future. I first learned this in seventh-grade science class. Astronomy and the periodic table stood out to me during those years. This course was my sixth class out of seven for the entire day. During the course, I would develop intense headaches, making it hard for me to concentrate. One day, I remember panicking because I couldn't see the periodic table on the chalkboard anymore. I told my parents and they took me to an eye doctor. I had inherited the hazy vision of my parents and a rather intense form of astigmatism.

I remember a lesson on color and our eyes' systems that give us the ability to see color on the day I returned to class with my new glasses. Light reflected off of objects creates the color we see, thanks to the technologies of our eyes. My teacher asked me to hand him my glasses to show the class. He explained that the need for prescription glasses is related to the ways eyes interact with light. Why he chose my glasses is beyond me—he, too, wore glasses. But I remember that particular moment: my seventh-grade teacher holding my glasses up before the class, as I watched the afternoon light shine through the lenses. Today, whenever I see sunlight shine through lenses or glass, I am reminded of that moment in that classroom when I learned that, because sunlight takes eight minutes and twenty seconds to reach the earth, the things we see are in some way a part of the past. Pasts, presents, and futures exist simultaneously.

There is a pond near my family's sheep corral. Whenever I see or remember the pond, I am reminded of many moments of my childhood, my past. The pond is a physical construction of my memory, much like sunlight passing through lenses. It's a memory field. The pond itself is small and sits at the entrance to the sheep corral. The pond also sits at the entrance to my childhood. It holds the moment my cousin stood in the pond with her overalls rolled up and dozens of tadpoles swimming around her ankles. She wore light and faded overalls with a stark-white shirt. Her hair was held back with a headband and flowed out in deep, dark curls. She covered her face with her hands as she squirmed at the touch of the tadpoles on her feet. Her clothes were new, and we both shuddered when we heard her father yell her name. We both knew the kind of trouble she would be in. I remember her slowly walking out of the pond, her head down.

She left footprints in the dark mud between us. I looked down and lifted my right foot slowly in an attempt to catch tadpoles on the top part of my foot. A few of them slid off as I lifted my foot out of the brown water. I heard yelling as the door shut behind my cousin. I didn't mean to get her in trouble. As I sit here typing, this moment of my past, the visceral experience of the moment is pulled from the past into the present (my child-self's future), and I feel these moments again. I feel the tadpoles swimming around my feet and the wind cooing as I watch my cousin walk toward her house. I sit back in my chair and think about the stories conjured from this pond, this physical and cognitive space.

Memory exists as a kind of spatiotemporal entity, because time, memory, and land are woven together. One cannot look at the Grand Canyon without conjuring the deep time needed to create it. We drive past restaurants, and maybe we remember that one time *that thing* happened. I grow weary of the word "spatial," because I am more interested in the idea of a terrestrial-temporal matrix. I call this terra-temporal matrix the "memory field" because of memory's unique engagement with time and land. Time is terrestrial and feeds our cognitive development and relationship to the universe itself. The word "terrestrial" also grows heavy; it has similarities with words like "sublunary," which place the terrestrial opposite a religious or spiritual space. The word "temporal" isn't adequate either. The memory field is a matrix of time, memory, and land. Land's connection to time feeds our development as human beings, and understanding this connection strengthens our relationship to the universe itself.

I talk often about the way energy conjured from landscapes finds its way into my poetry. Both the ponds near the sheep corral and the windmill enjoy an existence within my being as temporal, physical, and memory tools. Throughout our lifetimes, we develop many memory fields as we navigate humanhood in ever-changing times and environments. As we venture in and out of these fields, we are essentially participating in time and space travel. The act of remembering is a technology of the cognitive and physical parts of the human body. Radical remembering is the ability to travel through time, space, and existence. Radical remembering is connected to storytelling, which is an act of survivance for various Indigenous communities across the world. Radical remembering is a tool we hold deep within each of us that can help shape our lives, communities, and Nations. The memory field is the key to radical remembering.

In his book *Beyond Settler Time: Temporal Sovereignty and Indigenous Self-Determination*, Mark Rifkin argues that Native people exist in a timeless space, ever-changing between referential frames of time. Native people exist in a "precontact" past or within a "postcolonial" current, depending on which American consciousness and gaze are being employed. Native people are given the ability to transcend physical limitations of representation—they walk from spectacle to activist to spiritual to contemporary to dead. However, it is through memory that Native people reclaim a history both individual and collective, both personal and communal, both deeply intimate and extremely political. Memory is woven in a unique matrix with land, language, and time. Native people have already mastered time travel: they are able to conjure the deepest parts of humanhood through the act of memory. Radical remembering, then, has the potential to teach a way of being that isn't tied to a capitalist future but is instead reliant on the self's engagement with the natural world. I don't mean that we should return to precontact Native life, but we should push forward into a new realm of thinking about memory, time, and land. I can't provide an example of what this looks like, because there are no examples to pull from that exist in our physical reality. Instead, I turn to language and storytelling because of their connection to our memory fields.

Rifkin refers to the concept of simultaneity, which I've discussed before when addressing my own work within poetry. Chiastic structure in verse opens spatiotemporal reasoning within language. Within Standard American English (SAE), a sentence's syntax should be subject-verb-object: for example, "I am going to the store." Within Diné syntax, the sentence becomes "The store is where I'm going to." In fact, this sentence comes from Luci Tapahonso's poem "Hills Brothers Coffee." Within SAE, the subject is placed at the center and verbs into the world. Within Diné syntax, the spatial reasoning of the object is centered and therefore ignited within the reader's mind before the speaker and verb. In another example, "hello" is considered a standard greeting in SAE. "Hello" has a mixed past and is considered to be drawn from "hallo" or "hollo," which are words said to attract attention. However, according to a brisk Google search, "hello" is first referenced within the American West as a normal welcome when entering a house. One would utter, "Hello, the house," upon entering a home to announce themselves a friendly neighbor and not a savage Indian. Again, the subject verbs into the space. This space is then closed off from the frontier. The American home is immediately placed opposite the savage wilderness. Within Diné universe, *yá'át'ééh* is considered a standard greeting. However, *yá'át'ééh* has a much deeper translation that acknowledges the surroundings of the speaker and those around the speaker. Its loose English translation is "from the sky to the ground and everything in between we are here and it is meant to be this way." *Yá'át'ééh* acknowledges the landscape and offers back to the universe a sense of balance. This is needed now more than ever.

MEMORY FIELDS

> Pond, gill, reptilian green leather slick in brown hands
> A finger tracing a stucco wall
> a stubbled chin
> Blood rivering from the knees
> Like lightning striking a sheep corral
> A thousand tadpoles, looking like rain
> rattling the water

The memory field reveals a spatiotemporal existence through an acknowledgment of and engagement with time's physical self and the spatial contexts of that existence. When I introduce myself in Diné, I start first with my mother's clan. I've learned that it's also appropriate to identify where your mother's family is from both physically and historically. That is, one should always try to learn their family clan's stories and history. Then, I share my father's clan, my maternal grandfather's clan, and my paternal grandfather's clan. Again, you should always try to mention the homelands of these families and clans. This insight into the world and ways of introduction centers land and stories. Spatial contexts are centered in almost all ways of being within the Diné universe. There is order, and that order comes from a deep reverence for space. This spatial reverence is something I channel when I approach poetry on the page.

Poetry has a deep connection with the idea of the memory field. For me, a blank page becomes an altar where the memory field is teased into existence. The field of the page becomes a kind of physio-textual landscape, and it is the poet's job to render a blank page into a literal field using language. The job of the poet is to apply spatial reverence within both the field of the page and the physical constructions beyond the poem. I think of Diné weavers and the symbolism behind a loom. Diné weavers use organic materials found within nature to weave together a story, a memory field. The warp symbolizes rain, so Diné weavers are literally weaving time, memory, and land onto a rainstorm. Diné weaving holds an extreme reverence for the memory field. I argue that poetry should be no different. Poetry should have reverence for its land and landscapes. I'm not arguing that poetry should come with a land acknowledgment. Instead, I am arguing that the field of the page should do what the land does for us on a daily basis. One way to accomplish this feat is through radical remembering.

When one makes their way over the Chuska Mountains through Buffalo Pass—from Tsaile, Arizona, to Shiprock, New Mexico—they are met with the startling sight of Shiprock just over the summit point. The mountain sightline transitions into pink and orange sand stretched for miles in a flat plane of terrestrial glamour. Suddenly, the structure of Shiprock erupts from the surrounding flatness. There are many stories associated with Shiprock, and each time I make my way down I am reminded of those stories. I won't share them here, of course, but each time we pass Shiprock a story accompanies the geological phenomena. Shiprock, a holder of memories, becomes a memory field too. Each time we pass through these roads, my partner will mention a rock formation's name and explain the story behind its naming. He'll ask, "Do you know why they call those rocks that?" Then, as we drive either to or from the Chuskas, he will tell another story, and sometimes it's the same story about the rock formation and its name. Within the lexicon of Diné universe, Shiprock and similar images of snow, arroyos, and rock formations deal with the past, present, and future, because each comes with a story. If I were to name a few random images, such as reeds, knob, rainbow, corn pollen, virga, mesa, horse trough, chapter house, Burger King, and Lotaburger, Diné readers would each begin to travel through time and space into these memory fields, populating them and existing simultaneously in the past, present, and future.

Memory is a touchy thing, in that you can touch it. I often rub the scarring on my knees from when I jumped off a swing during the summer lunch program at Bread Springs Day School. My brothers, cousins, and I were swinging, and I jumped and landed knee first onto the side railing of the sandbox. I hopped up and looked at my leg; rivers of blood were gushing from both of my knees. I ran to the restroom to stop the bleeding. I remember thinking that if the cooks or caretakers saw me bleeding they would not let me go with the group into town. This summer lunch program would pick us up at our homes for a free breakfast meal. After, they would let us into the playground with giant swings and a really fast merry-go-round. Then, they would take us into town to watch a free summer movie at the theater or play at Ford Canyon Park. They would take us back to the school for a free lunch in the afternoon. After we finished, they would take us back to our homes. Today, I think about the blood gushing from my knees and my worry that I would be caught and punished for bleeding in the first place. That memory is literally scarred into my body; I am unable to forget it.

In a way, I am arguing for the recategorizing of land through radical remembering and the memory field. Today, we are faced with an onslaught of new challenges as wildfires roar into cities, hurricanes grow in the seas, and big freezes take entire communities by surprise. The American colonial project that marked much of the land as a wild frontier has led to this very moment. Through radical remembering, we are able to reclaim these wilds and frontiers as intimate parts of our very being. In that way, wilds and frontiers are transformed into homes and fields. They become part of the domestic, the intimate, and the spiritual. By reclaiming memory as a thing we can touch, we give a body to the memory machine that exists inside of our minds. It is this body that tells us stories. This body, our body, tells us stories. And sometimes our body listens for us to tell the stories of ponds, windmills, downtown buildings, apartment kitchens, dining tables, and tadpoles. We remember them and continue to remember them.

Note

First published in *Emergence Magazine.*

Shell Shaking Sisters
and Chain Cries Blues

Creole Tidalectics and Echolocative Self-Reflexive Rhetorical Praxis

Rain Prud'homme-Cranford and Carolyn M. Dunn

We whisper poems for navigation / make sure that we can find the way . . .
Because poems are a better map.
—Kim Shuck, "From Muscogee"

Part I. Ebbing Tides of Grief: From Tidalectics
to Echolocative Self-Reflexive Rhetorical Praxis

Stories

She dances with the storm itself, sorrow holds hands with hope . . . / Oya . . . /
becomes rain. / She tears it down to the dirt. / Clean for The People. A place to
build something better.
—Kelly Clayton, "Oya Dances the Bamboula: Congo Square, August 2005"

Ça fé inavé. Išak mon hoktiwe nakšo. We have a story to share.[1]

RAIN: Sitting looking out windows to the canal leading out to the Gulf of Mexico,
thunder rumbles in the muggy overcast sky. Palms bend in the wind as, an hour
and a half away, my mother sits, my father by her side having poison pumped
into her body—a body disabled by arthritis and radically compromised by
autoimmune illnesses. I have come to my parents' house by the Chassahowitzka
wetland preserve along the Gulf Florida coast. We are hoping to get another

year with my mother, who is battling lung cancer. When we first conceived of this chapter, Carolyn and I were navigating the loss of our Uncle-xukky, Papa Ken this spring and the loss of our Cane River Creole Matriarch, Mama Janet (Auntie-xukky), just two years prior.[2] Now, we have been watching my mother in the ferocious dance of radiation and chemo, as lung cancer attempts to tango her toward her ancestors. I am navigating waves, tides, of grief. Grieving is not finite. I am leaning on my sister-cousin, who continues the ever-ebbing and flowing process of grief—having watched both her parents cross the log decades earlier. My big sister sings me through this process, harmonizes, and tethers me in the tides.

CAROLYN: Grieving is a shroud worn in the midst of sun, chasing our ancestors home to the stars. Our people tend to die young, with some notable exceptions. Heart disease, cancer, all the various autoimmune disorders, particularly lupus SLE, which my child's pediatric rheumatologist told me impacts "Choctaw Indians at higher rates than any other tribe"—stalks us—claims us. Diseases of the heart/blood are churning waters that belie calm exteriors in the countenance of our kincestors.[3] Our elders, our parents' generation, are now passing the mantle to us, and sometimes, we are not ready. First, my sister, then my father and my mother walked on before their time should have allowed. This ever-present grief ebbs and flows like tides rolling against the land. Across Turtle Island from the Gulf of our ancestral homeland to the blue Pacific waters of California, across Creole-NDN diasporic lands, our grieving takes shape in ever-present waves of longing, loss, and hiraeth. We watch in uncertainty for my aunt's futurity as tides of grief, fear, and longing call a gathering song singing each one of us home to the stars—in time. The reality of losing our beloved elders brings us closer to becoming the generation who remembers—who follow our kincestors home.

RAIN: We echo from a place of water—the lands of Louisiana and Gulf of Mexico—like our ancestors who rose from salt shores. We mark ourselves through cartographic currents of land against water: "The ocean is a fact of life. One could say it is in our blood."[4] Water is a circuitry system carrying storied communications across Indigenous diasporas. In recent years, critics such as Tiffany Lethabo King, Stefanie Hessler, and Emilio Amideo have focused on the echolocative properties of Edward Kamau Brathwaite's (Barbadian Creole) tidalectics. Brathwaite exposes "hybridization is not restricted to land, but begins in maritime spaces and at the coast,"[5] wherein "tidalectics draws on" tidal movement, emphasizing "how cultural practices in the Black [and Indigenous] diaspora[s] have constantly been affected by both a going out and a returning movement."[6] Tidalectics as a neologism (tidal/dialectic) formulates "an oceanic worldview, a different way of engaging with" sea and sand/land. "Dissolving purportedly terrestrial modes of thinking and living, it attempts to coalesce steady land with the rhythmic fluidity of water and the incessant swelling and receding of the tides."[7] Tidalectics makes spaces for eco-intimacies between humans and more-than-humans, place/space, nonlinear circular currents, and circular time structures. It is foundational to Caribbean creolization and the cultural productions, histories, and epistemologies within Afro-Indigenous cultural diasporas.

Our poetic works speak to issues of cultural continuity through an embodied tribalography dependent on tidalectics of Gulf creolization. LeAnne Howe's (Choctaw Nation Oklahoma) tribalography upsets western constructs of time/place/space. Howe notes that within tribalography Indigenous peoples "pull all the elements together of a storyteller's tribe, meaning their people, the land, and multiple characteristics and all their manifestations and revelations" connecting "these in past, present and future milieus."[8] In essence, tribalography distills Indigenous story and geography into a neologism or philosophy of meaning-making inheritance. Event, geography (land), tribe/community, and memory, are interconnected. Further, Howe describes "embodied tribalography" as the ways we not only draw from our peoples, lands, and culture through intersecting time and space (tribalography), but also how those stories are carried *within* the body *and* the lands/waters (terrestrial/liminal spaces). Embodied tribalography "shows not only how one thing leads to another, but that movement across space and time, i.e., travel transforms us into something more than we are," so that we as Louisiana Creole people embody "the world and the land of the story" while our physical movements and manifestations "emplot[ted] the land with triumph, tragedy, renewal, and return."[9] And so we work as poets carrying not just our own weight but the weight of our kincestors and the land/waterscapes through the living stories embodied in our flesh. To Louisiana Creoles, this means an ebbing between sites of water (emergence, relocation, and arrival) and land (where creolization solidifies): tidalectics. Hence, story is foundational to our personal hermeneutics and also a lens or praxis inherent in our work. This storywork is educational and spiritual. Jo-ann Archibald (Sto:lo First Nation) defines storywork as:

> The four Rs of *respect, responsibility, reverence,* and *reciprocity* are traditional values and teachings demonstrated toward the story, toward and by the storyteller and the listener, and practiced in the storywork context. The other three principles of *holism, interrelatedness,* and *synergy* shape the quality of the learning process. Indigenous holism comprises the spiritual, emotional, physical, and intellectual domains of human development. holism also addresses the relationships among the self, family, community, wider world, and the environment. Effective storywork grows out of the actions of interrelatedness and synergy formed by the storyteller, the story, the listener, and the context in which the story is used.[10]

As Carolyn reminds me, storywork is connected to storyweaving: "the praxis of storyweaving also informs our work. Storyweaving is just as it sounds: piecing together of narrative and metaphor to tell a larger story, with text, image, sound, and movement, coming together in an echolocative tidalectic process carrying our collective stories from our kincestors home to us."[11] Storyweaving is a form of transrhetoricity. Rachel C. Jackson (Cherokee Nation Oklahoma) defines transrhetorical praxis as "the movement of rhetorics across multiple location categories—historical, spatial, temporal, cultural, local, regional, national, and global, as well as across disciplines . . . Transrhetorical analysis investigates relationships . . . between multiple sites of meaning making," linking across difference "ideas, issues, and events engage multiple groups and locations in the collective construction of meaning."[12] These processes of carrying (embodiment), building (storyweaving), and rearticulating (transrhetoricity) our embodied/inherited stories is what I have termed "echolocative self-reflective rhetorical praxis."

Echolocative self-reflective rhetorical praxis is a "way by which storied self-reflexivity creates a call-and-response pattern between personal story, community/familial/ancestral story, land, and language, towards recovery, resilience, restoration, and resistance. Through kinetic call-and-response transrhetorical processes we call ourselves into being by echolocating ourselves back to our kincestors in a continual circular ebb and flow between self, environs/

landbases, and our ancestors/kincestors."[13] Or, as Rachel Stubbs (Saulteaux descent) explicates, "It is the continual action of awakening narratives of our ancestors through our own storytelling. This framework allows me to consider my life as enacting the reciprocity of stories my ancestors told.... This suggests to me that there are proper and appropriate ways of both 'speaking back/with' and critically listening to my ancestors' stories."[14] This offers a way we poets situate our own embodied echolocative praxis of Louisiana Creole tidalectics on Turtle Island.

As a concept, this chapter weaves form, genre, theory, and practice as a call-and-response cowritten-dialogue in four connective parts. Moving from story to theory, conversation to applicable practice (creative production), we collectively seek to center narrative storytelling alongside methodological practices of storywork and storyweaving, in conversation with tidalectics and tribalography/embodied tribalography. Hence, this second section offers an "academic" articulation/definition of theory toward the storywork/weaving,[15] interview, and conversations explored in parts two and three. These middle passages offer a reflection of theory/praxis through conversational questions and stories between the authors, culminating in a sample of our cowritten creative praxis. Last, section four seeks to sing the story home, so to speak, uniting a personal-intellectual-creative-ecological scholar-poetics toward an understanding of "Creole Tidalectics & Echolocative Self-Reflexive Rhetorical Praxis."

CHORUS:[16] We have sought to be in conversation with other IBPOC poets, particularly Afro-Indigenous/Native/Creole/Caribbean and Global Indigenous poets, whose works we feel are in currents of conversation with our own themes, experiences, and whose works we write about, publish, and/or inform our own journeys: Kim Shuck (Cherokee Nation); Kelly Clayton (Louisiana Creole); Mona Lisa Saloy (Louisiana Creole/African American); Jenny L. Davis (Chickasaw Nation); and Junie Désil (African Canadian/Haitian-Kréyol). Thus, we model a communal call-and-response format exploring ways we, as poets, singularly and collectively, utilize Creole tidaletic poetics toward embodied echolocative self-reflexive rhetorical praxis. We offer through the water circuitry of tidalectics we navigate ourselves toward recovering ecological intimacies triangulating tidal ebbings between masses of land, language, and community toward Louisiana Creole kinships of resilience and resistance.

Part II. Relational Tributaries: Kinshipping Poetic Processes of Grief and Resilience

> Our names return / … / Saltwater Africans coupled to / Euro English, Irish, French
> … / Natives Choctaw, Houma, Natchez, and Alabama … / Families with roots like
> the / Live oaks firmly planted.
> —Mona Lisa Saloy, "Sankofa NOLA"

CHORUS: Louisiana Creole identity is a *culture* produced through forms of méstizaje, or as the late Janet Ravare Colson (Louisiana Creole/Tunica-Choctaw-Biloxi descent) has said: "an offspring of the Old world [Native] and New [African, European]."[17] Louisiana Creoles are a postcontact Afro-Indigenous *culture* tied to specific places and communities in what is now called Louisiana. Part of Latinidad *and* the Caribbean, Louisiana Creoles "recognize the totality of their ethnic/ cultural matrices, encompassing *specific* yet multiple American Indian tribes, African American, Caribbean, French-Indian, and European (usually French and Spanish) inheritance." We can situate Louisiana Creole peoplehood as a distinct culture, forming our own "distinct Indigenous-Afro (Red/Black Latinidad) Louisiana communities *grounded in a peoplehood matrix*—landbase (territory), language (Kouri-Vini), religion (ceremonial cycles), and sacred history." Further, Louisiana Creole is a language native to Louisiana, having its roots in French and Native American languages (Ishak, Choctaw, Caddo etc.) and West African (Wolof, Mandinga, Igbo, etc.) is listed on the international list of endangered Indigenous languages.[18] We think this also accounts for the languages we use in our creative works from English to Louisiana Creole and Haitian Creole to Choctaw and Ishak, French and Spanish, and Igbo, and so on.

RAIN: I think we continue to problematize stagnant notions of identity, anti-Blackness, and Indigenous erasure within conversations on Louisiana Creole peoples as a culture. Situating land/water, food/family, and story/ survivals alongside body (obesity/lupus/motherhood/menopause), and sex (love/sexualities) within Creole-Atakapa-Caddoan-Choctawan-Gulf landbases where survivals through abuse are linked to violences against kincestors and homeland-ecologies. In creating works that center the places/environments/ foodways, languages/soundscapes, and visual/musical arts, these works are a study in both echolocative self-reflexive rhetorical praxis and storyweaving.

CAROLYN: The works we write collectively oft focus on memory, survival, joy, and pain, while exposing critical issues of anti-Blackness in Indian country and Indigenous erasure within settler myths of Creole-country. Blacks and Indians have been intermarrying/gettin'-busy across Turtle Island for hundreds of years. Yet, governments/politics have created a climate of disenrollment, exclusion, racism, and erasure.[19] We also have generations impacted by the BIA, recognition politics, and diaspora. As a woman of Louisiana Creole/Gulf Indigenous descendant in California, I have learned to put my ancestral lands into conversation with lands on which I live/reside and the tribal peoples upon whose homelands I am a guest. In creating works that center blood memory across diaspora, colorlines, and visual arts, we expose embodied tidalectics and storyweaving.

CHORUS: Thus, the works we cocreate move from centering grief/sorrow alongside reclamation and recovery of communal story processes and the feminine through a living embodiment of Creole (Afro-Indigenous) diasporas/migrations. These storied poetic worlds speak into being the echolocative call-and-response of familial memory, ecologies, and histories held in body and land, creating generative recovery and resilience in the face of grief and intergenerational and ecological trauma. Our cowritten poems "Grandma's Zydeco Stomp Dance," "Singin' the Tides Home," and "Oxbow,"[20] resist violent ruptures of Louisiana Creole erasures, illustrating ecological and familial recovery and re-articulation through removals and landbase echolocations.

Conversations

"Know every grain of salt and sand meet where/ tiw aknakit tul hec hukinul. / Tidal ebbing refrains taught us how to sing in call and response—where sisters shell-shake zydeco."
—Rain Prud'homme-Cranford, Carolyn M. Dunn, and Maaliyah Papillion, "Hokišak Yokn"

RAIN: I want to circle back to grief. We have loss many relatives since 2020, from our Matriarch Mama Janet, to our brother's father, Grandpa Shawnee, cousins and friends, and recently, our uncle Papa Ken. Now, my mother is currently battling lung cancer and heart disease. I know a number of the poems in *Echolocation* were written during my Auntie-xukky's illness and passing. A time that also drew you into re-grieving for your father and sister. Could you talk about the role grief plays in this collection? How does grief work as both a genealogy and ceremony toward recovery and healing in your works?

CAROLYN: Most of the poems in *Echolocation* were written when my mother suffered from dementia/Alzheimer's—known as the "family curse." I've oft wondered if it is a curse or a blessing. My mother lost my sister quickly at thirty to cancer (lymphoma and leukemia), then my father to a heart attack nine months to the day later. She forgot she was a heavy drinker along with the folx she lost along the way. The collection that became *Echolocation* is about calling oneself home—utilizing the sounds of our voices to echo off the landscapes that help us find our way.

My sister's passing was tragic. My father's was sudden. My mother's was a long, slow decline into absentia that eventually robbed her of everything she was. Grief is a genealogical process, tracing backwards the moments that create who we are and forward to who we become. This is particularly reflected in the poem "Missing" where I write: "One soul./ Stolen / in the depths / of a dark night." Naming and honoring grief is a ceremony of not only the dead but also the living. "Missing" references both hiraeth (the longing for something within a place that can never exist again) and the reparation (or ceremony) inherent in grief/grieving: "I'm in a state of grieving . . . / asking / why / when there's no words / in either language / for it."[21]

RAIN: Audre Lorde writes: "For Women, then, poetry is not a luxury. It is a vital necessity of our existence . . . Poetry is the way we help give name to the nameless so it can be thought."[22] Your work oft centers female-identified experiences and creative writing as a process generative and dependent on mind, body, spirit, knowledge-making, ceremonies, and celebrations. Can you talk about how your collections speak broadly to how and why this work is a "vital necessity," particularly as Creole-Indigenous woman?

CAROLYN: As Louisiana Creole people, we speak in metaphor. Our languages (Indigenous, West African, French/Spanish) became merged, creating a new lexicon–new language, similar to a Mobilian-trade language. We think in metaphor, speak in metaphor, and live in the world trying to access and think in a language (English) that is very limiting. As poets, we make meaning of words that don't necessarily go together, forcing English into the way we make sense of it. It is both poetry and translation. This is especially true in my poem "Here the Earth Is Brown," where I write:

> A wavering soul
> wandered upon this scorched land,
> like a cricket across
> an asphalt highway . . .
>
> We talk a good song,
> wishing for light and
> stars to speak our
> names . . .
>
> a brown story told in red
> a whisper upon the breath
> of every living thing.[23]

Weaving together strands of word-worlds is like storyweaving or a basket made solid by creation and dreaming it into existence by its maker. It is "vital" to recovery and healing.

RAIN: I have written about your work "The Knot at the End of the World,"[24] and how your use of N. Scott Momaday's blood memory speaks to Louisiana Creole cultural traditions inherent in Louisiana Hoodoo/Voodoo as well as Muscogee creator/creation (Hesaketvmese). I think this is a prime example of what tidalectics and echolocative self-reflexive rhetorical praxis looks like. How do you understand/articulate these theories in your work?

CAROLYN: I, of course, talk about blood memory quite a bit as a Native in diaspora. I always say that I'm not a California Indian, but an Indian from California. We are settlers on Tongva land, recognizing displacement upon displacement and how we ended up in California is recognizing the complicity in settling stolen land in the first place. What Momaday calls blood memory is also a genealogy of our collective grieving.[25] Therefore, we Creoles carry our kincestors' stories, just as we carry their trauma in our blood—trauma of Removal and Relocation, and trauma of racialized gender roles in Louisiana. I'm talking for example of Marie Jeanne, an Indian woman, who carried her French owner's name and her daughter Cecilia ("India Libre"), who sued the French government for her freedom based on being a mixed-race Indian (also African by blood from her Congolese enslaved father).[26] I'm also thinking about the other female kincestors—who were "subjects/objects" of wealthy white men (also ancestors) who shared families and lives with them, sometimes in the shadow of their legal wives and legitimate children. "The Knot at the End of the World" tells those stories, moving like water from Louisiana to California:

> Each knot of a curse
> Formed long before
> *The Maker of Breath*
> Sang us into life . . .
>
> This world repeats
> The presence of spirits
> And the land that
> Speaks to the past . . .
>
> Crossing water . . . [27]

This echolocative praxis relies on spaces of water/land, or shoals—its tidalectics toward Creole reclamation and celebration through sites of trauma.

CAROLYN: We've spoken many times about the unique strands woven into our Creole culture, creating an Afro-Indigenous Louisiana culture. You address this in both your collections. How do you use/situate body as a map to and from historical to the contemporary Louisiana Creole Afro-Indigenous world?

RAIN: Louisiana Creole culture cannot exist if we remove the cultural practices/ embodiments of Indigeneity (African and Turtle Island) or European—the culture melds through the merging of practices/traditions/ancestries into something wholly itself—Louisiana Creole. In the poem "In the Key of Red," perseverance, family, and land work as a balm/medicine and a place of recovery despite violences and erasures: "blues tinged Mvskogean Creole / beaten cotton stepped Zydeco, / from Louisiana's Mississippi / soaked red clay."[28] This creolization/weaving is apparent in the culture and land, but also the weaving between mind, body, and spirit. I articulate my physical self by situating body—from beautiful to ugly, obesity to lupus, and sexual assault—markers in spirit/flesh. I often talk about how the spirit/spiritual or unseen/quantum-world—what Dr. Leroy Little Bear (Kainai-Blackfoot) calls "Indigenous physics" or "flux"—materializes from intangible to tangible. Our lodges-of-flesh have ways of creating cartographic maps/manifestations between intangibilities and tangibilities. This is a reason why keloids factor in so much of my work—Creole folx have a history of keloid scars. So even after an injury is healed, it writes a physical map onto the body. We create similar keloid markers within our spirits, connecting this to the ways intergenerational trauma and colonization mark our bodies through autoimmune disease. In "Love Letter to Lupus," I write:

> Muscles stage coup.
> Needles are painful.
> Pills don't do shit.
> Break your ankles.
> Take a bat to your wrist . . .
>
> You're a bully.
> Another rapist, slave master,
> abusive bastard husband—
> But me—I'm still a bitch.
>
> Fuck off—
> cuz I been walking with bloody steps for centuries.[29]

CAROLYN: You often speak of ways water creates kinship between memories/ histories, embodied rhetorics, and cultural praxis. I'm thinking especially of poems in "Miscegenation Round Dance." How do these poems create ways of kinship between language, body, and blood memory?

RAIN: In "Red River Moan," land and ancestry collide: "We emerged from this river, made of red / clay, broke from earth and water—struggled to / breathe."[30] Similarly, in "Jeanne and Marie Anne Therese de la Grand Terre to Marie Thérèse CoinCoin," ecology and ancestry/kinship are woven with blood memory: "We are tied to this land, our children work / return . . . rising tides / ghosts in blood. They conjure us."[31] We enter the world through water as we breach our mothers' birth canals, and we leave the world in water as our body releases fluids. For some, this might seem too medical, but in fact, it really is an act of beauty. That waters we inhabit have memory, particulates, energies, spirits from seven generations and more before us, and will carry, if we can learn to respect our ecologies, seven generations forward. I am brought to think of things like water ceremonies. Not just practices of "going to water" but also practices of taking the waters where we are birthed, for example—Gulf of Mexico or Red River or Cane River—and how these waters are used in our joining ceremonies/ marriages and in making ceremonies between community and land. What does it mean to bring the Gulf of Mexico and introduce it to the Elbow River—asking spirits and water permission to accept your gift of the waters that birthed you in an act of making kinship? I often mark myself in relation to waters where I live and how those waters are ingested, carried, and cycled through the body.

CAROLYN: What role do expressions of grief/trauma, rhetorics of rage/anger, and celebration/joy play in your creative and critical collections?

RAIN: I really started thinking about bell hooks's and Audre Lorde's rhetorics of rage/anger while teaching M. Carmen Lane's multimodal poem "Some Notes On Racism During A Global Pandemic" in my Red/Black Rhetorics graduate class.[32] It made me consider how anger works as a fire toward resilience and recovery in my own work. It has also led me to think about ways grief/trauma manifest. In the poem "Hatwan: Orison," this cycle comes together in a hatwan ("prayer" in Ishakkoy) ritual of resilience:[33]

> Flesh of mother
> flesh of father. . . .

> . . . seeds of pomegranate
> four black muscadines

Red river water colour of rust . . .

. . . roux made from
46 years of tears
pound of my belly fat
and moon time blood

This medicine is combustible[34]

There is this idea, particularly in western paradigms, that grief/trauma is this "bad" thing. But I've come to recognize the beauty of our resilience and power of our reclamation is about cyclical ceremonies—we cannot have triumph without trauma, joy without grief, birth without death. Particularly in a time like now, where there is anger and grief, I keep reminding myself that there is still beauty in these seasons of fire and rebirth.[35]

Part III. Singin' the Tides Home: Storying Intertextual Harmonies and Hermeneutics

We are the daughters of water. / Didn't you know all life comes / from and through us? These are the lands / we have brought into being and these / are the lands we will reclaim, / whether or not you acknowledge us.
—Jenny L. Davis, "Water Acknowledgement Statement"

RAIN: In spring of 2014, I traveled from Oklahoma City, OK to Saginaw Michigan to stay with Carolyn at her townhouse. She was working at Central Michigan University and we were preparing a presentation for the *Cultural Rhetorics Conference* at Michigan State University. Curled up on the couch late one night our conversation turned to our family and music. The conversation flowed in calls and responses–one of us questioning to the other on memory, song, cultural practices, and poetry. It was here that we started our first call-and-response poems. Over the course of this trip, we would draft the cowritten works "Grandmas' Zydeco Stomp Dance: A Patchwork Poem" and "Conversations: Eualie and Azelie."[36]

CHORUS:

I.
This Creole blood—
Mixed cultures of home
West Africa West Indies
disrupted along slave trade
French and Spanish traveling tributaries.
Mississippi red,
blood arteries
have long varied stories:
colonization and conquest.
Choctaw, Creek, Cherokee, Natchez, Caddo, and
Métis, Cree, Miq'maq come down
River Women—
by virtue of French exploitation and
expulsion of our ancestors
from Nova Scotia to Manitoba

II.
These cultures Ishak,
Choctaw-Biloxi, Mvskogean, Creole made
woven into my Grandfather—
his mother, my Great Grands.
Three is a sacred number for us:
three sisters, three worlds.
Three.
The number of strands it takes to weave.
Three.
The waters of Louisiana:
seawater
fresh water
brackish water.

III.
Memory

lives in body
stomach, heart,
throat, head.
Granma's holding court with family,
Grampa fiddle at chin
in the middle of bayou.
Place my grandmother and grandfather
emerged.
Where their Ancestors
emerged.
Our history along swath of *okhina oka*.

IV.
We are women who shorn
our hair in
grief—
spit bone shard arrow anger
at complacent parish priests.
Our souls burnt edges
from prayers form an
incendiary roux:
cedar,
blood &
cottonmouth venom.
Carry our Grandma's stories
on wide hips laughing
through split lips &
shuffle shake zydeco rhythms.

RAIN: "Grandmas' Zydeco Stomp Dance" came by pulling a few lines from an article I had written previously and a few lines Carolyn had written for the introduction to my first poetry collection. These lines became the seeds for a "Patchwork poem," or "found poem," integrating stanzas taken from these two previous works, reordered, and combined with new stanzas, and new writings. Call-and-response also known as question-and-answer is prevalent in both Native American and African American musical and poetic forms. Working in cohesive answer/question: piecing and writing one stanza at a time—me writing and handing it to Carolyn—her writing a stanza back. We followed this pattern with the second piece as well, the only difference being we started from scratch—meaning no seeds were gathered from previous contexts. This way of working for us is both transrhetorical and rhythmic—it draws upon the natural ebbs and flows within Creole tidalectics while also drawing from traditional forms of storymaking and music-making in both Southeast Indigenous and Afro-Indigenous/Creole cultural traditions. Mark Howell notes the ways Stomp Dance songs of the Choctaw, Chickasaw, and Creek and Ring Shouts within African American musical traditions both center question-and-answer structures relaying on active listening, innovation, and syncretism.[37] While kin we also embody different experiences within our homescapes/landscapes, ages, sexual identifications, and different experiences with parenting/motherhood.[38] My auntie-cuz and uncle-cuz (Carolyn's parents) were born in California, that side of the family having moved from Louisiana and Oklahoma during the dust bowl, while my side of the family stayed in Louisiana until the 1960s (staying within the Gulf south). I had different ecological landbase experiences being raised in the Gulf south while Carolyn was raised in urban Indian/Creole spaces outside of Los Angeles. These ecological intimacies are as much a part of how our parents (and we) carry culture, as are the songs they (and we) sing/play, and the stories they tell of "the home country."

CAROLYN: Storyweaving, according to Muriel Miguel of Spiderwoman Theater, tells us that in performance they use a "conscious, layered weaving of story," or "storyweaving," a process of an unfolding narrative informed by and created by the telling of multiple related story cycles, which reveal the dramatic action(s) of the original story.[39] In our call-and-response poem process, we tell multiple stories that replicate the storyweaving process—the dramatic action of a poem is revealed by telling stories of our kincestors in a vivid weaving, creating a unified story of healing, renewal, and of remaking our worlds. Storyweaving as a transrhetorical praxis is how we oft retell/reimagine/reclaim our kincestors' histories. Using storyweaving and echolocative call-and-response praxis, we reimagine and reanimate our ancestors' lives and their natal homelands within Louisiana. I see this patterned storyweaving practice likewise take form in our poem "Oxbow." The story in "Oxbow" is of our connection to and with our ancestral homelands (our love) and the ecological devastation (abuse) of the land. In telling our kincestors' stories (and their homescapes) through this call-and-response practice, we reveal—with each call/question and each response/answer—the larger story of how we came to be in this world.

CHORUS:

This line here it breaks
like a road given to sinkhole
I am left behind,
stagnating like an oxbow lake
or a memory held too tightly.

Heat rises off brackish waters.
Blood turning inward churning upon
itself to where warring tribes enter
my body, taking their rage and
momentary blindness to differences
between them, undiluted pathways—
in blood to killing fields.

In early evening anhingas
sun themselves, their wings
move softly, necks arched
as to the point of breaking—
They turn like this lake.
I curve inward wading
in forgetting.

Where can I hide? Where there is
no blood churning, no smoke rising,
lungs taking in air from dark waters
claiming skin and taking names?
To forget is to ease pain of dying—
And the names etched upon my heart

flow away, rippling at edges
of breath and longing.

In morning egrets ease silt heavy
shallows surfing for crawfish and minnows.
The birds and I watching you flow, winding
slowly flowing out further and further from reach,
until they too, fly away. Leave me to
darkness and mocking calls of night crickets.

I have learned to weave blankets
from split cane and snake skins—
To blend with the rise and fall of
red river water, mask my anger with
ochre clay and mosquito swarms,
lay pregnant and silent like
a waterpanther at the pool of a river.

I gaze into deep pools of eyes, silent,
waiting under water where their breath
gives way to mine. Waterpanther, there is no
such thing as a ghost. Silt underneath
your nails like the earth from where we emerged,
you keep water count of each life stolen.

Red dirt turns black under water. The
wor'd you have built contains my heart,
mending the tear with skin and bones.
Towers rise to the sky but lay trapped,
like my breath, underwater world and I
can't breathe.

I want to carve a canal.
Dig us back into being.
Sift the land and damns

and histories in unmaking
this oxbow.

That we might unite to this river
and resume our journeys home.

CAROLYN: Whether called poetry, prose, or theory—story is the core—and at the core of story is the ceremonial act of reifying our place in this world. The late Paula Gunn Allen (Laguna Pueblo descent) argues that traditional narratives (whether couched in poetry or prose) are literary recordings of ceremony and ritual.[40] Citing Allen, Hanay Geiogamah (Kiowa/Delaware) explores Indigenous performative praxis as engaging in remaking the world through singing and dancing. In this sense, then, Indigenous story as performative praxis calls into existence world renewal.[41] World renewal ceremonies, like the Jump Dance (Karuk/Yurok/Hupa peoples) and the Green Corn Dances (Choctaw/Chickasaw/Ishak/Muscogee, and many other nations within the Southeastern Ceremonial Complex), predate John L. Austin's theories of performativity. "Saying is as doing,"[42] Austin notes—Indigenous communities (and, we argue, Afro-Indigenous cultures as well), have always been remaking the world through saying and doing via call-and-response as an echolocative praxis. "Native stories are power," LeAnne Howe reminds us, "they create people. They author tribes."[43] Our stories have the power to renew, heal, reconstitute, and to make something by saying and/or doing. Our stories revive languages and metaphors, and sustain our Indigenous ways of thinking and responding to the world around us.

RAIN: Dale Shackleford (Choctaw) writes extensively on the impact of "Hilhlha or Stomp Dancing," on Delta Blues within African American musical traditions,[44] while Muscogee Creek poet Joy Harjo notes: "What you hear first is the calling, a call and response, Where the leader calls out and then the men answer. When you hear that up against blues, rock, jazz, its part of the origin."[45] In this sense, our application of Jackson's transrhetoricity can be understood as a storyweaving call-and-response that "engages listeners as collaborators in meaning making across multiple sites . . . work[ing] together with storytellers to construct and sustain cultural knowledge by building storied connections across difference."[46] I have oft said we sing or call ourselves into being by tracing where we come from. "Creolization is cultural creativity in process. When cultures come into contact, expressive forms and performances emerge from their encounter, embodying the sources that shape them yet constituting new and different entities. Fluid in their adaptation to changing circumstances and open to multiple meanings, Creole forms are expressions of culture in transition and transformation."[47] Like "Oxbow," our poem "Singin the Tides Home" forms at the intersections of both familial cultural genealogies and ecological genealogies/inheritances. If call-and-response as a structure is tied to both Stomp Dance songs and Ring Shouts, then the question-and-answer musical composition within the poem only reinforces the connectivity between form, function, ceremonial performativity, and echolocative self-rhetorical praxis.[48]

CHORUS:

This box was locked, filled with water
where scent, sound, and breath preserved
essences of us, and place, and journey.
She birthed me from northern Bittern Lake and Irish seas
fertilized by southern Bok Homma and Gulf waters

This box was locked, filled with blood
and bone where despair, rage and solitude
sang us home. Following diasporic lines on map,
ringing sorrow into joy, the sweetness of
ocean air, and Pimu singing her traveling songs.

Oh oh sister—help-me-pray
Oh oh sister—help me make it through the day

I have watched her shed hair and weight.
Her eyes gone hollow as her smile wains,
the lines they deepen and crack—As if her spirit will slip its lodge of flesh
rising to ancestors on other side—Singing to call their daughter back.

The light in her eyes has faded and borne
her grief is marked in loss of skin and hair and

slipping away—she lays on threshold
between ocean and stars. Her breath formed of
clouds, nebulas, dust, and ash. Her Ancestors
Sing. Following their voices to the other side.

Oh oh sister—help-me-pray
Oh oh sister—help me make it through the day

Her words are what is left. I can hear songs
of earth and sky. Her feet rise and fall within
paths of dust and ash—We follow where she will
walk amongst stars. Sound of her voice,
her breath reaching across oceans, suns, and worlds,
a distant whisper to light a thousand years.

And yet, her arms still hold me.
Her voice still my conscience—
Her spirit still my guide—
Her breath moves like wind over water.
Her soul a moon pulling tides.

Oh oh sister—help-me-pray
Oh oh sister—help me make it through the day

How can I sing you home?
Sister, oh beloved one—
Tether me with memories—
anchor me with our songs.

Oh oh sister—help-me-pray
Oh oh sister—help me make it through these days Make it through————these days
Hold my hands—and pray . . .
Weyah weya wi ho
Weyah weya wi ho
Weyah weya wi ho
Weyah weya wi ho-o!

CHORUS: For us, this process of transrhetoricity through tidaletic waves of call-and-response illustrate Louisiana "Creole formulations . . . remain intimately grounded and entwined in the everyday exigencies of their own Creole communities."[49] In this sense, using call-and-response methods in our writings emphasizes that stories "survive not just through the telling, but through communities listening to them together, adding to them, building them into larger narratives that connect us in relationship with each other, and telling them again."[50] It is the tidal ebb and flow of carrying (embodying), building (storyweaving), and rearticulating (transrhetoricity) our stories through acts of echolocative self-reflective rhetorical praxis.

IV: Echolocative Currents and Tidal Cartographies

to answer where are you / from i must tell you i come from the ocean.
—Junie Désil, *Eat Salt / Gaze at the Ocean: Poems*

Stories

RAIN: Carolyn and I began writing this work in summer of 2022. In the editing and reediting of this chapter, we have had ups and downs, watched mom's weight, hair, and spirit dwindle as she fights cancer. Yet, *every day* has been and continues to be a blessing. Through grief, we are strengthened in our love, our family, and our belief that prayer is power. Now, Mom has finished her rounds of chemo and has recently begun a second round of radiation, had five stints put in her heart arteries, and survived pneumonitis, which made her ineligible for immunotherapy treatment. Through it all my family, and my big sister-cuz Carolyn have heard my call of "*Oh oh sister- help-me-pray / . . . help me make it through these days.*" My sisters have answered, held "*my hands- and pray[ed].*" It is now 2024 and my mother's scalp reminds me of the current springtime . . . Her white hair returns like wavy-wispy grasses after a barren winter—signs of life, perseverance, and renewal. I watch the sun setting here on the canal, Gulf saltwater in my nose, and a crane calls out from the side yard. So, as the sun sets I am strengthened by family, these Gulf circum-Caribbean lands, and the healing power of poetry—so we will rise kakau' iye'tsne u't ińi[51]—we will rise "to look to sunrise."

CHORUS: "Tidalectics allows us to think of hybridity, cross-cultural syncretism, incompleteness, and fragmentation. It holds a flexible approach to geography that accounts for land forming."[52] Moreover, these formations are demarcated in language. As LeAnne Howe reminds us: "Choctaw place names were the memory aids of their day . . . Nearly every Choctaw town name reveals another story," this encodes "place names with embodied meanings."[53] Our Louisiana Creole homescapes are demarcated through tribal language-memories in Choctaw and Ishakkoy: Abita (Chahta ibetap, creek or spring); Atchafalaya ("long river" from hacha falaia); Catahoula ("beloved Lake" from okhata, lake and hullo, love), Calcasieu (from Ishak chief Katkošyok "Eagle Chirping"),[54] Mermentau (from Ishak chief Nementou), and countless others. This chapter is tidal storyweaving. A song unfinished. "In her essay 'The Site of Memory,' Toni Morrison centers "the words 'flooding' and 'remembering,' the idea that water has memory, an emotional memory embodied in the nerves and the skin of human anatomy."[55] And so, through this flood of embodied memory, we have sought to articulate how we poets situate our own embodied echolocative praxis of Louisiana Creole tidalectics; modeling a communal call-and-response format centering Creole tidaletic poetics toward embodied echolocative self-reflexive rhetorical praxis. Through this water circuitry of tidalectics, we navigate definitions of grief toward recovering ecological intimacies, triangulating tidal ebbings between masses of land, language, and community, illustrating our shared Red/Black/ Creole kinships of resilience and resistance. Wi cit yinco. Mon hoktiwe kakau' iye'tsne u't ińi.

Notes

1. "Ça fé inavé" signals a story is to be told or a tale in Louisiana Creole, while "Išak mon hoktiwe nakšo" asks us to all listen together in Ishakkoy, and finally we offer collectively in English that we have a story. Taken together we signal in different ways in different languages (each associated with Louisiana Creole culture) a time to share and listen to story. We use similar ways of signaling story in other works as well using plays of

Louisiana Creole alongside Choctaw, Ishak, and Tunica, each associated with Louisiana Creole gulf culture. We open the title of this essay with a line from our poem "Mimi's Paper Magnolias," in *Louisiana Creole Peoplehood: Afro-Indigeneity and Community*, edited by Rain Prud'homme-Cranford, Darryl Barthé, and Andrew J. Jolivétte (Seattle: University of Washington Press, 2022), 263–269.

2. "Xukky" is a gender-neutral term in Ishakkoy (Atakapa-Ishak language) meaning cousin or familial relation. With thanks to the Atakapa-Ishak community for their language work. Our use of "Creole" and variations thereof in this essay is specifically Louisiana Creoles.

3. We use kincestors here to mean our Ancestors in the totality of their relational connectivity: blood, marriage, those born "on the wrong-side of blankets (or colorlines)," adoptions (legal, historic, traditional, etc.), and our own blood relations who might be related to one of us but not the other, who are non-the-less our kin because of our familial connectivity.

4. Cresantia F. Koya Vaka'uta, Lingikoni Vaka'uta, and Rosiana Lagi, "Reflections from Oceania on Indigenous Epistemology, the Ocean and Sustainability," in *Tidalectics: Imagining an Oceanic Worldview through Art and Science*, ed. Stefanie Hessler (London: TBA21-Academy, 2018), 127.

5. "Tidalectics Group Exhibition, TBA21–Augarten, Vienna 2017," Stefanie Hessler, 2017, http://stefaniehessler.com/entries/tidalectics.

6. Emilio Amideo, *Queer Tidalectics: Linguistic and Sexual Fluidity in Contemporary Black Diasporic Literature* (Evanston, IL: Northwestern University Press, 2021).

7. Stefanie Hessler, *Tidalectics: Imagining an Oceanic Worldview through Art and Science* (London: TBA21-Academy, 2018), 31.

8. LeAnne Howe, "The Story of America: A Tribalography," in *Clearing a Path: Theorizing the Past in Native American Studies*, ed. Nancy Shoemaker (New York: Routledge, 2002), 42.

9. LeAnne Howe, "Embodied Tribalography," in *Choctalking on Other Realities* (San Francisco: Aunt Lute Books, 2013), 173–174.

10. Jo-ann Archibald, "An Indigenous Storywork Methodology," in *Handbook of the Arts in Qualitative Research: Perspectives, Methodologies, Examples, and Issues*, ed. J. Gary Knowles and Ardra Linette Cole (Los Angeles: SAGE, 2008), 373.

11. Embodied by Spiderwoman Theatre and Safe Harbors Indigenous Collective in New York, Spiderwoman Theatre is the longest-running Indigenous women's theatre company on Turtle Island. The Miguel sisters—Gloria Miguel, Muriel Miguel, and the late Lisa Mayo—started the company in the basement of the family brownstone in Brooklyn, and much of the company's early work was filmed in the family living room. Muriel Miguel's

daughter, Muriel Borst Tarrant, and granddaughter, Henu Josephine Tarrant-Richardson, have carried on the family legacy and praxis with Safe Harbors Indigenous Collective. Carolyn Dunn, conversation with Rain Prud'homme-Cranford, 2022.

12. Rachel C. Jackson, "Locating Oklahoma: Critical Regionalism and Transrhetorical Analysis in the Composition Classroom Author(s)," in "Locations of Writing," special issue, *College Composition and Communication* 66, no. 2 (December 2014): 305.

13. Rain Prud'homme-Cranford, "'Gather at the River': Spiritual Ecologies in Red/Black Literatures" (Research presentation, California State University Los Angeles, April 2022).

14. Rachel Stubbs, "Rebellion in Every Movement: Women Writing Indigenous Girlhood in Twentieth-Century Western Canada" (dissertation proposal draft, Calgary, AB. 2023), 3; Rain Prud'homme-Cranford and Rachel Stubbs, discussion, May 2021. I began working on the concept of echolocative self-reflexive rhetorical praxis (along with "Indigenous rhetorical transubstantiation") for "Gather at the River." However, as theory/praxis, this concept has grown toward a *co-conceptualized articulation* through work and conversations with my graduate student and future colleague Rachel Stubbs (Saulteaux descent) in the writing and theorizing of her dissertation and the role familial, spiritual, artistic, and intellectual recovery and resilience plays in both her creative (poetry and art) and critical dissertation, "Rebellion in Every Movement." I am *honored* to work with and witness this young, brilliant, and compassionate/carrying Indigenous scholar who carries the mantle forward. So I offer Rachel my heartfelt thanks: hiwéw/mési/yakoke— as she reminds me that we are better as we work, talk, counsel, and grow communally rather than individually. I must also add I am grateful to *all* my graduate students and future colleagues I have been blessed to think with over the last seven years: Dr. Kaitlyn Purcell, Maryam Gowralli, Mahmoud Ababneh, and Omar Ramadan.

15. We use "storywork/weaving" to signal the interdependent relationship between storywork and storyweaving that is united praxis in our methodology.

16. We use "chorus" to denote our cowriting.

17. Janet Ravare Colson, *The Creole Book* (Natchitoches, LA: Creole Heritage Foundation; Raleigh, NC: Lulu Publishing, 2012), 7.

18. Rain Prud'homme-Cranford, Darryl Barthé, and Andrew J. Jolivétte, eds., *Louisiana Creole Peoplehood: Afro-Indigeneity and Community* (Seattle: University of Washington Press, 2022), 38.

19. This is what bothers me specific to Louisiana Indigenous peoples because of the cultural and racialized mixing that has been going on since Louisiana first became colonized. This is also an issue because this happens in other states but specifically to Louisiana because of cultural mestizaje creating a *completely new postcontact Afro-Indigenous*

culture from the strands of *all three of its parent cultures*: Indigenous peoples of Turtle Island and Africa as well as settlers (Europeans). We continue to struggle against anti-Black racism and Indigenous erasure and misunderstandings of who/what Louisiana Creoles are. Louisiana Creoles are a culture and communities, not a "race." Moreover, the records, historic, oral, material, etc. are complex, and those not well-trained in the area are oft more likely to perpetuate erasure and settler myths around Louisiana Creole identity and Creole culture. From the ways Catholic baptisms and marriages of Indian women (to white men) were demarcated and afforded them political racial passing while Blackness created another erasure, (where racial designations have been changed based on phenotype, baptisms, and enslavement) and the ways the *code noir* and Jim Crow impacted how Creoles are/were perceived makes *working with and listening* to our communities directly extremely vital. Scholars such as Gwendolyn Mido Hall, Julia Barr, Elizabeth Shown Mills, and Gary B. Mills have written as has Jeffrey U. Darensbourg. Jeffrey as well as Leila Blackbird, Christophe Landry, Andrew Jolivétte, and Darryl Barthé have all written about this process, noting that the identities of folks change over time in historical records. For Louisiana Creole, the romance and tragedy of the mulatto has created both Indigenous erasures and assigned racial designations as white, Black, and mulatto—we Creoles know that lots of misinformation is out there regarding our identities and culture—so listening to our communities should be a priority.

20. From Rain Prud'homme-Cranford, Carolyn Dunn, and Maaliyah Papillio, *Singin' the Tides Home: Poems in Call, Response, and Chorus* (Lafayette, LA Bayous & Byways Books, 2025).

21. Carolyn M. Dunn, "Missing," in *Echolocation: Poems From Indian Country, L.A.* (Tucson: Fezwig Press, 2013), 4, lines 1–4, 12, 17–21.

22. Audre Lorde, "Poetry Is Not a Luxury," in *Women's Voices, Feminist Visions: Classic and Contemporary Readings*, 2nd ed., ed. Susan M. Shaw and Janet Lee (New York: McGraw-Hill, Education, 2015), 372.

23. Carolyn M. Dunn, "Here the Earth Is Brown," in *Echolocation*, lines 6–9, 11–14, 21–23, 25–27.

24. See Rain P. Cranford Goméz, "Hachotakni Zydeco's Round'a Loop Current: Indigenous, African, and Caribbean Mestizaje in Louisiana Literatures," *Southern Literary Journal* 46, no. 2 (2014): 95–96.

25. See N. Scott Momaday, *The Way to Rainy Mountain* (Albuquerque: University of New Mexico Press, 1976).

26. See Gwendolyn Midlo Hall, *Africans in Colonial Louisiana: The Development of Afro-Creole Culture in the Eighteenth Century* (Baton Rouge: Louisiana State University Press, 1995); Julia Barr, *Peace Came in the Form of a Woman: Indians and Spaniards in the Texas*

Borderlands (Chapel Hill: University of North Carolina Press, 2009).

27. Carolyn M. Dunn, "The Knot at the End of the World," in *The Stains of Burden and Dumb Luck* (Norman, OK: Mongrel Empire Press, 2017), 63, lines 1–4, 5–8.

28. Rain C. Goméz "In the Key of Red," in *Smoked Mullet Cornbread Crawdad Memory* (Norman, OK: Mongrel Empire Press, 2012), 93, lines 2–6.

29. Goméz, "Love Letter for Lupus," in *Smoked Mullet*, 52, lines 53–65.

30. Rain Prud'homme, "Red River Moan," in *Miscegenation Round Dance: Poèmes Historiques* (Norman, OK: Mongrel Empire Press, 2021), 7, lines 21–23.

31. Prud'homme, "Jeanne and Marie Anne Thérèse de la Grand Terre to Marie Thérèse CoinCoin," in *Miscegenation Round Dance*, 10, lines 2–5.

32. See this visual poem at https://vimeo.com/430919765.

33. I want to recognize the 2023 version of the Ishak dictionary written with community updates of the orthography for hatwan to hawtén (prayer).

34. Prud'homme, "Hatwan: Orison," in *Miscegenation Round Dance*, 2, lines 1–2, 6–8, 19–23.

35. Jeffery U. Darensbourg reminds us in his work/lectures that it was among the Louisiana Ishak and Choctaw, in particular, that French settlers first recorded witnessing slash-and-burn ecological management. For more, see Jeffery Darensbourg and John DePriest, "The Music of the Rivercane Exploring the Indigenous Origins of Hill Country Fife and Drum Music, and the Instrument at Its Heart," *Country Rounds Magazine*.

36. A "patchwork poem" is a found poem. This poem pieces together writing by Dunn and Prud'homme-Cranford to form a new poetic conversation in call-and-response. It was first published in *World Literature Today: Native Renaissance Third and Fourth Wave Special Collection*, 91, no. 3–4, 2017.

37. These poems have since evolved into an addition of our younger kin-sister into the collection *Singin' the Tides Home*. Mark Howell, "African American Native American Music Syncretism," in *Field Hollers and Freedom Songs: The Anthology Featuring the Collected Works from the Sweat Equity Investment in the Cotton Kingdom Symposium*, ed. C. Sade Turnipseed (Wilmington, DE: Vernon Press, 2022), 179–181.

38. I identify as a queer pansexual/sapiosexual while my sister-cuz identifies as hetero and has raised three awesome children, two of whom are Two-Spirit. While Carolyn has given birth and raised children, I have never been able to carry a pregnancy to term. Rather, I have been a tremendously active coparent Auntie-mom in the raising of my younger sister's children—as well as the adopted parent to two adult nonbinary kiddos, who are loved and as much a part of my life and family as any of our kiddos in the extended Dunn/Prud'homme-Cranford/Shawnee family.

39. Muriel Miguel cited in Carolyn Brave Heart, "[Workshop Reflection] from Storytelling to

Storyweaving: Muriel Miguel, a Retrospective," Oral History Master of Arts, December 6, 2013, oralhistory.columbia.edu/blog-posts/People/workshop-reflection-from-storytelling-to-storyweaving-muriel-miguel-a-retrospective. For more on storyweaving and performative praxis, see Sarah Dangelo, "Indigenous Placemaking and Storyweaving An Interview with Murielle Borst-Tarrant (Kuna, Rappahannock)" in *Decentered Playwriting: Alternative Texts for the Stage*, ed. Carolyn M Dunn, Eric Micah Holmes, and Les Hunter (New York: Routledge, 2024).

40. See Paula Gunn Allen, *The Sacred Hoop* (Boston: Beacon Press, 1986).

41. See Hanay Geiogamah, *Ceremony, Spirituality, and Ritual in Native American Performance: A Creative Notebook* (Los Angeles: UCLA American Indian Studies Center, University of California, 2011).

42. See J. L. Austin, *How to Do Things with Words* (Eastford, CT: Martino Fine Books, 2018).

43. LeAnne Howe, "Tribalography: The Power of Native Stories," *Journal of Dramatic Theory and Criticism* 14, no 1 (1999): 118.

44. See Dale Shackleford, "Muskogean Tribes Musical Influence on the Genre of Delta Blues" (Thesis, Honors College, Middle Tennessee State University 2021).

45. Catherine Bainbridge and Alfonso Maiorana, dirs., *RUMBLE: The Indians who Rocked the World* (Montreal: Rezolution Pictures, 2017), 19:43.

46. Rachel C. Jackson and Dorothy Whitehorse DeLaune, "Decolonizing Community Writing with Community Listening: Story, Transrhetorical Resistance, and Indigenous Cultural Literacy Activism," *Community Literacy Journal* 13, no. 1 (2019): 41.

47. Robert Baron and Ana C. Cara, "Introduction: Creolization as Cultural Creativity," in *Creolization as Cultural Creativity*, ed. Robert Baron and Ana C. Cara (Jackson: University Press of Mississippi, 2011), 12.

48. Original melody and lyric refrain R. Prud'homme-Cranford; original harmonies and shakers C. M. Dunn.

49. Baron and Cara, "Introduction: Creolization as Cultural Creativity," 13.

50. Jackson and DeLaune, "Decolonizing Community Writing," 52.

51. Ishakkoy (Atakapa-Ishak language) for "to look toward sunrise."

52. Hessler, *Tidalectics*, 34.

53. Howe, "Embodied Tribalography."

54. While many settlers have translated this as "Crying Eagle," Jeffery Darensbourg (council member of the Atakapa-Ishak Nation of SWLA) and linguist David V. Kaufman have noted the correct translation as "Chirping Eagle."

55. Amideo, *Queer Tidalectics*.

Bibliography

Allen, Paula Gunn. *The Sacred Hoop*. Boston: Beacon Press, 1986.

Amideo, Emilio. *Queer Tidalectics: Linguistic and Sexual Fluidity in Contemporary Black Diasporic Literature*. Evanston, IL: Northwestern University Press, 2021.

Archibald, Jo-ann. *Indigenous Storywork: Educating the Heart, Mind, Body, and Spirit*. Vancouver: University of British Columbia Press, 2014.

———. "An Indigenous Storywork Methodology." In *Handbook of the Arts in Qualitative Research: Perspectives, Methodologies, Examples, and Issues*, edited by J. Gary Knowles and Ardra Linette Cole, 371–386. Los Angeles: SAGE, 2008.

Austin, J. L. *How to Do Things with Words*. Eastford, CT: Martino Fine Books, 2018.

Bainbridge, Catherine, and Alfonso Maiorana, dirs. *Rumble: The Indians Who Rocked the World*. Montreal: Rezolution Pictures, 2017.

Baron, Robert, and Ana C. Cara. "Introduction: Creolization as Cultural Creativity." In *Creolization as Cultural Creativity*, edited by Robert Baron and Ana C. Cara, 3–19. Jackson: University Press of Mississippi, 2011.

Barr, Juliana. *Peace Came in the Form of a Woman: Indians and Spaniards in the Texas Borderlands*. Chapel Hill: University of North Carolina Press, 2009.

Brave Heart, Catherine. "[Workshop Reflection] from Storytelling to Storyweaving: Muriel Miguel, a Retrospective." Oral History Master of Arts, December 6, 2013. oralhistory.columbia.edu/blog-posts/People/workshop-reflection-from-storytelling-to-storyweaving-muriel-miguel-a-retrospective.

Clayton, Kelly. "Oya Dances the Bamboula: Congo Square, August 2005." In *Mother of Chaos: Queen of the Nines*. Harrah, OK: That Painted Horse Press, , 2019.

Colson, Janet Ravare. *The Creole Book*. Natchitoches, LA: Creole Heritage Foundation; Raleigh, NC: Lulu Publishing, 2012.

Cranford Goméz, Rain P. "Hachotakni Zydeco's Round'a Loop Current: Indigenous, African, and Caribbean Mestizaje in Louisiana Literatures." *Southern Literary Journal* 46, no. 2 (2014): 88–107. https://doi.org/10.1353/slj.2014.0001.

Davis, Jenny L. *Trickster Academy* Tucson: University of Arizona Press, 2022.

DeLoughrey, Elizabeth M. *Allegories of the Anthropocene*. Durham: Duke University Press, 2019.

Désil Junie. *Eat Salt / Gaze at the Ocean: Poems*. Vancouver: Talonbooks, 2020.

Dunn, Carolyn M. *Echolocation: Poems from Indian Country, L.A.* Tucson: Fezwig Press, 2013.

———. *The Stains of Burden and Dumb Luck*. Norman, OK: Mongrel Empire Press, 2017.

Geiogamah, Hanay. *Ceremony, Spirituality, and Ritual in Native American Performance: A*

Creative Notebook. Los Angeles: UCLA American Indian Studies Center, University of California, 2011.

Glissant, Édouard. *Poetics of Relation.* Ann Arbor: University of Michigan Press, 1997.

Goméz, Rain C. *Smoked Mullet Cornbread Crawdad Memory.* Norman, OK: Mongrel Empire Press, 2012.

Hall, Gwendolyn Midlo. *Africans in Colonial Louisiana: The Development of Afro-Creole Culture in the Eighteenth Century.* Baton Rouge: Louisiana State University Press, 1995.

Hessler, Stefanie, ed. *Tidalectics: Imagining an Oceanic Worldview through Art and Science.* London: TBA21-Academy, 2018.

———. "Tidalectics Group Exhibition, TBA21–Augarten, Vienna 2017." Stefanie Hessler, 2017. http://stefaniehessler.com/entries/tidalectics.

Howe, LeAnne. "Embodied Tribalography." In *Choctalking on Other Realities.* San Francisco: Aunt Lute Books, 2013.

———. "The Story of America: A Tribalography." *Clearing a Path: Theorizing the Past in Native American Studies,* edited by Nancy Shoemaker, 29–50. New York: Routledge, 2002.

———. "Tribalography: The Power of Native Stories." *Journal of Dramatic Theory and Criticism* 14, no 1 (1999): 117–126.

Howell, Mark. "African American Native American Music Syncretism." In *Field Hollers and Freedom Songs: The Anthology Featuring the Collected Works from the Sweat Equity Investment in the Cotton Kingdom Symposium,* edited by C. Sade Turnipseed, 179–209. Wilmington, DE: Vernon Press, 2022.

Jackson, Rachel C. "Locating Oklahoma: Critical Regionalism and Transrhetorical Analysis in the Composition Classroom Author(s)." In "Locations of Writing," special issue, *College Composition and Communication* 66, no. 2 (December 2014): 301–326.

Jackson, Rachel C., and Dorothy Whitehorse DeLaune. "Decolonizing Community Writing with Community Listening: Story, Transrhetorical Resistance, and Indigenous Cultural Literacy Activism." *Community Literacy Journal* 13, no. 1 (2019): 37–54.

King, Tiffany Lethabo. *The Black Shoals: Offshore Formations of Black and Native Studies.* Durham: Duke University Press, 2019.

King, Tiffany Lethabo, Jenell Navarro, and Andrea Smith, eds. *Otherwise Worlds: Against Settler Colonialism and Anti-Blackness.* Durham: Duke University Press, 2020.

Koya Vaka'uta, Cresantia F., Lingikoni Vaka'uta, and Rosiana Lagi. "Reflections from Oceania on Indigenous Epistemology, the Ocean and Sustainability." In *Tidalectics: Imagining an Oceanic Worldview through Art and Science,* edited by Stefanie Hessler, 127–132. London: TBA21-Academy, 2018.

Lorde, Audre. "Poetry Is Not a Luxury." In *Women's Voices, Feminist Visions: Classic and*

Contemporary Readings, 2nd ed., edited by Susan M. Shaw and Janet Lee, 517–527. New York: McGraw-Hill, Education, 2015.

Momaday, N. Scott. *The Way to Rainy Mountain*. Albuquerque: University of New Mexico Press, 1976.

Prud'homme, Rain. *Miscegenation Round Dance: Poèmes Historiques*. Norman, OK: Mongrel Empire Press, 2021.

Prud'homme-Cranford, Rain. "'Gather at the River': Spiritual Ecologies in Red/Black Literatures." Research presentation, California State University Los Angeles, April 2022.

Prud'homme-Cranford, Rain, Darryl Barthé, and Andrew J. Jolivétte, eds. *Louisiana Creole Peoplehood: Afro-Indigeneity and Community*. Seattle: University of Washington Press, 2022.

Prud'homme-Cranford, Rain, and Carolyn M. Dunn. "Grandma's Zydeco Stomp Dance: A Patchwork Poem." *World Literature Today: Native Renaissance Third and Fourth Wave Special Collection*, 91, no. 3–4, 2017.

———. "Mimi's Paper Magnolias." In *Louisiana Creole Peoplehood: Afro-Indigeneity and Community*, edited by Rain Prud'homme-Cranford, Darryl Barthé, and Andrew J. Jolivétte, 263–269. Seattle: University of Washington Press, 2022.

Reckin, Anna. "Tidalectic Lectures: Kamau Brathwaite's Prose/Poetry as Sound-Space." *Anthurium A Caribbean Studies Journal* 1, no. 1 (2003): 1–15. https://doi.org/10.33596/anth.4.

Saloy, Mona Lisa. "Sankofa NOLA." In *Second Line Home: New Orleans Poems*, 5–7. Kirksville, MO: Truman State University Press, 2014.

Shackleford, Dale. "Muskogean Tribes Musical Influence on the Genre of Delta Blues." Thesis, Honors College, Middle Tennessee State University, 2021.

Shuck, Kim. "From Muscogee." In *Exile Heart: Collected Poems*, 47. Harrah, OK: That Painted Horse Press, 2021. 47.

Simpson, Leanne Betasamosake. *As We Have Always Done: Indigenous Freedom through Radical Resistance*. Minneapolis: University of Minnesota Press, 2019.

Stubbs, Rachel. "Rebellion in Every Movement: Women Writing Indigenous Girlhood in Twentieth-Century Western Canada." Dissertation proposal draft, University of Calgary, Calgary, AB, 2023.

Walcott, Rinaldo. *The Long Emancipation: Moving toward Black Freedom*. Durham: Duke University Press, 2021.

Weinberger, Eliot, and Edward Kamau Brathwaite. *Written Reaction: Poetics, Politics, Polemics, 1979–1995*. Venice: Marsilio Publishers, 1996.

Poetry as Performance of Language

Beth Piatote

Years ago, the course of my writing life changed when I heard the Māori poet Robert Sullivan say that we should use our Indigenous aesthetics in our writing.[1] As a scholar, I had encountered this strategy in the works of generations of Indigenous writers, from Simon Pokagon and Zitkala-Ša to Leslie Marmon Silko and Esther Belin. But as a writer, I found this prospect somewhat daunting—I didn't quite feel authorized to use Nez Perce/Niimíipuu aesthetics in my own work. In thinking about our aesthetics, I turned to a corpus of traditional stories recorded in the language.[2] Through my study of these stories, I could identify specific characteristics: the use of direct discourse, the dominance of the number five, the motif of the youngest/littlest one as the hero, the animacy and agency of the land and living beings, among other things. I thought about community stories and rituals that honored other living beings, such as salmon, deer, roots, and rivers. The night that I heard Sullivan's advice, I wrote about our relationship with eels, and it was not easy. I was afraid of being misunderstood, or worse, being criticized by my own community. At the same time, I recognized the power of our aesthetics, the powerful beauty of Nez Perce intelligence, and the deep wisdom of Sullivan's challenge.

Up to that point, my life as a creative writer, a scholar, and an Indigenous language activist had been moving along as parallel streams. Implicitly, these projects had informed each other, but this new commitment caused them to merge. In my 2019 mixed-genre collection, *The Beadworkers: Stories*, Nez Perce aesthetics appear in various ways: a ceremonial feast as a literary structure, the repetition of the number five, explicit intertexts with traditional stories, and dreams of eels, among other things. I knew that my readers would not necessarily understand what I was doing. But the process became one in which I was able to connect my own work to a longer genealogy of Nez Perce literary and linguistic aesthetics. As I increasingly turned to my Indigenous language and literature to shape my creative writing, I came into a deeper relationship and facility with my titooqatímt, my people's language. The language brought me closer to my homelands, my ancestors, and my Nez Perce relatives. In this essay, I express the importance of using creative writing to support language revitalization work, and reflect upon the unique capacity of poetry to convey the structural and sonic aesthetics of Indigenous languages and grammars of meaning. Poetry performs language, and when we perform poetry in our language, we gain capacity for speaking and carrying the language forward. In these intertwined ways, poetry as performance of language is a powerful tool in language revitalization work.

Language Play in the Context of Endangerment

Indigenous language revitalization almost always emerges out of a context of endangerment, usually defined by a decrease in language use. According to UNESCO's World Atlas of Languages, Nez Perce is "critically endangered," with fewer than ninety-nine speakers.[3] The term "language endangerment" is an effective phrase for bringing attention to a critical issue—the language needs more speakers to thrive—and yet this call to action can also be immobilizing. When one is in danger, or close to someone else in danger, a trauma reaction is likely to occur: fight, flight, or freeze. When our languages are endangered, it impacts us as though we ourselves are in danger—because we are. Our languages contain the sounds, grammar, and thought-worlds of our lands, ancestors, and cultures. It's a difficult paradox that the languages most in need of revitalization can also be the most difficult to engage, in part because of the extremely high stakes of the relationship. As the Tlingit linguist and poet Nora Dauenhauer, with her co-author Richard Dauenhauer show, the product of decades of colonial attacks on Indigenous languages and cultures has left individuals and communities "plagued and haunted with anxieties, insecurities, and hesitations about the value of their indigenous language and culture." In their extensive essay that explores the spiritual and psychological barriers to revitalization, they state that "many people are afraid of the traditional language. It is alien, unknown, and difficult to learn. It can be a constant reminder of a deficiency and a nagging threat to one's image of cultural competence. For others, the mere thought of the language stimulates a fear of unplugging evils of the past, real or imagined."[4]

Fear is the enemy of language. My teacher, Haruo Aoki, would remind me that the context of language revitalization, in which most learners are adults, requires great generosity and kindness for language to emerge. He would say: think of how toddlers begin to speak—we encourage them for every utterance that's even close to a word. He encouraged me to treat my language learning with the same gentleness and support, and I could heed his advice when working on my own, but I often experienced difficulty and terror in speaking with others. I was immobilized by fear that other members of my tribe would criticize me for making mistakes in grammar or pronunciation or usage. I was terrified of making mistakes, even though I knew from my experiences of taking foreign language classes in school that mistakes were one of the most productive (and humorous) ways of learning language. I was also afraid to play with the language—to do anything that deviated from "authorized" language use, such as translating popular songs into the language. Because of the state of language endangerment, I feared that any mistakes or variations I made would be evidence that I could not be *trusted* with the language.

Language play, or creative writing, emerged as a path out of fear and immobilization, and should be central to language revitalization efforts. The process of bringing one's own creative vision to the work is a process of language authorization. And a creative writing workshop—or any format engaging the arts—can be a laboratory for exploration and a safe place to make mistakes. In 2020, I cofounded, with my relative Phillip Cash Cash, a collective of Nez Perce writers devoted to using creative writing and performance for language revitalization. Our collective is called luk'upsíimey, and our weekly meetings have become a regular site where we can practice our language and explore poetic forms and playwriting. Within the group, we share or perform our works, and through these regular performances of poetry, we perform the language. As creativity and language have flowed through us, we each have gained more confidence in speaking the language.[5]

Grammar as Poetics of Language

Our language is naturally poetic. And it is naturally performative in the sense that it is verb-based and thus constantly expressing action; it is constantly *doing*.[6] Nez Perce is a verb-based polysynthetic language, which means most of the words in the language are formed by placing verbs at the center of the word, with prefixes explaining the *who* and the *how* and suffixes defining the *when* and the *where*. It is a highly specific, highly relational language; verbs don't exist on their own, as infinitives, but rather must express who/what is doing what to whom/what and how and when and where and for how long and for what reason. For example, consider the word we'npíse (I am singing). At the center of the word is the verb, 'inipí, which means *to take hold of, to seize, to hold*. The prefix, we-, means *with mouth* or *with song*, and the suffix -se is first- or second-person present tense. Naturally poetic ways to express "I am singing" emerge directly from the grammar: *I am holding song*; *I seize song with the mouth*; *I am holding with song*. To this basic construction, any number of morphemes can be added, such as the prefix for *angry*: wéetxwe'npse (I am singing in anger, or, *I seize anger in the mouth*). Add a suffix that indicates the action is for the benefit of another: 'uu'nipéey'se (I am singing for someone, or, *I hold another with song*). When I think the phrase *I hold another with song*, I feel the flow of medicine songs through the body of one who is suffering. I think of honor songs that elevate the good deeds of a person. I think of mothers rocking their babies with lullabies. In these examples, I have used roman font to indicate the word's translation as it appears in the dictionary, and *italics* to express my own translation of the word's poetics and ontological meaning.[7] It is in this gap, between the usage meaning of a word or phrase (the dictionary entry) and the aesthetic/ontological meaning, that I find the medium of poetry most promising for language revitalization.

Poetry has the capacity to illuminate not only the power of words but also the power of systems of thought. In the Tohono O'odham homelands of Arizona, the phrase "there is no O'odham word for wall" has been a rallying point against the border wall and a powerful intervention into the so-called logic of border thinking. The slogan claims a limit: the wall is unthinkable in this language, in this entire grammar of being. Rhetorically, "there is no word for X" is powerful, yet it is limited in the sense that it focuses on words, and words evolve in language. Languages are alive and constantly adapt to name new things. New words can enter a language with some degree of ease, but to change the grammar—the underlying structure of the language—is much more difficult. More frequently than I've heard "we don't have a word for X," I've heard "we can't say *this* without *that*." In her poem, "The First Water Is the Body," Natalie Diaz writes, "I carry a river. It is who I am: 'Aha Makav. This is not a metaphor," and in a later stanza, "'Aha Makav means the river runs through the middle of our body, the same way it runs through the middle of our land."[8] Her poem embodies the ways in which our rules for speaking are bound up with our rules for living and our systems of interrelations. As much as we need to say "our language doesn't have a word for that," we need to say "we don't have a *grammar* for that." Our world is not ordered in that way.

So grammar is important and it is also beautiful. The usage meaning of Nez Perce words is essential, but in order to build independence in the language, speakers must understand the construction of verbs and how to create words with morphemes. To that end, poetry provides an excellent medium to demonstrate not only how grammar works, but also the beauty that embodies. In my own work, I've endeavored to show the aesthetics of our grammar, and here I offer short excerpts from my six-poem cycle, "I Cause My Heart to Pour Out is how to say *remember*," which is structured after a dictionary entry and uses sample sentences/ words directly from the dictionary. Each poem in the cycle takes a different form, highlighting the role of *morphing* in morphology, and seeks to present images and phrases that will underscore usage. The cycle as a whole links the words through the central verb, pin'i (to come out or pour out) to teach a pattern of thought. This poetic structure of the cycle maintains the centrality of the verb as an organizing force. Words that are not conceptually or linguistically related in English—to come out, to sew, to question, to flow as a river, to remember—are all linked through the central Nez Perce verb pin'i. The poem cycle, as the dictionary entry, performs this set of relationships and reflects how the language thinks.[9]

The second poem in the six-poem cycle, "cúupn'ise/I sew," receives its title from the sample usage sentence in the dictionary, then repeats the morphology of the word (prefix: with sharp object; verb: to come out) in the line of the poem. The poem ends with single string of the letter "I," which is both a refrain of longing and a visual representation of a line of stitches.

CÚUPN'ISE

I SEW.

I sew a red dress to bring my sister home.
I seam a red dress to sew her to myself.
I see; I fight: sharp object comes out.
I sew a red dress to seam my sister home.
I sew a red dress to seem my sister.
I seam a red dress. I sew for redress.
I so want my sister home
I see red
I sew dress
I sew red; eyes so red
I sew
I sew
I
I
I
I
I

In the third poem of the cycle, "séepn'it / asking, question, inquiry" employs the form of a question to express the concept of "question" as the combination of the causative prefix with come out and a nominalizing suffix.

SÉEPN'IT

ASKING, QUESTION, INQUIRY

séepn'it is the word for *question,*
the thing we cause to come out—

and why would we think of it

any other way?

The poem strives to capture the beauty and significance of the grammatical and epistemological structure of the concept—a question is a thing that has to come out, that we cause to pour out or flow out of ourselves. In this poem cycle and other works, I draw on the method of translanguaging, or working across two languages in a single piece. Thus, the tools of English and poetic structure allow the aesthetics, grammar, and intelligence of our titooqatímt to shine. My aim is to give the reader something conceptually that will help them bring the language into their bodies and consciousness. In my poetry manuscript, I make use of footnotes (the "feet" upon which we stand) to provide morphological analysis that will maximize the benefit to the language learner; I imagine these footnotes as their own grammar commentary, running along with the poems. In some poems, I use interlinear notes and contextual definitions to highlight the morphology.

Often, I find it difficult to write a poem with our language, which is so naturally poetic. But this, too, is one of the joys of bringing the practice of creative writing to our language learning; it gives us license to savor the poetics inherent in the language, and to contemplate the beauty through which the grammar orders the world. Our language both describes and embodies an animate universe. One may say the language is verb-centered, or life-centered, or body-centered; all of these descriptions are true. The intersubjectivity and inter-relationality expressed through the grammar of our language gives life to our titooqanáawit, our ways of knowing and doing. Among the many morphemes that shape our words and thought are those that express spatial relationships; the grammar insists that we identify where we are, where we are from, where we are going, and so on. Just as there are no stand-alone infinitives—no way *to make* or *to do* something in the abstract, but always with subject, object, adverb, and tense specificity—the locative and directional suffixes place action in specific spatial relation. The language is performative in that its grammar distributes relationships by requiring the articulation of a speaker's relationship to other beings as well as to time and place. The language constantly maps social and geographic relationships. Just as the verb is central to the creation of a word, these elements of relationship are central to Nez Perce cukwenéewit (knowledge or understanding) and aesthetics.[10]

Poetry as Performance of Language

Our languages emerge from and belong to our homelands, and poetry, which emphasizes form, movement, and the sonic properties of language, can bring the intimacy of the land to the page. The connection to land is a significant aspect that supports language revitalization efforts. In the essay "Indigenous Language Use Impacts Wellness," co-author Jaeci Hall, a Tututni descendant, describes a sense of balance that comes through the connection of land with language. "When I go down to our Rogue River where our language is, there's trees, there's rocks there that were there that heard this language back when many people spoke it there. The sounds that our language makes resonates within the body. We have xh and ł and ts.' I really believe that this vibration of the language is still there in the land as well."[11] Poetry offers an opportunity to convey the vibrational energy of place through the page.

In a recent podcast for the Poetry Foundation, Diné poets Esther Belin and Orlando White discuss concrete poetry as a form that highlights the sonic and performative properties of Diné concepts.[12] "Our relationship to language, it's a real relationship that we have with our grandparents. And I think it's that same relationship . . . we have with the land," White says.[13] He cites a concrete poem by Diné writer Sherwin Bitsui, "tó," which repeats the Diné word for water in a single line down the center of the page.[14] "It's really about the sound," White says. "It's that sound that, when water is dripping, like after a rainstorm, right, a water droplet dripping from a leaf." The concrete poem form visually and sonically performs the language and its conceptual world as it emerges from Diné homelands. White is currently working on one-word concrete poems in Dinébizaad, and in his own water poem uses the technique of translanguaging to infuse the onomatopoetic structure of tó with the English word, water.[15] His poem, "water," places a single word on the page.

wä tó ər

The poem insists on the primacy of Diné aesthetics and conceptual categories. The embedded tó at the center sonically and genealogically connects the poem to the Diné land as well as to Bitsui's work and the creative force of tó itself. The poem performs the language, not as a static presence but as an energetic being.

Poetry has the capacity to embody movement, to perform the animacy of Indigenous words and concepts. In their conversation, White comments on this characteristic in Belin's poem, "bundles are bundling," which repeats "názbas" or the word for *circle* four times, forming a circle on the page.[16] The poem is encircling, it is bundling; it represents circle as verb. "I always saw that poem as moving on the page," Belin says. "It wasn't just kind of an anchor."[17]

In a similar fashion, Nez Perce readers can experience the movement embodied by words as morphemes click into place. Unconstrained by the line, poems can perform this movement and reveal the aesthetics of grammar and thought. In my poem below, I experiment with representing movement in the English translation of a poem written in Niimiipuutímt. "C'éewc'ew'/ Ghost" was inspired by a poetic expression that Phillip Cash Cash identified in the papers of X̣íluX̣in/Charlie McKay, a Nez Perce/Cayuse intellectual of the twentieth century. McKay's piece is a found poem that Phil and I each sought to imitate on our own. The strategy in the exercise was to apprentice oneself to the poem and learn directly from it. In each line, I imitate the categories of the found poem by McKay; the first line is concerned with temporality, the second with the movement of hunters, and the third with the movement of the Ghost. Each line of "C'éewc'ew/Ghost" has movement embodied within the words, and to capture the aesthetics of the grammar, I attempt to show how the language *moves* and orders spatial relationships by representing the lines in a visual fashion. In the poem below, I attempt to capture the movement within the word itself, as the Ghost hi'yalahtq'iyóoya ("rose up and went out after") the hunters.

C'éewc'ew/Ghost

AFTER X̣ÍLUX̣IN CHARLIE MCKAY

kaa wáaqo' seX̣liweynéekitx
and now it was turning toward fall
hipetkuulíixne meX̣sémkex
they went out hunting toward the mountains
c'ewc'éewnim hi'yalahtq'iyóoya
the Ghost rose up and went out after them

Here, I clarify the movement of the third line through visual representation, not a concrete poem but rather a concrete translation:

<pre>
                                                    ya *past tense*
                                      yóo   toward (hunters)
                                  and OUT (v)
                            UP
                 lahtq'i. *MOVE*
            a.   *air*
          y   *the*
 c'ewc'éew.nim   hi. '   *in*
 Ghost.subject   *3rd person subject*
</pre>

The poem, by speaking directly with an ancestor through an archival fragment, participates in a process that Maliseet linguist Bernard Perley has termed "*re-membering* ancestral voices." He argues that reanimations of archival materials produce "emergent vitalities" that reorient language in place and time, working against the dismembering and vitiating practices of linguistics as a science. In his creative practice, Perley reclaims Maliseet language through the graphic novel, drawing contemporary characters speaking the language while moving through the land, thus remembering the language to the living beings and places to which it belongs.[18]

In the discussion above, I've emphasized poetry's capacity to reveal the performance of language, to demonstrate how the language acts and moves and organizes the world. Poetry is a genre that brings attention to form and aesthetics, and thus is well-suited to highlighting the beauty and unique characteristics of our Indigenous languages. In our language, we have a beautiful word for song (we'nipt), but we also have a grammar that makes our word for song even more profound and compelling. Poetry is a welcoming entryway into the thought world of the language and the culture, and a gentle method of learning grammar that supports language revitalization. Further, creative writing's emphasis on invention and re-creation grounds the work of revitalization in life-centered activity, pushing against narratives of endangerment, scarcity, and death (although, thanks to efforts by language activists, the terms "extinction" and "death" are no longer dominant terms). Creative writing is an occasion for celebrating the intelligence, beauty, and on-goingness of Indigenous languages and peoples.

In the context of language revitalization, poetry is not an exclusive realm that belongs only to wordsmiths and those with particular facility in language. It is a methodology that places creation and life-generation at its center; it values individual genius and expression as a gift to the collective. Creative writing is a method first and an outcome second. In conventional approaches to poetry, language is at the service of the poem; in language revitalization, that relationship is reversed and the poem is at the service of the language. This is not a strict formula, of course, but simply a distinction that addresses the context of language revitalization that utilizes poetic forms and expressions as ways to express the beauty and structure of language itself. That is, language is the primary subject of the poem, even as a poem speaks of wider external and internal worlds. Creative expression is a process through which one can, through the language itself, develop a sense of authority as a speaker and writer. Put most directly, the penning of poems, songs, and stories is a process of *author*izing language use.

In our Nez Perce collective, luk'upsíimey, an aspect of that authorization, has come through our opportunities to perform our work, both within our group and for external audiences. Recitation is built into the weekly process of sharing work, and poems and other works give us specific words and phrases to master for and through performance. Moreover, the occasions upon which we have performed as a collective for external audiences have had a bonding effect that has strengthened our relationships to our language, our land, and each other. The performance of poetry creates a context for speaking, and speaking enhances our performance of the language. Like learning the lines for a play, we memorize the elocution of our words and perform them until they become part of us. The performance of poetry and other creative works is a means through which our language can be brought into the body, and ultimately, a means through which our language can be carried forward.

Notes

1. For a related discussion, see Robert Sullivan, "A Poetics of Culture: Others' and Ours, Separate and Commingled," *Landfall* 211 (2006): 9–18.

2. My aunt, Theresa Eagle, and my uncle, Raymond Eagle, were both first-language speakers. I learned some words and phrases from them. In 2002, I began to study the language with Dr. Haruo Aoki, the linguist who wrote the *Nez Perce Dictionary, Nez Perce Grammar,* and translated several volumes of Nez Perce texts. He taught me how to translate the stories on my own, so that the texts would be my teachers. I am forever grateful to my dear teacher Haruo Aoki, and the path that he made for me and others to return to the language.

3. "Nez Perce," *World Atlas of Languages,* UNESCO, https://en.wal.unesco.org/languages/nez-perce.

4. Nora Marks Dauenhauer and Richard Dauenhauer, "Technical, Emotional, and Ideological Issues in Reversing Language Shift: Examples from Southeast Alaska," in *Endangered Languages: Language Loss and Community Response,* ed. Lenore A. Grenoble and Lindsay J. Whaley (New York: Cambridge University Press, 1998), 63, 65.

5. In addition to myself and Phillip Cash Cash, the original members of luk'upsíimey include Ines Hernandez-Avila, Angel Sobotta, Kellen Lewis, Julian Ankney, and Sarah Hennessey. The word luk'upsíimey means *without movement* and it refers to the North Star.

6. This sense of performative language—that the language itself is doing things through its grammar, rather than causative of other phenomena—is a departure from J. L. Austin's concept of performative speech/language in which certain speech acts create new conditions (i.e., "I do" seals a marriage covenant). See J. L. Austin, *How to Do Things with Words,* 2nd ed. (Cambridge: Harvard University Press, 1975).

7. Haruo Aoki, *Nez Perce Dictionary* (Berkeley: University of California Press, 1994), 1050–1051.

8. Natalie Diaz, *Postcolonial Love Poem* (Minneapolis: Graywolf Press, 2020), 46.

9. Beth Piatote, "I Cause My Heart to Pour Out is how to say *remember,*" in *Emerge/ncy* (Berkeley: Arts Research Center, 2022), 46–50. This poem cycle riffs on just six entries from the dictionary. There are hundreds of combinations possible for this one verb; the *Nez Perce Dictionary* lists more than eighty.

10. A bonus grammar lesson. The word for *smart* or *bright* is wepcúuk, possibly a combination of the prefix wep- for *hand,* and cúukwe, the same verb for *know,* as in the word cukwenéewit/knowledge. Intelligence is located in the hands, not the head. That should give Descartes something to think about. Aoki, *Nez Perce Dictionary,* 853.

11. Alice Taff, Melvatha Chee, Jaeci Hall, Millie Yéi Dulitseen Hall, Kawenniyóhstha Nicole Martin, and Annie Johnston, "Indigenous Language Use Impacts Wellness," in *The Oxford Handbook of Endangered Languages,* ed. Kenneth L. Rehg and Lyle Campbell (New York:

Oxford University Press, 2018), 6.

12. Diné language is not endangered, but listed as "potentially vulnerable," with about one million speakers, according to UNESCO's language map. "Navajo," *World Atlas of Languages*, UNESCO, https://en.wal.unesco.org/languages/navajo.

13. "Esther Belin in Conversation with Orlando White," *POETRY Magazine* podcast, June 21, 2022, https://www.poetryfoundation.org/podcasts/158222/esther-belin-in-conversation-with-orlando-white.

14. Sherwin Bitsui, *Flood Song* (Port Townsend, WA: Copper Canyon Press, 2021), 3.

15. Orlando White, "Water," *POETRY Magazine*, June 2022, 256.

16. Esther Belin, *Of Cartography* (Tucson: University of Arizona Press, 2017), 3.

17. "Esther Belin in Conversation with Orlando White."

18. Bernard Perley, "Remembering Ancestral Voices: Emergent Vitalities and the Future of Indigenous Languages," in *Responses to Language Endangerment: In Honor of Mickey Noonan*, ed. Elena Mihas, Bernard Perley, Gabriel Rei-Doval, and Kathleen Wheatley (Amsterdam: John Benjamins Publishing, 2013), 243–270.

Bibliography

Aoki, Haruo. *Nez Perce Dictionary*. Berkeley: University of California Press, 1994.

———. *Nez Perce Grammar*. Berkeley: University of California Press, 1965.

———. *Nez Perce Texts*. Berkeley: University of California Press, 1979.

Aoki, Haruo, and Deward E. Walker Jr. *Nez Perce Oral Narratives*. Berkeley: University of California Press, 1988.

Belin, Esther. *Of Cartography*. Tucson: University of Arizona Press, 2017.

Bitsui, Sherwin. *Flood Song*. Port Townsend, WA: Copper Canyon Press, 2021.

Diaz, Natalie. *Postcolonial Love Poem*. Minneapolis: Graywolf Press, 2020.

Dauenhauer, Nora Marks, and Richard Dauenhauer. "Technical, Emotional, and Ideological Issues in Reversing Language Shift: Examples from Southeast Alaska." In *Endangered Languages: Language Loss and Community Response*, edited by Lenore A. Grenoble and Lindsay J. Whaley, 57–98. New York: Cambridge University Press, 1998.

Perley, Bernard. "Remembering Ancestral Voices: Emergent Vitalities and the Future of Indigenous Languages." In *Responses to Language Endangerment: In Honor of Mickey Noonan*, edited by Elena Mihas, Bernard Perley, Gabriel Rei-Doval, and Kathleen Wheatley, Gary Simons, and M Paul Lewis, 243–270. Amsterdam: John Benjamins Publishing, 2013.

Piatote, Beth. "I Cause My Heart to Pour Out is how to say *remember.*" In *Emerge/ncy*, 46–50. Berkeley: Arts Research Center, 2022.

Sullivan, Robert. "A Poetics of Culture: Others' and Ours, Separate and Commingled." *Landfall* 211 (2006): 9–18.

Taff, Alice, Melvatha Chee, Jaeci Hall, Millie Yéi Dulitseen Hall, Kawenniyóhstha Nicole Martin, and Annie Johnston. "Indigenous Language Use Impacts Wellness." In *The Oxford Handbook of Endangered Languages*, edited by Kenneth L. Rehg and Lyle Campbell, 1–25. New York: Oxford University Press, 2018.

"Esther Belin in Conversation with Orlando White." *POETRY Magazine* podcast, June 21, 2022. https://www.poetryfoundation.org/podcasts/158222/esther-belin-in-conversation-with-orlando-white.

White, Orlando. "Water." *POETRY Magazine*, June 2022, 256.

Our World Was Born from Poetry

Koʻihonua as ʻŌiwi Poetic Praxis

kuʻualoha hoʻomanawanui

In ʻŌiwi (Hawaiian) culture, the concentrated, rhythmic form of mele (song text, poetry) is shaped across generations of oral tradition through performative practices (recitation, song, chant, prayer, ritual, ceremony, dance).[1] For millennia, mele recorded ʻŌiwi history in distinct poetic genres like koʻihonua (genealogical chants of cosmic origins), meta-moʻokūʻauhau (genealogy) recounting our familial pilina (relationship) as Indigenous people with our ʻāina (land, environment, lit., that which feeds) and natural elements, including native flora and fauna born into our world like us. Thus, koʻihonua are our first expressions of aloha ʻāina, love for the environment and everything in it as cherished ʻohana (family) and kūpuna (elders, ancestors). Beginning in the politically tumultuous late 1880s, aloha ʻāina became the foundation of Hawaiian nationalism. Since that time, aloha ʻāina remains political, affirming the continuity of the shared moʻokūʻauhau between ʻŌiwi and ʻāina. In this relationship, mālama (care) is enacted in the present by remembering the past while simultaneously keeping an eye always toward fostering abundance for future generations to inherit. Thus, koʻihonua are a starting point of aloha ʻāina as ʻŌiwi poetic praxis, reflecting our worldviews and enacted in our language, practices, and being.

Writing and printing were first introduced by American Calvinist missionaries in the 1820s–1830s with the intention of converting Hawaiians to Christianity. However, ʻŌiwi utilized writing for their own purposes, despite haole (white) settler insistance on assimilation.[2] From that time forward, moʻolelo (story, history) and mele could be recorded and shared outside the body, broadening their transmission across place and time.

Mele ʻŌiwi (Hawaiian poetry) is a culturally derived praxis rooted in oral and performative traditions that influence ʻŌiwi poetics in all forms. Koʻihonua demonstrate methodologies and praxis of our kūpuna that continue today, particulary in genres such as mele aloha ʻāina (Hawaiian nationalist poetry). In this chapter, I explore how mele aloha ʻāina embody ʻŌiwi epistemologies and is inscribed in our political, educational, and activist practices, culminating in ʻŌiwi self-determination and Land Back movements.

Mai ka Pō mai (From the Ancient Past): Mele Koʻihonua and Pilina as Praxis

For ʻŌiwi, all life emerges from pō (night, darkness, chaos) and genealogically unfolds through mele koʻihonua, poetic compositions detailing the ʻŌiwi understanding of the origins of the cosmos, earth, and life forms. Because koʻihonua were originally composed verbally, memorized, and chanted, composition practices emerged that aided memorization and recall. For example, meiwi (ethnopoetic devices) such as ʻēkoʻa (diads), pīnaʻi (repetition), and helu (recounting, listing), are embedded in the kino (form) and organization of the mele as a whole, and within interior sections, such as paukū (stanzas). These can also function as mnemonic devices, along with other meiwi such as kaona (metaphor), hoʻomaoe (allusion), and hōʻailona (symbolism).

Moʻolelo are generally considered prose narratives, a genre distinct from mele. However, mele are often packed with moʻolelo revealed through figurative language like kaona, hoʻomaoe, and hōʻailona. The use of key words in a mele work like hypertext links, where one "click" opens up myriad relevant associations. In an oral cultural, memory is crucial to recording and transmitting valuable history and knowledge, which provide a foundation for cultural continuity. Writing, print, and later digital technologies have expanded the ability of Indigenous cultures to continue remembering, telling, and creating our own moʻolelo and mele, which accomodates both the transmission of traditional knowledge and the incorporation of contemporary experiences as living peoples with living cultures—thus countering the colonial trope of an imagined "authentic" culture of the past that is no longer attainable, meaning Indigenous peoples are not who we know we are.

Mele koʻihonua articulate ʻŌiwi identity and our genealogical connection to our ʻāina. Thus, they "are crucial to understanding a Kanaka worldview, and through these cosmogonic genealogies we learn of the formation of the ʻāina, the first living organisms, and the birth of the akua (gods) and the people."[3] Many koʻihonua provide differing accounts of origin. Such diverse points of view demonstrate the cultural concept of makawalu (lit., eight eyes), or multiple perspectives. Moʻokūʻauhau literally means the succession (moʻo) of descendants that stand (kū) on the leg bones (ʻauhau) of the ancestors, and koʻihonua protruding or prominent (koʻi) earth or foundation (honua).

Kumulipo details the birth of the Hawaiian universe from the deep dark night, or kumu (source) of deep darkness (lipo). At 2,108 lines in legnth, it is by far the most comprehensive koʻihonua. It is evenly divided into sixteen wā (epochs, sections), from which all elements emerge, beginning with slime, mud, and corals. These are followed by pairs of native flora and fauna in the sea and on the land, culminating in lengthy ʻŌiwi lineages that include the earth mother, Papahānaumoku (lit., the foundation that births islands); her primal partner, Wākea (lit., vast expanse of sky), the sky father; and their aliʻi (chiefly) descendants, down to Kaʻīamamao, for whom Kumulipo is composed circa 1720s. The intent of Kumulipo was to demonstrate Kaʻīamamao's birthright to rule because of his genealogical connections to his illustrious human ancestors, pre-human life forms, and ultimately, to the earth, sea, sky, and universe.

Mālama ʻāina (cherishing the land) is a foundational concept rooted in ʻŌiwi kinship to nature. Kanaka are the youngest descendants of the Hawaiian universal family tree, offspring of Papahānaumoku and Wākea, and the younger siblings of flora and fauna. In a kinship framework, the kuleana (responsibilities) of the elder generations and siblings is to mālama—care for, nurture, cherish, and protect—the younger ones so they may flourish. Our environment does that by providing for all of our needs, wants, and desires, including food, shelter, clothing, medicine, and pleasure. The reciprocation expected from the younger siblings is to respect, honor, cherish, and care for the elders. ʻŌiwi do this by working to balance the ecosystem by following strict regulations on growing and harvesting to ensure abundance for all. Thus aloha ʻāina dictates a cultural practice of living pono—in harmony and balance *with* the land, and is harshly critical of those who waste or overextract resources.

Such praxis visibly juxtaposes the heteropatriarchial Christian creation story of Genesis in the Bible, where Adam, a human male, is create by God, a singular male deity, and given jurisdiction over all of the deity's creation to do with as he pleases for his own benefit. A human female, Eve, is created by God from Adam's rib as a companion for him, relegating her to an inferior position within the hierachical patriarchial framework established in the narrative. Moreover, as Eve is tempted by a (male) serpent and enticed to eat from the forbidden tree of knowledge, the human pair is evicted from the Garden of Eden, and a narrative of sin, punishment, constant lack, and longing because of a forced separation from nature by their punitive creator emerges. A foundational philosophy of western capitalism, that nature (and its resources) is for the benefit of humans to do with what they desire, is established in Genesis—Adam/man is the "master" of all (including Eve/women), and those who benefit in extracting excess for profit are "blessed" by God.

The poetic praxis that emerges from mele koʻihonua is central to ʻŌiwi society, culture, values, and poetics. Cultural concepts such as aloha—love, respect, compassion, mālama, and pono—are core values that come from pilina between people (individuals, families, communities, society), between people and nature, and between elements of nature. For example, the root of the word for family, ʻohana, is ʻoha, the way the kalo (taro) plant grows, where keiki (baby, child) corms emerge as clusters around the makua (parent) corm. Kumulipo and other sources recount that the first born keiki of Papahānaumoku and Wākea is Hāloanakalaukapalili (lit., long breath with leaves that quiver [in the breeze]), a stillborn fetus who is lovingly buried just outside their home. After the grieving parents inter the child's body, they discover the next morning that a kalo plant, the very first one and the main vegetal carbohydrate for ʻŌiwi, has grown from the place that Hāloa was buried. Later, when their next son is born healthy, he is named Hāloa (long breath) in memory of his elder kalo brother. The kuleana of Hāloanakalaukapalili is to mālama Hāloa and his human descendants by providing nurishing food—the entire kalo plant, leaf, stem, flower, and corm, is edible and highly nutritious; kalo is a domestic crop that thrives under human cultivation, and thus the kuleana of Hāloa and his ʻŌiwi descendants is to cultivate kalo, and by extension, the ʻāina, caring for and protecting it, their elder. This is a loving relationship, upon which 'Ōiwi writer Kepelino Keauokalani elaborates:

He mea maikai loa ka mahiai kalo ma na aina maloo. He hoaloha oluolu loa ia ano, a he kumu paipai mai i ka puuwai o kanaka. He ea ala ka lau, ka ha, ka pua ma na kihapai kalo. He mea aloha, a he mea makemake maoli, ke ike aku i ka ulu a ke kalo, a me na ano huli he nui wale, ke noho oe, a hoomaha paha iloko o napuepue kalo. I ka wa kahiko, he mea ue na ka poe mahiai ka hana, ke loohia ko lakou mau kino i ka mai; nolaila, ue maoli lakou i ka minamina i ka hana, a me ke aloha i na mea kanu. "He keiki aloha na mea kanu," wahi a ka poe mahiai.

Cultivating taro on dry lands is a most excellent endeavor, the kalo a beloved companion, one delighting the hearts of the people. The leaves, stems, and flowers have a pleasing scent in the garden. It is a beloved thing, truly delightful, to see taro growing and the replanted kalo flourishing when you linger and relax amongst the heaps of kalo. In the past the kalo farmers wept if they became disabled and couldn't farm, because they loved their plants. "Plants are beloved children," the farmers said.[4]

The form and devices of mele 'Ōiwi are found throughout ko'ihonua, starting with helu and pīna'i. This is evident in the following example, excerpted from Kumulipo's third wā, which is typical throughout:

	KA WĀ 'EKOLU	THE THIRD ERA
285.	Hānau ka *huhu* he makua	The *termite* is born, a parent
286.	Puka kāna keiki he *huhu lele*, lele	Its child, a *flying termite*, emerges and flies
287.	Hānau ka *pe'elua* he makua	The *caterpillar* is born, a parent
288.	Puka kāna keiki he *pulelehua*, lele	Its child, a *butterfly*, emerges and flies
289.	Hānau ka *naonao* he makua	The *ant* is born, a parent
290.	Puka kāna keiki he *pinao*, lele	Its child, a *dragonfly*, emerges and flies

291.	Hānau ka *'unia* he makua	The *cricket* is born, a parent
292.	Puka kāna keiki he *'ūhini*, lele	Its child, the *grasshopper*, emerges and flies
293.	Hānau ka *naio* he makua	The *pinworm* is born, a parent
294.	Puka kāna keiki he *nalo*, lele	Its child, a *fly*, emerges and flies
295.	Hānau ka *hualua* he makua	The *double egg*[5] is born, a parent
296.	Puka kāna keiki he *manu*, lele	Its child, a *bird*, emerges and flies[6]

The birth order and relationship between the smaller winged, flying species are recounted through helu, culminating in the emergence of manu (birds), and the helu of native bird species commences. Repetition of key phrases, "Hānau ka ___, he makua" (a ___ is born, a parent) and "Puka kāna keiki he ___, lele" (Its child, a ___, appears and flies) is indicative of pīna'i found throughout Kumulipo that changes when needed; for example, when fish are born, they don't lele (fly), they holo (lit., go; to travel in water, sail). At another level within this section, pīna'i is evident in the high concentration of repeated consonant (h, k, l, m, n, p) and vowel (a, e, i, o, u) as well as sounds and morphemes (ha, ka, hu, he, nao, nau), words (hānau, lele, puka), and phrases (he makua, kāna keiki). Slant rhyme is also evident (hānau/naonao, hua/'unia), and as is a rhyming pattern between lines common in mele 'Ōiwi, linked assonance, where the end of one line rhymes with the beginning of the next line ("makua / Puka").

Helu and pīna'i are both poetic methods and mnemonic devices integral to oral cultures that aid memorization. The kind of repetition evident in mele 'Ōiwi is dependent upon 'ōlelo Hawai'i, where sounds of letters, syllables, and morphemes are highly prevalent, in part because 'ōlelo Hawai'i contains fewer consonants than English—h, k, l, m, n, p, w, an the 'okina (') or glottal stop, a consonant not found in English.[7] Next are the *'ēko'a* pairings of makua (parent) and keiki (child) species: pe'elua and pulelehua, naonao and pinao, 'unia and 'ūhini, and naio and nalo, all of which contain assonance, alliteration, and slant rhyme. Collectively, the kaona of the parent/child diads illustrates an intelligent imagining of species evolution embedded in the poetics of Hawaiian language—a flying termite may be related to a termite, and a butterfly does metamorph from a catepillar; a cricket and a grasshopper look similar, and a fly transforms from wriggling larvar but the rhythmic poetry of 'ōlelo Hawai'i (huhu/huhu lele, pe'elua/pulelehua, nao/naonao, naio/nalo) is lost, and a connection between ant and dragonfly, in English (and western thinking), is equally absent.

Moreover, the repeated birthing (hānau) process indicates mo'okū'auhau, and further solifies the kinship connection of nature with 'Ōiwi, and our mutual kuleana to respect and care for each other.

As wā three continues, bird species are recounted, beginning with seabirds, then moving inland to the native forest birds, before returning to the seabird species. Again, the same meiwi are present, with similar layering of repeated sounds, rhythms, and images throughout the lines. Lines 323–328 reveal the proliferation of bird species populating the land and sea, reflecting a world of abundance. Each named species provides immediate sensory imagery, starting with the visual—the color, sizes, and shapes of the birds; auditory—the calls of the various species and sounds of movement, such as flapping wings; kinesthetic imagery—through the flight and movement of the birds on and above the 'āina and kai (ocean); tactile imagery—recalling the softness of feathers; organic imagery—the feeling of delight and being mesmerized by the birds; and perhaps gustatory imagery—as some species were eaten. There is also a connection to hō'ailona, or the symbolism of specific bird species, associated with being excellent navigators and land finders revered by long-distance ocean voyagers ('iwa, mōlī), those expert at detecting rotten tree logs that would not make suitable canoes or watercraft if felled ('elepaio), those with red and yellow feathers prized for featherwork symbolizing high-ranking royalty ('ō'ō, mamo, alawī, 'akikiki, 'apapane), and so forth. The 'iwa (frigate) bird also symbolizes an attractive person, as in the poetic lines, "He 'iwa ka hoa e like ai" (a companion who resembles the 'iwa bird [one who is dressed up in finery]) and "Ka 'iwa ālai maka" (the 'iwa bird that dazzles the eyes).[8] It is also a hō'ailona used as metaphor for admired ali'i, and a powerful chiefly symbol of political acumen and military prowess applied to powerful ali'i, like Kamehameha I.[9]

However, some traditional symbolism and allusions regarding birds have been lost. Kumulipo was not recorded in writing until the 1880s, a century after initial western intrusion.[10] The onslaught of colonialism through haole explorers and settlers over the next century resulted in a population collapse of up to

90 percent, and wrought catastrophic harm on the environment, including extinction and threat to many native species of plants and animals.[11] The impact of colonial exploitation is evident in Kumulipo, which lists five bird species (the alawī, 'e'ea, 'alaiaha, 'ukihi, and unana) we no longer know anything about; Kumulipo is the only record of their existance, and all poetic symbolism and associations with them have been lost as well.

This is another way ko'ihonua demonstrate the cultural value of hali'a (memory). It is also a way to recount pilina of all kinds, and related mo'olelo from the personal to the national, an aspect of mele composition (and themes) embedded in a genre of mele that emerged in the politically turbulent 1890s, mele aloha 'āina—the songs, chants, and poetry that expressed love for the land as Hawaiian nationalism and political resistance to haole interference, governance, and oppression of the lāhui Hawai'i (Hawaiian people, nation).

Mele 'Ai Pōhaku (Rock-Eating Song): Aloha 'Āina and Memory as Poetic Praxis

On January 17, 1893, the peaceful Hawaiian Kingdom was illegally overthrown by a cabal of haole men assisted by the U.S. Marines. Despite strong 'Ōiwi resistence, Hawai'i was transformed into a republic governed by the same haole implicated in the overthrow; it was illegally annexed to the United States in 1898, and in 1900 Hawai'i became a U.S. Territory, followed by statehood in 1959. During these politically tumultuous years, many 'Ōiwi composed mele vehemently protesting the vile actions of the haole settlers, and encouraged the lāhui to remember and support their own lāhui, land, and leaders. Traditionally, mele kālai'āina (political poetry) touted the attributes or leadership of particular ali'i, or alluded to possibilities of conflict. While political in nature, mele aloha 'āina brought another dimension to mele kālai'āina, as they were explicitly supportive of Hawaiian self-governance and sovereignty, and specifically critical of haole actions and interference.

'Ōiwi scholars, including myself, have written about the mele "Mele 'Ai Pōhaku" (rock-eating song) composed in this period by Ellen Kekoahiwaikalani Prendergast.[12] But Prendergast was hardly alone. In 1895, F. Testa published *Buke Mele Lāhui* (Hawaiian National Songbook), a compilation of nearly one hundred mele aloha 'āina, including "Mele 'Ai Pōhaku."

Countless mele aloha ʻāina were published in the Hawaiian language newspapers as well. Viewed collectively, these mele reveal a staunch aloha ʻāina nationalism by ʻŌiwi and their supporters, other Hawaiian Kingdom citizens, who vehemently objected to the forced overthrow and later annexation of the Kingdom to the United States, deep support and admiration for those who tried to protect, defend, and later restore Hawaiian governance, and a fierce love for the ʻāina. During this period, the concept of aloha ʻāina took on an additional meaning of nationalism and enduring matriotism, which also deeply contradicted and interrogated the western concept of monotheistic patriotism. On one hand, mele aloha ʻāina express love for the land that can be very specific to and meaningful to the individual poet. On the other, mele aloha ʻāina also express ʻŌiwi nationalism and unity with the lāhui (people) who are loyal to and take great pride in our pilina with our ʻāina.

Ua Mau ke Ea o ka ʻāina i ka Pono (The Sovereignty of the Land Is Linked to Justice): Mele Aloha ʻĀina and Decolonial ʻŌiwi Futurisms

These thoughts continue in contemporary compositions by ʻŌiwi poets in ʻōlelo Hawaiʻi, English, and sometimes other languages, and in traditional and introduced genres of poetry and music. The diversity of "Hawaiianized" poetic and musical styles challenge haole perspectives that "authentic" cultural praxis is relegated to a pre-colonial past that denies ʻŌiwi agency. On the contrary, we continue to create and participate in a dynamic, thriving culture influenced by the larger world around us.

On July 31, 1843, after a brief breach of Hawaiian sovereignty, King Kamehamaha III proclaimed, "Ua mau ke ea o ka ʻāina i ka pono." The state of Hawaiʻi has appropriated it as the state motto, often translated with Christian influence as "the life of the land is perpetuated in righteousness." However, the terms mau, ea, ʻāina, and pono should be interpreted within the political context of the time period.[13] The alternative translation "the sovereignty of the land continues [has been restored] because justice was served" is more fitting. Interpreted this way, aloha ʻāina is understood within ʻŌiwi cultural praxis inherent in koʻihonua, specifically Kumulipo.

Hundreds, perhaps thousands of mele aloha ʻāina have been composed between 1843 and today, crossing multiple generations and genres. Many of these mele incorporate or allude to Kamehameha III's famous words.[14] Despite the loss of political sovereignty in 1893, which has had severe and long-lasting deleterious effects on the lāhui Hawai'i as a politically independent, self-determining nation, 'Ōiwi today continue the struggle of our kūpuna, the po'e aloha 'āina, and remain kūpa'a ma hope o ka 'āina (ever steadfast and loyal to our homeland). The themes, the kaona, and symbolism of these beloved mele aupuni continue to resonate. The phrase "ua mau ke ea o ka 'āina i ka pono" alone is found in dozens of compositions from 1906 to 2023.[15]

Two recent Kumulipo-inspired mele aloha 'āina are "Kumulipo" by the Ho'okupu hip-hop collective, led by Hano and Maile Naehu (Paniolo Prince and Queen Maile) (2023) and "'Āina Hānau" by Brandy Nālani McDougall (2023). "Kumulipo" is eighty-five lines long; the first twenty and last twelve lines of the mele are the opening and closing lines of the original Kumulipo (lines 1–20 and 1991–2002). The first twenty lines represent the beginning of the ko'ihonua and birth of the universe, which culminates in the birth of Kalani'īamamao (line 2002). In between, sixteen couplet paukū represent the sixteen wā. While highly condensed in length from the original, each paukū encapsulates the original wā through meiwi (helu, pīna'i, kaona, and hō'ailona, as previously discussed). Each paukū uses ho'omaoe to the breadth of information contained in the original. Before concluding, ko'ihonua poetics as 'Ōiwi cultural praxis is emphasized:

> Let the rhythm scatter rhyme
> Pattern line data with the evidence we battle minds
> Perfect in design I'm not the only one who saw the signs
> Called upon to tell it from the stories of the oldest ones
> Spoken in Golden times
> With the knowledge of the world's wind
> Inner working outer sky
> Cosmic creation and constant constellations align
> the 'ike [wisdom] resides
> For Kānaka [Hawaiians] from pō we climb
> primordial slime
> Evolution the tree of life.[16]

After stressing mo'okū'auhau as a core of 'Ōiwi being, pilina to 'āina, and poetic praxis, the poets link traditional 'Ōiwi ko'ihonua knowledge to that of the Middle East, the cradle of civilization in the western world: "From the land of two rivers / To the plateau of Giza, Gobelki Tepe pillars / Enuma Elish, it started with the darkness / Emerge from the source with the mixing of waters."[17] Giza, of course, is the site of a massive pyramid complex, while the oldest known megaliths are located in Turkey's Göbelki Tepe; both are UNESCO World Heritage Sites. Enuma Elish, the Babylonian creation epic that reflects Mesopotamian cosmology paralleling Old Testament biblical passages becomes a parallel of exquisite cosmology exalted in the West, and the poets draw an intentional comparison between sacred Hawaiian koʻihonua and ʻāina recognized in Middle Eastern traditions.[18] The allusion to the "tree of life" is an image central to many old religions around the world, extending the comparison so as to validate traditional Hawaiian knowledge at the global level. The mele then return to ʻŌiwi moʻokūʻauhau as a central focus before concluding with the lines from Kumulipo culminating with the birth of Kaʻīamamao, "Straight from the piko like the maile [vine] umbilical / Connected to the source like a vine with the ebb and flow / Interlocked like a dragon [moʻo] spine, moʻokūʻauhau / Genealogy of the koko [blood]."[19] Maile (*Alyxia olivaeformis*) is a fragrant native vine with four types "believed to be sisters with human and plant forms" who are also akua hula.[20] Here, a hōʻailona represents all the pre-human plant kūpuna listed in Kumulipo whose umbilical cord-like vine ties ʻŌiwi genealogies to our pre-human lineage. The root word of moʻokūʻauhau, moʻo, has many meanings, primarily referencing lizards and reptiles, here represented by the dragon; the "interlocked spine" is the genealogy; symbolically the dragon is a hōʻailona, representing all the pre-human animal kūpuna who come before Hawaiian people in Kumulipo. The mele uses synecdoche, with the term koko (blood) to refer to Hawaiian people.

McDougall's poem "ʻĀina Hānau" (birth land) also uses the Kumulipo structure in that it is divided into sixteen paukū that represent Kumulipo's sixteen wā. However, each paukū moves between different themes related to pregnancy (hāpai) and birth (hānau) as experienced by an ʻŌiwi mother. The mele shifts between the individual (the poet's personal experience with pregancy, motherhood, colonialism, and decolonialism) and the collective (the experiences of the same as a lāhui). Thus, the poet draws from the second wave feminist slogan of the 1970s, "the personal is political." Yet this concept is presented within an ʻŌiwi context of koʻihonua, in which the individuals (mother, daughters) are also part of ʻohana, lāhui, and ʻāina. Moreover, as

'Ōiwi nationalist, scholar, and poet Haunani-Kay Trask argues, Indigenous women and men are affected by colonialism, and white feminism is a part of this political construct.[21] Therefore, understanding 'Ōiwi feminism or mana wahine (lit., female power) is critical: the lāhui stands together as a collective, as men (grandfathers, fathers, brothers, cousins, sons, etc.) are an integral part of 'ohana, and everyone is together in the struggle to decolonize and thrive. Thus, the mele describes the experiences of hāpai and hānau in pre-colonial and colonial contexts. McDougall juxtaposes the traditional experience of hāpai and hānau within the context of cultural wisdom and a supportive community with the demeaning modern experience of medical colonialism, which embodies racism and misogyny against native women and mothers (and their families). She also, however, shares her process of decolonization, as the mother/narrator/poet reconnects herself—and thus her daughters—to 'āina through the ancient pre-colonial wisdom of ko'ihonua, specifically Kumulipo.

In paukū thirteen, the narrator reveals a miscarriage, and speaks to her unborn, never to be born child, "You were in the dark / waves for a time, your body a / pearl of flesh, hands and feet / formed . . . / Something in the dark / called and you followed, / leaving / only your body to come / into light. You were / wrapped and held before you / were buried. You are loved and / missed."[22] The imagery recalls the sacred dark night (pō) of Kumulipo, when the first ancestors are born in the water; the fetus is a pearl, a treasure, the child's spirit called to the realm of the akua and kūpuna, only its fragile body born into ao (light, time of people). In this way, another important mo'olelo in Kumulipo is recalled, the stillborn birth of Hāloanakalaukapalili, the first kalo plant, who is followed later by his human brother, Hāloa, who establish the concept of mālama 'āina. This loving recollection (hali'a) juxtaposes the clinical coldness of her experience as a Native mother:

> In another time, you
> would have had 'ohana around you
> who knew what to say and do
> to help you. A Hawaiian
> medical doctor would hāhā
> your 'ōpū as you describe what happened
> and told you *he keiki*
> *he'e wale* or *he keiki hā'ule wale,*

a child who has flowed away,
a child who has fallen like rain.
You would be given tea to drink
and time to grieve, pray, reflect,
and dream, and you and your
ʻohana would be asked to share feelings
to heal you, and when it was time
for your keiki to flow from your body, your keiki would be wrapped
in kapa and planted as songs fell like
rain . . .
We tried our best to give that to you, kuʻu
keiki aloha. You sank down from us like
water, our love for you lossening the earth
beneath the lauaʻe, its cradling roots.[23]

The literal and metaphorical reconnection to Kumulipo is a part of the decolonizing process for for the grieving mother (and family) to heal by remembering
and reconnecting with their familial relationship as ʻŌiwi with our ʻāina.

Later in the mele, the narrator/mother speaks to her daughters. She also
speaks to us all as as our mothers (also grandmothers, aunties) do:

E kuʻu mau ʻōmaka i ke kīhāpai [my beloved young buds of my garden]:
may you always know these
islands, like you, daughters, are more
than enough, know that like you,
they are everything beautiful,
everything bouyant. Their winds
and rains and mountains, ravines
and valleys love without
question. Like our islands, may you
give birth first to yourselves then
love always with green tenderness,
thrusting
your hands into mud, opening
your body into ocean, knowing
these islands are here for you,

for your children and their
children, knowing we are these islands . . .
. . . even when you think
you are alone, that you feel the ocean
in your sweat and tears, that
you watch rain wash the hillsides
into a dark steam and see your
skin, that the sun, moon and stars,
dark underwater caverns, underground
rivers, all you see and don't see of
'āina, are your kūpuna, your 'ohana
in your every breath, that something of
you, something of all of us before, and
something of all of us to come are these
islands. May this always be with you:
E ola mau, e ola nō.[24]

Like mele aloha 'āina of the past, the narrator addresses her daughters directly and with much love, and weaving nature imagery and evoking beauty and pilina. Throughout the mele, the narrator repeats a reminder to her daughters that "like you, these islands were born." The final paukū summarizes the familial pilina to 'āina that the daughters have, and provides a final reminder that "we are these islands." Perhaps more importantly, this concept is imbued with mana, that the islands "birthed themselves," and are thus powerful akua with great agency, a practice of mana wahine the daughters are encouraged to emulate as the newest generation of the lāhui. The final line, "E ola mau, e ola nō" (long life, long life indeed), alludes to the call for long life to ali'i as beloved leaders of the people, and works here as a desire for the mother to see her daughters live a long and happy life, but also for the future generations of 'Ōiwi they represent to continue as well, a thought reflected from the beginning of 'Ōiwi culture, expressed through our mele.

"'Āina Hānau" is a brilliant example of contemporary 'Ōiwi poetic praxis that draws directly from Kumulipo, as many 'Ōiwi poets have done across genres and generations. Aside from its use of kino and meiwi like traditional ko'ihonua, the mele functions as a personal ko'ihonua for the daughters incorporating the rich history and poetics that are as intricate in thought and meaning as Kumulipo for the infant Kaʻīamamao.

My own poetic praxis is highly influenced by koʻihonua and aloha ʻāina, in that I strive to center many of the same themes, highlighting my relationships to my ʻāina using ʻŌiwi perspectives that also disrupt, interogate, and refute (settler) colonialism and its continuous oppression and destruction of our Native lands and people. One example appears in the poem "ʻĀina Kūpuna: Waipā":

Kūpuna mountains surround us
verdant green fingers of red earth
stretched longingly ma kai
to touch kūpuna sea
Kua uli arched towards ka lani
touch kūpuna clouds and sky
hold us in their nurturing embrace
beneath kūpuna sun
illuminating our path in radiant light
Caressed by kūpuna wind
who teases, refreshes us
plays with kūpuna trees who
conversate
in
ancient
kūpuna language overhead
still foreign to our modern ears
protecting us i kō lākou malu

One day we will return
as we travel the relentless path
from birth to youth to old then ancient
rebirth
our bodies will sink
dissolve into Papa's muddy kūpuna embrace
our spirits uplifted on kūpuna winds

> add our voices of wisdom
> to the chorus of ancients.[25]

Waipā is an ahupuaʻa in the moku of Haleleʻa, near my kulāiwi (ancestral family lands). Traditionally used primarily for kalo cultivation, it is an important site for loʻi kalo. Much of the ahupuaʻa is managed by Waipā Foundation, a nonprofit community-based organization whose mission is "to restore Waipā's vibrant natural [ʻāina] systems and resources and inspire healthy, thriving communities connected to their resources."[26] Part of what they do is grow kalo, and process poi every Thursday, with free delivery to kūpuna on the island. I composed this poem in 2005 as part of a writing and art workshop held at Waipā for the Nā Pua Noʻeau Native Hawaiian Gifted and Talented program for middle school students. Part of my poetic praxis is composing alongside and with my haumāna (students) as we cocreate. In this process, there is nothing more inspiring than to be out on our ʻāina, surrounded not just by nature, but by all the elements—the mountains, trees, clouds, sun, and wind, named as our ancient but ever-present ancestors (kūpuna) who watch over and still provide for us. In this context, a kaona of kūpuna is also wisdom; our wise elders are our teachers who pass their wisdom on to us, their moʻopuna (descendants, lit., grandchildren). These elements are personified (hoʻokanaka) as living elders who communicate with each other all around us, each tracing their moʻokūʻauhau back to Kumulipo. In other contexts, the elements often carry personal names of specific locations in which they are found; in other contexts, elements like the sun carry the name of one of the four main akua kāne (male deities) Kānehoalani (Kāne, heavenly or royal companion).

Structurally, the mele follows a traditional ʻēkoʻa (opposite but balancing diads) in moving from the inland and upland (mountains) to the sea (ma kai), and then from the uplands (kua uli, lit., dark [green] back) of the mountains to the lani (sky, clouds, sun) back down to the earth (trees, us [as Kānaka ʻŌiwi], Papa[hānaumoku]). While Kumulipo (and, by extension, moʻokūʻauhau) appears linear, a helu of names, in essence, each generation is a rebirth and a renewal; a circular understanding of time is viewed through naming offspring after illustrious elders, in essence keeping the elders alive, similtaneously calling and recalling them—their mana, aloha, ʻike, and presence through their namesake. Thus, the second part of the mele reminds us that one day we, too, will pass on to the next world and be kūpuna, as the cycle and circle of life is e mau ana—ever continuing.

The mele "Wanini" is titled for my ʻohana's specific kulāiwi, not too far from Waipā. While there is some descriptive imagery about the ʻāina itself, it is a mele that speaks more about how that ʻāina is alive and continues to nurture my ʻohana across generations by referencing their and my moʻolelo and memories of their experiences there. The mele is written in two parts, divided like the wā in Kumulipo—the first is poetic snapshots of moʻolelo I've learned over my life from and about my kūpuna there, the second is a helu of how "My life at Wanini is captured in pictures" (line 66, which is also the year I was born), with selected images from age one to age fifteen.[27] This is predicated on a reference to the photos of kūpuna framed and placed throughout the house:

> A melange of photos are scattered on the walls:
> large portraitures mixed with snapshots
> tined hues and sepia tones fresh, faded,
> documenting a century's worth of moʻokūʻauhau
> Lives of the living memorialized alongside the lives of the dead.
> The watch us from the walls, these kūpuna:
> our guardians, our collective memory of this place.[28]

There is a critique of modernity, imposed by colonialism, as no one in the ʻohana can afford to live here full time, all of us employed on the neighboring island of Oʻahu, the economic hub of the state:

> There is a spring in the backyand, which feeds the taro loʻi on the hill, now grossly
> overgrown and neglected, hidden by the banana trees gone wild.
> Aunty would be disappointed that no one has time anymore
> to care for the once manicured and highly productive gardens
> which fed our family for generations.[29]

Yet rather than be overwhelmed by colonialism, the next paukū celebrates the abundance of the ʻāina, which is still accessible to current generations:

> They were wise, the kūpuna, they were self sufficient: every imaginable
> edible plant
> Is somewhere in that yard: mango, papaya, guava, avocado, banana, citrus;
> bamboo, hōʻio, pōpolo, and mint; mamake, laukahi, and kokoʻolau for tea

> Taro, of course, and coconut. Dad says his Tūtū [grandmother] planted the
> watercress / and choi sum in the 'auwai to suit her Chinese taste buds.
> All of it still there. Even the pens for the pigs, although they've been gone
> for at least a decade. The fish [dry] box and fish safe are safely stored on
> > the back lānai.
> But we don't use them as often as we used to, as often as we should.[30]

Food is such a crucial component of cultural identity, and the helu of edible plants is reletively specific to Hawai'i and the previous three generations of my Hawaiian-Chinese 'ohana as well as a mix of native and introduced plants in postcolonial times. A knowledgeable (Hawaiian) audience understands the use and preparation of the kaona of each plant listed as food or medicine; these balance the main protein source, i'a (fish), alluded to in reference to the dry box and safe, used to salt, dry, and store excess catches for lean times or for off seasons. Fronting the beach and an enormously productive reef, there is 'ēko'a between the land food plants (lā'au mea 'ai) and complementary protein from the sea (i'a).

A mele I am currently working on laments the devastation of a 2013 molasses spill in Honolulu Harbor, which resulted in the mass suffocation and death of an estimated twenty-six thousand fish and marine life, along with seventeen thousand corals. Over 1,400 tons of molasses being transferred by ship from Hawaiian Commercial Sugar on Maui to the United States was spilled when a faulty pipeline ruptured; because molasses is not regulated, there was no contingency plan in place by either Matson Navigation or any government agencies from the local to federal level. As corals and aquatic life are the first born in Kumulipo (wā one and two), the mass death of sealife in the harbor horrified me beyond its ecological and environmental impacts—it was a direct example of settler colonialism and capitalism literally destroying our 'āina, and metaphorically devastating our nonhuman and more-than-human kūpuna, the eldest of our 'ohana in Kumulipo. The mele is a kanikau (lament), a traditional Hawaiian genre expressing both grief and affection for the subject. The mele begins:

> This is not another Kumulipo poem
> Where life unfolds from the depths of pō
> A spark, a flash, intense heat, swirling
> Where born is the cosmos
> Kumulipo, Pō'ele

Nā ʻākoʻakoʻa populate the seas
Build coral reefs, coral kingdoms
Sea pulsing with life
Iʻa and limu, limu and iʻa
All born in the sea, swimming—
no.

It then transitions to the context of the spill, and incorporates a quote (in italics) from Roger White, a local news station (KGMB) videographer who went into the harbor waters to film.

No one knew in 2013
A massive molasses spill could massacre
marine life
Everything down there is dead
Auē, e luluku wale ē!

The final line of this section, "Auē, e luluku wale ē!" (Alas, only devestation!) is a line found in other Hawaiian mele to convey immense grief at the destruction of our ʻāina. White's longer quote is woven throughout other parts of the mele:

It was shocking because the entire seafloor is covered with dead fish. Small fish, small crabs, mole crabs, eels. Every type of fish that you don't usually see—But now they're dead. Now they're just laying there. Every single thing is dead. Hundreds, thousands—I didn't see one single living thing underwater.[31]

Large sections of the mele draw directly from the helu of species of fish, sea, and plant life from wā one and two in the order they are listed in Kumulipo. However, instead of species being hānau, born, here their hoahanau (cousins, others born in Kumulipo alongside them) mourn:

Uē no nā *heʻe*, nā *ʻoʻopukai,*
Uē ka *walaheʻe,* ka *ʻoʻopuwai,* ke *kauila,*
Uē no ke *kauila,* ka *umaumalei,* ka *pākuʻikuʻi,*
Uē ka *ʻulei,* ke *kukui,* ka *milo,* ke *kou,* ka *uhi,*
Uē no ka *laumilo,* ke *kūpoupou,* ka *hāuliuli.*

> Cry for the *octopus*, the *sea gobies*,
> The *walahe'e shrubs*, the *fresh water gobies*, the *kauila trees* lament,
> Cry for the *kauila eel*, the *umaumalei eel*, the *pāku'iku'i sturgeon fish*,
> The *'ulei shrubs*, the *kukui nut trees*, the *milo trees*, the *kou trees*, the *yams* lament,
> Cry for the *laumilo eel*, the *cigar wrasse*, the *snake mackerel.*

Yet, despite the immense devastation, it is not within cultural poetic practice to end on such a depressing note. As Noelani Arista writes:

> Though these laments come from moments of grief, these songs for the soul, as Hawaiian scholar Rubellite Kawena Johnson called them, were oli to aid the soul on its traverse from this world into the place of akua and 'aumākua ... A kanikau could be a spontaneous expression of grief heard at funeral gatherings, or an oli labored over by skillful chanters to later be performed in public–kanikau told stories, honored the deceased, and in more recent times, expressed the deep affection and aloha felt for a beloved member of the family or community.[32]

Kanikau have a purpose, as Arista points out, to aid the soul in its journey from our living world of ao to the realm of the gods, guardians, and ancestors (pō), which is also where life begins in Kumulipo. When horrific environmental losses such as the massive aquatic deaths from the molasses spill occur, mele assist us, the grieving community, in having hope in recovery, and inspire us to perservere. Therefore, the end of the mele draws from mele aloha 'āina that is kūpa'a (steadfast) in our survivance as people who continue to be ever loyal to our 'āina:

> Ua mau ke ea o ka 'āina i ka pono
> E ola, e ola, e ola nā kini ē!

> The life of the land continues when justice prevails
> Life, life, life to the multitudes indeed!

Ha'ina 'ia mai ana ka Puana (The Story Is Told): Concluding Thoughts

Ha'ina 'ia mai ana ka puana is a common refrain signaling the conclusion of a mele with a brief summary of it. Thus, it is an appropriate way to conclude a discussion on ʻŌiwi poetic praxis. Because our world was born in poetry, ʻŌiwi ways of being and knowing are forever informed by it. This is why poetic expression is so critical in our activism, because koʻihonua are the foundation of our worldview: we are one ʻohana with our ʻāina. ʻŌiwi praxis traverses language, although there is a renewed determination to highlight ʻōlelo Hawaiʻi and avoid translations. Yet English is still a dominant language of everyday life, and communicating messages of aloha ʻāina in English are still valuable in reaching broader audiences.

In the introduction to her book on ʻŌiwi knowledge, Emalani Case cites reknown African American queer wahine writer Audre Lorde in an opening epigraph:

> The farthest horizons of our hopes and fears are cobbled by our poems, carved from the rock experiences of our daily lives. As they become known to and accepted by us, our feelings and the honest exploration of them become sanctuaries and spawning grounds for the most radical and daring of ideas.[33]

In centering the role of poetry—figuratively and literally carved from our experiences with and on our ʻāina—Case reflects on her physical presence on Mauna Kea during the 2019 occupation of poʻe aloha ʻāina intent on halting the settler colonial project of a thirty-meter telescope (TMT) on the sacred summit of our most sacred mauna (mountain). She explains how she was invited to speak there, and how her presence on the mauna inspired her to compose a mele while sitting on the smooth pāhoehoe lava: "Begining a poem, I scribbled, ʻLet me be your sanctuary / a place to find comfort when your soils have been dispersed / roots unearthed, left hanging.ʻ" She continues:

> I didn't fully understand these words, carved from the lava beneath me, until I stood there, adorned in mist and my brother's heavy camouflage jacket, the mauna cloaked in clouds, a group of kiaʻi [protectors] listening, and the words finding shape and meaning as they came out of my mouth . . . That moment and that poem became the spawining ground for the "radical and daring" hope [of her work].[34]

What Case clearly articulates is a revelation of ʻŌiwi poetic praxis literally born from and centered on our ʻāina. She then discusses the puʻuhonua (place of refuge) established at Puʻuhuluhulu (a nearby cindercone at the base of the

Mauna Kea access road) as a "place of awakening, a place of rising" for the many people who felt the *need* "to be *at* and *with* the mountain, wanting to support the growing movement, and, I suspect for many, wanting to be in a place where they could find comfort in standing for something larger than themselves." For Case, the occupation "pulled me to purchase a plane ticket, to fly back to my 'āina . . . from Aotearoa, where I live and work, to find sanctuary in my place, my mountain, my people, and our never-ending commitment to aloha 'āina (love of place)."[35] My experiences on Mauna Kea had a similar effect, inspiring me to compose new mele.[36] Case reveals that her time on Mauna Kea showed her new directions for her writing, and as an 'Ōiwi scholar, poet, and cultural practitioner, she believed it was her kuleana "to provide new/renewed concepts, to be ready to tackle the issues of our current and shifting worlds."[37]

I am inspired by Case's vision for her own work. She argues that Kahiki, both Tahiti and the ancient homeland 'Ōiwi ancestors sailed from to discover Hawai'i, "is a symbol of both ancestral connection and the potential that comes with remembering and acting upon that connection"; moreover it "has always been a sanctuary."[38] Ko'ihonua like Kumulipo connect us to our Kahiki kūpuna as well, and to the larger oceanic region Tongan anthropologist 'Epeli Hau'ofa aptly described as "our sea of islands," as our moana nui (great ocean) does not divide us, but, as seafaring voyagers, unites us across vast distances.[39]

Poetry is one way to reaffirm such larger kinship connections, both in reading and being inspired by the work of other Indigenous poets, and by composing our own work that embodies these connections. Like Case and many others, I have had the privilege of visiting other lands across the Pacific and beyond, and have been inspired by these lands and seas, traversed by our ancestors, their beauty and the aloha and resilience of our Indigenous cousins. It is awe-inspiring to consider one's Indigenous knowledge of our 'āina viewed from the 'āina of another culture. In the mele "Matavai Wedding," which I composed on a 2013 trip to Tahiti, the first paukū reflects on this:

> a midnight wedding
> on Matavai bay
> young love, celebration
> under a young moon
> the night of Hua in the month of Welehu
> life blossoms, time turns.[40]

Welehu roughly corresponds with November, the time of Makahiki or rest from hard labor, a time to relax and celebrate. Hua is the thirteenth night of the month, an unlucky number in western thinking. But the kaona of Hua is that it means fruit or seed, and alludes to fertility, children, and abundance, and is found in this context throughout Kumulipo. In addition, it is the name of a star used by our common Polynesian wayfaring ancestors, named in line 1874 of Kumulipo, connecting ʻŌiwi to our ancestral Kahiki homelands, kūpuna, and cousins who are still celebrating weddings, anticipating new generations, and living on our ancestral ʻāina.

The conclusion of the mele "Nā Pua Purau o Vaimā" (the hau blossoms of Vaimā) also reflects on encountering the ʻāina kūpuna (ancestral lands), as this mele is:

> no kahi ʻāina aloha kūpuna ē
> nā pua purau o Vaimā
> e lanaau i ka ʻili wai.
>
> for a beloved ancestral place where
> the hau blossoms of Vaimā
> float serenely on the water.[41]

ʻŌiwi poetic praxis is rooted in our pilina ʻāina (relationship to land) and is one of social action. As Manulani Meyer underscores, relationships are about action, as "relationship as verb infers the intentional quality of connection that is experienced and remembered."[42] In this way, we continue to compose mele aloha ʻāina while simultaneously practicing aloha ʻāina activism, collectively contributing to our decolonial future. Koʻihonua as ʻŌiwi poetic praxis highlights pilina ʻāina and aloha ʻāina as active and continuous, mai ka pō mai, mai nā kūpuna mai, mai ka waha mai a mau loa. E ola, e ola, e ola nā kini ē!

Notes

1. "'Ōiwi" is a shortened Indigenous Hawaiian language reference to ethnic or Native Hawaiians, the original inhabitants of the Hawaiian Islands born from the land or who voyaged here centuries before western incursion. The terms "'Ōiwi" and "Hawaiian" are used interchangably in this context. Within an ʻŌiwi context, the terms "song text" and

"poetry" are the same.

2. While haole originally meant "foreigner," Hawaiians quickly became aware of ethnic difference and applied different names to various peoples. Thus, haole became specifically associated with "white," primarily western Europeans and Americans, who were also the first permanent settlers to the islands.

3. Katrina-Ann R. K. N. Oliveira, *Ancestral Places, Understanding Kanaka Geographies* (Corvalis: Oregon State University Press, 2014), 3.

4. Z. Kepelino, *Kepelino's Traditions of Hawaii*, ed. Martha Beckwith (Honolulu: Bishop Museum Press, 1932), 155. English translation by ku'ualoha ho'omanawanui.

5. "Hua lua" also refers to twins.

6. Hawaiian text adapted from *He Pule Hoolaa Alii, he Kumulipo no Kaiimamao a ia Alapai Wahine* (Honolulu: Hui Pa'ipalapala Elele, 1889), 12. Diacritical marks, line numbers, and English translation by ku'ualoha ho'omanawanui.

7. Samuel H. Elbert and Noelani Māhoe also discuss this in their work. See *Nā Mele o Hawai'i Nei, 101 Hawaiian Songs* (Honolulu: University of Hawai'i Press, 1972).

8. Samuel H. Elbert and Mary Kawena Pukui, *Hawaiian Dictionary*, rev. ed. (Honolulu: University of Hawai'i Press, 1986), 104; see also, Mary Kawena Pukui, *'Ōlelo No'eau, Hawaiian Saying and Poetical Expressions* (Honolulu: University of Hawai'i Press, 1986).

9. One example is found in the mo'olelo of Ha'inakolo. See "Ka Moolelo Walohia o Hainakolo," *Ka Holomua*, January 14, 1914, 2; "Ka Moolelo Walohia o Hainakolo," *Ka Holomua*, September 26, 1914, 2. One example is found in a history of Kamehameha I. See Joseph M. Poepoe, "Ka Moolelo o Kamehameha I," *Ka Na'i Aupuni*, December 27, 1905, 4.

10. British Naval Captain James Cook is credited with being the first English-speaking haole explorer to enter and map the Pacific; he arrived in Hawai'i in 1778.

11. See David Stannard, *Before the Horror: The Population of Hawai'i on the Eve of Western Contact* (Honolulu: University of Hawai'i Press, 1989).

12. See ku'ualoha ho'omanawanui, "Mana Wahine: Feminism and Nationalism in Hawaiian Literature," *Anglistica* 14, no. 2 (2010): 27–43; Amy Ku'uleialoha Stillman, "'Aloha 'Āina': New Perspectives on 'Kaulana Nā Pua,'" *Hawaiian Journal of History* 33 (1999): 83–99; Noenoe Silva, "Hawaiian Literature in Hawaiian," in *The Oxford Handbook of Indigenous American Literature*, ed. James H. Cox and Daniel Heath Justice (Oxford: Oxford University Press, 2014), 102–117; Leilani Basham, "I mau ke Ea o ka 'Āina i ka Pono: He Puke Mele Lāhui no ka Lāhui Hawai'i" (PhD diss., University of Hawai'i at Mānoa, 2007).

13. For example, *mau* refers to, in part, always, steady, constant, unceasing, permanent, continual; to continue, persevere, preserve, endure, last; preservation, continuation. Ea (life) is also sovereignty, rule, and independence, all political concepts. 'Āina provides

everything necessary for an abundant, joyous life; as a cherished ancestor, ʻŌiwi self-governance and Land Back movements are struggles to provide for the lāhui by protecting our kūpuna. Pono has many meanings, including correct or proper procedure, excellence, prosperity, benefit, true condition, accurate, completely, exactly, or carefully; in this context, it implies justice. Elbert and Pukui, *Hawaiian Dictionary*, 36.

14. Examples include the first Hawaiian national anthem, "Mele Lāhui Hawaiʻi," composed by Princess Liliʻuokalani in 1866 at the request of King Kamehameha V, who reigned from 1863 to 1872. It contains a repeated (pīnaʻi) emphasis on ola (life) that also alludes to the aliʻis genealogical ties back in time to Kumulipo. It also looks forward, as long life is also tied to the birth of heirs. When Liliʻuokalani's brother David Kalākaua became Mōʻī in 1874, he replaced "Mele Lāhui Hawaiʻi" with his own mele aupuni, "Hawaiʻi Ponoʻī" (Hawaiʻi's own [people]). The new mele aupuni continued to direct Hawaiians as individuals and as a lāhui (nation) to look to the aliʻi of the past, their moʻokūʻauhau, the source of political mana. The message of the final paukū is a call to action, reminding the lāhui that their most important duty (hana nui) is "E ui ē" (to rise up). The irony of "Hawaiʻi Ponoʻī" is that it, too, like Kamehameha III's proclamation of enduring political soveignty, has been coopted by the State of Hawaiʻi as the state song.

15. Some notable examples include "Ka Naʻi Aupuni" (William Kaniho, 1906), "E nā Kini" (Ernest Kalā, circa 1920s), "E Mau" (Alvin Kaleolani Isaacs, 1941), "All Hawaiʻi Stand Together" (Liko Martin, circa 1976), "Hawaiʻi ʻ78" (Micky Ioane, 1978), "Ua Mau (ke Ea o ka ʻĀina i ka Pono)" (Dennis Pavao, 1986), "Keep Hawaiian Lands in Hawaiian Hands" (Walter Aipolani, 1990), "Hawaiians Look to Your Cozmogany" (Mapuana Hayashida, 2001), "Couldn't take the Mana" (Kalei Caceres, 2001), "Huki ʻia" (Kakaʻe Kaleiheana, 2011), "Hawaiʻi 3000" (Sudden Rush, 2013), "All Hawaiʻi (Stand Together)" (Sudden Rush, 2018), "ʻOnipaʻa" (Ikaakamai, 2021), and "Kumulipo" (Paniolo Prince and Queen Maile, 2023).

16. Tanya Maile Naehu, Kapiliʻula Naehu-Ramos, and ʻIhilani Laconia, "Kumulipo," in *Hoʻokupu Learner and Teacher Resource Guide, a Hip Hop Anthology of Hawaiian History* (Kumimi: Hui o Kuapā Molokaʻi, 2023), 18.

17. Naehu, Nehu-Ramos, and Laconia, "Kumulipo," 18.

18. Alexander Heidel, *The Babylonia Genesis, the Story of Creation* (Chicago: University of Chicago Press, 1951).

19. Naehu, Naehu-Ramos, and Laconia, "Kumulipo," 18.

20. Elbert and Pukui, *Hawaiian Dictionary*, 223.

21. See Haunani-Kay Trask, "Pacific Island Women and White Feminism," in *From a Native Daughter, Colonialism and Sovereignty in Hawaiʻi* (Monroe: Common Courage Press,

1993), 263–277.

22. Brandy Nālani McDougall, "ʻĀina Hānau," in *ʻĀina Hānau, Birthland* (Tucson: University of Arizona Press, 2023), 128.

23. McDougall, "ʻĀina Hānau," 129.

24. McDougall, "ʻĀina Hānau," 136–138.

25. kuʻualoha hoʻomanawanui, "ʻĀina Kūpuna: Waipā," *Native Literatures—Generations* 1, no. 1 (2010).

26. "Mission Statement," Waipā Foundation, https://waipafoundation.org/about-us.

27. kuʻualoha hoʻomanawanui, "Wanini," *Native Literatures—Generations* 1 no. 1 (2010).

28. hoʻomanawanui, "Wanini," lines 35–41.

29. hoʻomanawanui, "Wanini," lines 46–50.

30. hoʻomanawanui, "Wanini," lines 51–58.

31. Mark Memmott, "Massive Molasses Spill Devastates Honolulu Marine Life," NPR, Hawaiʻi Public Radio, September 12, 2013, https://www.npr.org/sections/thetwo-way/2013/09/12/221709158/massive-molasses-spill-devastates-honolulu-marine-life.

32. Noelani Arista, "Kanikau Lament the Loss of Loved Ones," *Ka Wai Ola o OHA*, February 1, 2018, https://kawaiola.news/hehoomanao/kanikau-lament-loss-loved-ones/.

33. Audre Lorde, *Sister Outsider: Essays and Speeches by Audre Lorde* (Berkeley: Crossing Press, 2007), qtd. in Emalani Case, *Everything Ancient Was Once New: Indigenous Persistence from Hawaiʻi to Kahiki* (Honolulu: University of Hawaiʻi Press, 2021), 14.

34. Case, *Everything Ancient Was Once New*, 14.

35. Case, *Everything Ancient Was Once New*, 14.

36. One such poem is "He Lei Māmane no Maunakea," *Broadsided*, November 1, 2021, https://broadsidedpress.org/?p=5172&post_type=jjm_articles&preview=1&_ppp=e59a6f8714.

37. Case, *Everything Ancient Was Once New*, 14.

38. Case, *Everything Ancient Was Once New*, 14.

39. Epeli Hauʻofa, "Our Sea of Islands," in *A New Oceania: Rediscovering Our Sea of Islands*, ed. Eric Waddell, Vijay Naidu, and ʻEpeli Hauʻofa (Suva: University of the South Pacific, 1993), 2–17.

40. kuʻualoha hoʻomanawanui, "Matavai Wedding," *Litteramāʻohi* 22 (March 2015): 118.

41. Vaimā is a fresh water spring in Taravao on the island of Tahiti where Māʻohi (Indigenous Tahitian) people often swim, as the fresh clear water is thought to have healing properties. kuʻualoha hoʻomanawanui, "Nā Pua Purau o Vaimā," *Litteramāʻohi* 22 (March 2015): 121.

42. Manulani Meyer, qtd. in Case, *Everything Ancient Was Once New*, 70.

Bibliography

Arista, Noelani. "Kanikau Lament the Loss of Loved Ones." *Ka Wai Ola o OHA*, February 1, 2018. https://kawaiola.news/hehoomanao/kanikau-lament-loss-loved-ones/.

Basham, Leilani. "I mau ke Ea o ka ʻĀina i ka Pono: He Puke Mele Lāhui no ka Lāhui Hawaiʻi." PhD dissertation, University of Hawaiʻi at Mānoa, 2007.

Case, Emalani. *Everything Ancient Was Once New: Indigenous Persistence from Hawaiʻi to Kahiki.* Honolulu: University of Hawaiʻi Press, 2021.

Elbert, Samuel H., and Noelani Māhoe. *Nā Mele o Hawaiʻi Nei, 101 Hawaiian Songs.* Honolulu: University of Hawaiʻi Press, 1972.

Elbert, Samuel H., and Mary Kawena Pukui. *Hawaiian Dictionary.* Rev. ed. Honolulu: University of Hawaiʻi Press, 1986.

Hauʻofa, ʻEpeli. "Our Sea of Islands." In *A New Oceania: Rediscovering Our Sea of Islands*, edited by Eric Waddell, Vijay Naidu, and ʻEpeli Hauʻofa, 2–16. Suva: University of the South Pacific, 1993.

Heidel, Alexander. *The Babylonia Genesis, the Story of Creation.* Chicago: University of Chicago Press, 1951.

He Pule Hoolaa Alii, he Kumulipo no Kaiimamao a ia Alapai Wahine. Honolulu: Hui Paʻipalapala Elele, 1889.

hoʻomanawanui, kuʻualoha. "ʻĀina Kūpuna: Waipā." *Native Literatures—Generations* 1, no. 1 (2010).

———. "He Lei Hoʻoheno no nā Kau a Kau, Language, Performance, and Form in Hawaiian Poetry." *Contemporary Pacific* 17, no. 1 (Spring 2005): 29–81.

———. "Mana Wahine: Feminism and Nationalism in Hawaiian Literature," *Anglistica* 14, no. 2 (2010): 27–43.

———. "Matavai Wedding." *Litteramāʻohi* 22 (March 2015): 118.

———. "Nā Pua Purau o Vaimā." *Litteramāʻohi* 22 (March 2015): 121.

———. "Wanini," *Native Literatures—Generations* 1, no. 1 (2010).

Kepelino, Z. *Kepelino's Traditions of Hawaii.* Edited by Martha Beckwith. Honolulu: Bishop Museum Press, 1932.

Liliʻuokalani. *Hawaiʻi's Story by Hawaiʻi's Queen.* Boston: Lee and Shephard, 1898.

McDougall, Brandy Nālani. *ʻĀina Hānau, Birthland.* Tucson: University of Arizona Press, 2023.

Memmott, Mark. "Massive Molasses Spill Devastates Honolulu Marine Life." NPR, Hawaiʻi Public Radio, September 12, 2013. https://www.npr.org/sections/thetwo-way/2013/09/12/221709158/massive-molasses-spill-devastates-honolulu-marine-life.

Naehu, Tanya Maile, Kapiliʻula Naehu-Ramos, and ʻIhilani Lasconia. *Hoʻokupu Learner and*

Teacher Resource Guide, a Hip Hop Anthology of Hawaiian History. Edited by kuʻualoha hoʻomanawanui and Noelani Goodyear-Kaʻōpua. Kumimi: Hui o Kuapā Molokaʻi, 2023.

Oliveira, Katrina-Ann R. K. N. *Ancestral Places, Understanding Kanaka Geographies.* Corvalis: Oregon State University Press, 2014.

Poepoe, Joseph M. "Ka Moolelo o Kamehameha I." *Ka Naʻi Aupuni,* December 27, 1905.

Pukui, Mary Kawena. *ʻŌlelo Noʻeau, Hawaiian Proverbs and Poetical Sayings.* Honolulu: Bishop Museum Press, 1983.

Silva, Noenoe. "Hawaiian Literature in Hawaiian." In *The Oxford Handbook of Indigenous American Literature,* ed. James H. Cox and Daniel Heath Justice, 102–117 (Oxford: Oxford University Press, 2014).

Stannard, David. *Before the Horror: The Population of Hawaiʻi on the Eve of Western Contact.* Honolulu: University of Hawaiʻi Press, 1989.

Stillman, Amy Kuʻuleialoha. "'Aloha ʻĀina': New Perspectives on 'Kaulana nā Pua.'" *Hawaiian Journal of History* 33 (1999): 83–99.

Testa, F. J. *Buke Mele Lahui.* Honolulu: Halepai Makaainana, 1895.

Trask, Haunani-Kay. "Pacific Island Women and White Feminism." *From a Native Daughter, Colonialism and Sovereignty in Hawaiʻi.* Monroe: Common Courage Press, 1993.

After the Before Time

Mapping the Temporal in Poetry by Jennifer Foerster,
Allison Adelle Hedge Coke, and Karenne Wood

Janet McAdams

> Space is not static, nor time spaceless.
> —Doreen Massey

> Time it was / And what a time it was.
> —Paul Simon

> So here we float in time among
> the stars.
> —Carter Revard

As I write this, I'm acutely aware of the recent temporal shift in the world around me, around all of us, a legible—painfully remembered—Before Time, which suggests an After. I suppose we now inhabit that After, although its borders are not so sharply defined. And as I write this, hospitals are once again filling up, even as we're encouraged by our leaders to unmask and breathe in each other's faces. Yes, it is some sort of After, but one neither delimited nor uncontested. It seems akin to another After, the post of postcolonial, which scholars in the field insist means after colonialism has begun, not after it has ended.

Everyone I know speaks of time differently these days, and it isn't just that we speak of events pre- or post-COVID. I think we understand time differently. I hope it means we understand how much of time is constructed and political, purposeful in the way it's narrated. Which is to say we are faced with how poorly we have understood time, how willfully we misunderstood it.

"So here we float," my late friend the Osage poet Carter Revard wrote. "So here *we float in time.*" "So here we float *in time among the stars.*"[1] I admit to having read this line longing for a helpful comma or two. Ultimately, I read this line grateful for the way it resists stasis, how the phrase "in time" floats back and forth between the line's two ends. How it enacts and celebrates floating. How time can be both a space stable enough to make floating possible. How the phrase "in time" might be read as eventually or inevitably. The both/and/or of this.

Poetry, of course, has never been the site where time runs in a linear or orderly fashion, where it is stable. As in dreams, events can occur before or after or simultaneously or all three at once, and dreamers float among pasts and presents, prophetic futures, ancestral memories. I am hardly unique in confessing that my own dreams trouble me. Like other poets, I write them down, make poems of them, search for clues. When I look back over my own work, I see the many ways the temporal has worried me, worried me in a more archaic sense of the word, meaning to harass or bother. The lone—and seemingly immortal—mosquito that creeps into my bedroom at night. Was I thinking specifically of the prophetic when I wrote the sequence of speculative poetry, "The Thousand-Year War," that appears in my first book? I don't know how I could have avoided it, yet the poems of that sequence, and the various voices that inhabit its post-apocalyptic landscape, resist prophesy, resist warning. The characters inhabit a certain *what-if?* Their concerns are with the quotidian: *how* will we live? rather than *what* do our lives mean? I returned to the speculative in my chapbook *Seven Boxes for the Country After*, a group of prose poems mapping a world which now feels all too present.

But more recently, perhaps given the looming uninhabitability of our world, I find myself pondering how language can help us not just to remember what happened, not just to map what has been lost, but to know what time was like then—how it felt, how we lived it. How poetry forges and uncovers worlds not readily available to us, how it maps times lost to us, the temporalities of those worlds.

Jennifer Elise Foerster, Allison Adelle Hedge Coke, and the late Karenne Wood are poets whose work I've admired for any number of reasons but perhaps especially for the ways they write time, for how they construct and uncover spaces, claim and reclaim land. While the focus of my essay is not the Indigenous south, it's worth noting that all three have strong ties to ancestral homelands in the Southeast. All three have experienced diaspora, even if the diasporic manifests differently for each of them. In relation to their work, I'm interested in thinking through the way a poem opens a field for temporal and spatial logics not easily discoverable in the overly secular world of late capitalism. I've invoked the spatial and temporal logics of dreams, since that seems the place alternative formations of time and space are available—to most of us, anyway—and because they are instructive to poets, particularly in the unlearning we need to do. I want to unsettle naturalized "settler-time" logics and to do so without eliding into mystification, which I think—as far as Indians are concerned—there's been more than enough of.[2]

I've long been interested in maps and their economies. And surely that's why I'm drawn to other poets whose work seems cartographic, whose own figurations of place and land teach me new ways to understand the spatial, to see how time constructs space, how the spatial figures its own temporalities. Poets like Foerster, Hedge Coke, and Wood.

The geographer Doreen Massey has written, in the same article from which one of the epigraphs to this essay is taken, "Space and time are inextricably interwoven. It is not that we cannot make any distinction at all between them but that the distinction we do make needs to hold the two in tension."[3]

The poetics of that tension—that is what I wish to explore here.

I hope readers . . . find a flicker of recognition of their own in-between space, of timelessness. A lot of it is about searching, following intuitions, not reaching a conclusion, and this constant process of clarifying oneself, and trying to find a story that is a mystery . . . I hope [the poems] will feed that part of the human mind which is shadowy. I think that part of our lives always needs to be explored, and poetry can help that.

—Jennifer Elise Foerster

A citizen of the Muscogee Nation of Oklahoma, Jennifer Elise Foerster has published three collections of poetry, including her first book, *Leaving Tulsa*, in 2013. As its title suggests, Foerster's closely woven collection is relentlessly peripatetic, comprising themes of travel, home, return, odyssey. It is possible, even easy, to read *Leaving Tulsa*, as a single long poem, with frequent recurring images and motifs of travel. More quest than journey, Foerster's speaker (or speakers) tracks hoof-prints through the long grass, gathers, sifts, collects. She travels in search of something, and yet travels *with* something and often with instruction: "You will gather the seeds/ and continue to travel." Even in the intertwined origin stories of her long poem "Genesis," the seemingly resistant traveler who "hadn't wanted to remember" cannot finally turn away from the search before her.[4]

Foerster is interested in writing about the histories one might expect to find in a millennial poet from a displaced Indigenous nation, that is, the literal documentation of and witnessing to land theft, inflected by the ways Muscogee cosmologies figure in a world encroached upon by settler colonialism. Her poems reference and sometimes detail the personal and family story of growing up in various international settings, with her grandparents' farm and land in Oklahoma as homeland.

In his review of *Leaving Tulsa*, Dean Rader writes: "Foerster uses the trope of cartography to illustrate how the past is always the territory of the present."[5] These territories and their attendant spatialities are especially dynamic and resistant to stasis, and as Foerster's persona moves through and across the volume's multiple spaces, she travels sometimes as witness, as an observer who seems to be passing through but not *of* a particular landscape. Notably, Foerster's landscapes are not only or even primarily literal, material ones, and, more importantly, they are never fixed. They may be discovered, even uncovered, but they always contain the capacity for change. The plot of *Leaving Tulsa* may feature—albeit not exclusively—a twenty-first-century persona moving through tribal, familial, and personal landscapes, but its *story* is that of the dynamism of various landscapes. I would argue, following Rader, that Foerster deploys a resistant cartography to uncover another space or spaces, the sites edging a seemingly entrenched and hegemonic center to include the interstices between and among and around sites of colonial power, including what she calls "the outskirts." Her poem of that name is useful for thinking about the temporal and spatial possibilities the volume opens up:

THE OUTSKIRTS

Each day is a threshold of the same dream.
I awake to the clatter of leaves,
a frayed dawn cawing in its wooden cage.
Each day the same street. Each street
the same name. Surfacing from a cut bank
the sketch of your face—or only my reflection

streaking the glass, a train
tunneling through morning fog.
I skirt the park into the city-blocks.
Green glass and bottle caps
collect along the curb, newspapers
tumble under blusters of boots.
I walk the crooked wind
under thick bougainvillea,
call back horses from the corridors of hours
then climb to the meadow and lie on my back
as the old men tiptoe among the bones.
Below the traffic is a crushing river.
Somewhere between wanting to be found
and not wanting to be found,
I bury my hands, turn in the grass.
Late light filters through a canopy
of leaves. The greening
hills seal themselves,
shut around the graves.[6]

The poem opens by announcing its temporally liminal location. The image following is suggestive of a landscape contained, and violently so, but not erased—the bird-like "frayed dawn cawing in its wooden cage." Foerster's traveler moves through the detritus of a fraught, vaguely dystopic landscape until the thirteenth line, when the poem takes a major turn. The traveler walks "through crooked wind / under thick bougainvillea" and seems to enter a different space. But as the sentence continues and she "call[s] back horses from the corridors of hours," it appears that Foerster's traveler has not so much entered new space but invoked it, called it into the world and displaced the landscape of "newspapers," "green glass and bottle caps," of "the same street [with] the same name." The traveler reiterates her liminality, as "somewhere between wanting to be found / and not wanting to be found." Tafisha Edwards has pointed out the importance of that comma in the penultimate line, which tempers the final image into something suggestive of safety, of shoring up the space of the greening hills; they seal themselves, resist becoming frayed like the dawn of the poem's opening, and shut *around* the graves.[7]

It's tempting to characterize what happens here as the movement of outskirts to center, thus relegating the center to the margins. But I think what happens is more interesting. Foerster's move tends much more toward an uncovering, of seemingly hidden away histories, of landscapes that seem yet alive and dynamic but are merely in flux, waiting, ready. What's crucial here, though, is that Foerster's outskirts are not predicated upon or extant via opposition to an entrenched hegemonic center. I speak here of an other space, not the other space or the space of the other. When the "greening/hills seal themselves," the resulting circumscribed space seems largely interested in itself, however figured the mapping of its sovereignty, and not as a counterspace opposed to a colonialist center.

We haven't slept since September. Some of us, since we remember. Not the real sleep, the deep-down cloud dreams. We do dream loaded maze of meaning, circling consciousness, streaming before we are wakeful to undo, rearrange perspective, begin seeing. It is reason, dreaming.
—Allison Hedge Coke

A writer of mixed Eastern Tsa la gi (Cherokee), Huron, Creek, Métis, French Canadian, Portuguese, English, Scots, and Irish descent, Allison Adelle Hedge Coke is the author of six collections of poetry, chapbooks, and the memoir *Rock, Ghost, Willow, Deer*. Her most recent collection of poetry, *Look at This Blue*, was a finalist for the 2023 National Book Award.

Critics have praised Hedge Coke's massive 2014 collection *Streaming* for its ambition and scope.[8] Reviewing the collection for *World Literature Today*, Jeanetta Calhoun Mish characterizes it as "epic" and writes of "the breadth, the depth, the historical and cultural reach" of *Streaming*.[9] The first section of *Streaming*, "Prelude," comprises a single, shorter lyric poem, an elegy for her mother titled "A Time."[10] Its narrative arc is complex, as the poem opens with the speaker reflecting upon her mother's death, an event that has "not been written yet" and is thus incomplete, and an event that then unfolds in real time later in the poem. Self-reflexive, performative, the poem describes what has not yet been written, even as it *is* the elegy to be written; it is situated, especially its first half, in the liminal space between living and dying. Beginning in the prophetic first stanza, with its catalog of omens—"the headless owl, the bobcat struck / the red wolf where she could not be"—the poem is rife with temporal markers. Notably, the word "yet"—an adverb indicating a period of waiting for something expected—is repeated in each of the poem's first three stanzas, heightening its liminal siting, its sense of unfixed betweenness.

Structurally, the poem marks time through its frequent turns; a particularly striking one is the move from the prophetic first stanza to the single-line second one, a resigned—and temporally paradoxical—statement: "None of it done and yet it's over." Although the poem's overall movement is forward—toward the mother's death, funeral, the rituals of mourning her—the frequent turns continually unsettle stasis, mirroring and reinforcing the space of the poem as a liminal one. The poem not only hovers and moves between life and death, spatially, but also its setting is caught between her mother's Alberta childhood homeland and its reproduction, that is, the photograph propped by the mother's shoulder of Chief Mountain—"Old Chief"—sacred to Indigenous people.

Time in this poem is never not also always about space. The omens that appear in the first stanza signal slippages between worlds, a fluidity made explicit in the stanza's final line: "the red wolf where she could not be." Structurally—and thematically—the poem seems to circle its subject, unwilling—or not yet willing—to engage fully with the grief at hand. It is interesting how temporally laden this resistance is. The omens presaging the death of the speaker's mother beckon from an other space, the red wolf, in particular, who is "where she could not be." Perhaps only in its final meditation on death, loss, and the passing of time—on "whatever / it was that held us human / in this life" does the poem effect any sense of rest, that is, come to a resting place. The poem's concluding lines suggest both resignation and regret:

> all I know   is what you know
>
> when it is over said and done
> it was a time
>   and there was never enough of it

I've returned to this poem perhaps more than any other in *Streaming* and especially to these quiet, heartbreaking lines. I first read the poem when I, too, was mourning my mother. The article preceding "time" in the penultimate line resists any sentimentalized mystification of time, and the final one recasts time *as* material, rife with thingness, and therefore renderable into something scarce. When I spoke with Allison on the phone about this poem, about the "never enough time" fact of our lives and so many others, we talked about how it's a brutal given under late capitalism that if work necessitates living away from our families, that's just how it is. It is only one of the ways capitalism produces a milieu of lateness, of too-lateness, where time, now made material, can be both doled out and parceled out.[11]

Thus, the mother's request, in the poem, for her crow painting and, especially, the photo of Chief Mountain in Alberta, which figures here as a simulacrum of the place where she grew up, is even more poignant. That the mountain—Old Chief—is with her, "still watching," is reassuring and shows the mother's immutable and deeply felt connection to her own homelands but it does not mitigate being away from them.

As both a Native poet and a historical researcher, I am often caught in this dilemma, aware that the mainstream stories of our people are deeply flawed but unable to find more authentic accounts, usually because the American Indians remain voiceless or were deliberately silenced. This is particularly true for Native women.
—Karenne Wood

A member of the Monacan Nation, Karenne Wood died in 2019 at the age of fifty-nine. She published two collections of poetry, *Markings on Earth* and *Weaving the Boundary.* She was an activist Indigenous poet, for her nation, for her language, for Virginia Indians. I believe her work in repatriation and museum studies influenced her later poetry, including her long poem "The Naming." I have thought of this poem often since I asked Karenne to send it to us at the *Kenyon Review* (I was then an editor there), where it first appeared in print, and I am glad for the opportunity to delve into it a little more deeply. We published it online, as a running sequential poem. In Wood's second and final poetry collection, *Weaving the Boundary*, "The Naming" appears as the final poem in the book, with each section appearing on its own page. Given its length and scope, I'll say a few things about the poem's overall structure, especially as it pertains to the temporal, and then focus on the final section.

Wood's chief concern in the poem—what drives it thematically—is the loss of language. In the poem, language serves as both index to and synecdoche of what has been lost. As Tara Causey has noted, "Wood connects the loss of language to the loss of the land."[12] Language is also what conjures, just as storytelling does, more than describe the world: it brings it into being, it constitutes and reconstitutes it. Thus, the poem's title points to the naming that "calls you from a maelstrom, / . . . imagines you, molded from words." The title is also self-referential, making explicit that the poem itself *is* the naming—the calling out—of genocide and diaspora. Notably, in Wood's essay "Prisoners of History," her exploration of the lives of Pocahontas and Mary Jemison, she attends carefully to the ways naming is an act that participates in the "deeply flawed . . . mainstream accounts of our people." Discussing Pocahontas's embodiment as "an American mother figure," she writes: "Even her name, Amonute, disappeared, along with her sacred name, Matoaka, and her Christian name, Rebecca. She remains Pocahontas, a nickname given to a child by her father that meant 'wanton' or 'mischievous.'"[13]

Naming and renaming, thus, constitute critical acts of personhood and cultural sovereignty. In the origin story that unfolds in the first two sections, the "storyteller," the "man so old he has never / not been among us" calls one into being by speaking "your first language, your name." Language is defined broadly in the poem, inclusive of all the ways speaking can take place. She writes: "the land speaks, its language arising / from its own geography," until, as from that language, "mortal lives" are woven into being, "the storyteller shift[s] the present." The poem shifts, too, into the imperative, as section two opens with a call for the reader to "imagine" fully that different map, that different "arrangement of stars." This is an origin story, one in which "utterance" is what makes us "come into being."[14]

The poem is lyrical, meditative, personal, collective, and—I would argue—its arc tilts toward the apocalyptic. The poem casts a wide net—Wood's accountings may be rooted in a Monacan tribal perspective but they are inclusive of the ancestral homelands and languages of many Indigenous nations, Muscogee, Pima, Koyukon, just to name a few. Wood in no way collapses the differences between. Rather, the poem's theoretical outlook is trans-Indigenous, as critic Chadwick Allen frames the term in his book of the same name. Allen writes:

I have begun to turn from both *ands* and *comparative* to the prefix *trans-*, experimenting with the idea of global literary studies (primarily) in English that are *trans*-Indigenous. The point is not to displace the necessary, invigorating study of specific traditions and contexts but rather to complement these by augmenting and expanding broader, globally Indigenous fields of inquiry. The point is to . . . acknowledge the mobility and multiple interactions of Indigenous peoples, cultures, histories, and texts. Similar to terms like *trans*lation, *trans*national, and *trans*form, *trans*-Indigenous may be able to bear the complex, contingent asymmetry and the potential risks of unequal encounters borne by the preposition *across*.[15]

While Allen's focus is on a critical methodology, poets, to paraphrase Barbara Christian in her groundbreaking essay "The Race for Theory" have always theorized. Wood is, thus—following Christian—theorizing broadly in this poem about the trans-Indigenous, mapping a specifically Indigenous version of end-of-times, figured as the heap of detritus. Just as I, following Wood, deploy her poem here to theorize about time and space. Wood's vision clearly sweeps *across*—Indigenous nations, locations and temporalities, colonial encounters—and seems both infused with the eschatological and headed toward a profound change of world.

Or perhaps I just longed for that.

Instead, something quite different happens in the final section:

> Now the wind lifts a circling dust
> and all that has been rises—ancestors'
> chipped flints and potsherds,
> photographs, cartridge shells,
> acorns and jerky, buffalo dung,
> cavalry uniforms, medals from Washington,
> antlers, notched arrowshafts, shoulder
> bones, discarded tires, smashed bottles ,
> ashes in fire pits, dry-rotted baskets,
> tin cans, commodity wrappers,
> Indian names and the names
> strung before us, cavern walls
> painted with red petroglyphs,
> the pressed forms of insects and fish
> gone to rock, and the rocks

> to air swirling, settling again
>
> into the silence we become.[16]

The first few lines lead us to expect revelation, even *prevail*ation, a change of world. But the catalog that follows, its dozen or so lines constituting the heart of this section and comprising artifacts and detritus across historical moments, finally can't be recuperated. Earlier, in discussing the poem's second section, I quoted a phrase from the poem, "As he calls you from a maelstrom."[17] The word "maelstrom" initially seemed akilter to me, an odd, perhaps even overly poetic choice. But when I investigated its etymology, I understood. Both parts of the word are of Dutch origin, "maalen"—grind or whirl—and "stroom"-stream. "Maelstrom" thus, literally, means "grinding stream." Here, at the poem's end, all the stuff of lost history rises, time runs backward. It rises, caught in history's grinding stream, only to settle once again, and what it settles into is silence, the place where even language has been destroyed.

"Maelstrom" was also used by cartographers to mean "whirlpool," for a particularly forceful whirlpool off the coast of Norway. *Whirlpool* figures as the aquatic version of a black hole, an inverse force pulling one world into another, a potent image of the spatial as destabilized and mutable. While the originary histories recounted in Wood's poem confirm and reconfirm essential connections between a land and its peoples—and not just its human people—modernity is the site of the "dismembered," of a profound ungrounding.

It's not my intention to delimit the spatial only to issues of land *possession* any more than I intend to abstract historic land loss—and theft—into the sort of intellectually engaging and thoroughly apolitical analysis that trended in the 1990s when I was an often-puzzled PhD student. Of the three poems discussed in this essay, Wood's is perhaps the most markedly concerned with material culture, and, in particular, with what Mark Rifkin calls "temporal sovereignty." He asks: "What does it mean to be recognized as existing in time?" I might extend his question so as to ask, "What would it mean to have the temporality in which a people exist recognized?" Because just as the final section catalogs what has been collected, damaged, museumified, and closed off into a "simulacrum of pastness," so too are Indigenous temporalities contained or precluded.[18]

But, so, too, are there other stories to be told—of time and temporality, space and geography. Wood and Hedge Coke and Foerster all tell these stories, as do so many Indigenous women poets. How poetry unwords our received metaphors and offers us, if we choose to listen, deeper, more layered understandings of worlds we inhabit, grieve, celebrate, reconstitute. We float in time. In time we float. Time geographizes and space ticks by.

Notes

1. The line is from Revard's poem "A Giveaway Special." Thanks to Eric Gary Anderson whose article "Carter in Space" reminded me of this poem. Carter Revard, *An Eagle Nation* (Tucson: University of Arizona Press, 1993), xi; Eric Gary Anderson, "Carter in Space," *Studies in American Indian Literature* 15, no. 1, In Honor of Carter Revard (Spring 2003): 26–31.

2. I borrow this phrase from Mark Rifkin's illuminating study *Beyond Settler Time: Temporal Sovereignty and Indigenous Self-Determination* (Durham: Duke University Press, 2017), passim.

3. Doreen Massey, *The Doreen Massey Reader*, ed. Brett Christophers, Rebecca Lave, Jamie Peck, and Marion Werner (Newcastle upon Tyne, UK: Agenda Publishing, 2018), 271.

4. Jennifer Foerster, *Leaving Tulsa* (Tucson: University of Arizona Press, 2013), 20.

5. Dean Rader, "Poems That Contain (and Critique) History: Three First Books," *HuffPost*, December 6, 2017, https://www.huffpost.com/entry/poems-that-contain-histor_b_5830112.

6. Foerster, *Leaving Tulsa*, 8.

7. Foerster, "Intrigue of the Heart."

8. In "Allison Adelle Hedge Coke: Constructing Southern Working Class Indigeneity," Ellen Arnold characterizes Hedge Coke as "a versatile poet and memoirist of the Southern Native diaspora whose roots in Cherokee homeland are not only historical and cultural but also intensely personal and physical." In her overview of Hedge Coke's writing, Arnold points to her 2014 *Streaming* as a turning point, a work "more complex formally and linguistically than Hedge Coke's previous work, *Streaming*'s contrasts are more violent, the achievement of balance less harmonious, more painfully won. Yet the thematic centers that emerged from her early life in the South—the intensely personal interrelationship of individual with place made through labor, the value of labor as anchor and prayer—remain at its heart." Ellen Arnold, "Allison Adelle Hedge Coke: Constructing Southern Working-Class Indigeneity," in *PostIndian Aesthetics: Affirming Indigenous Literary Sovereignty*, ed. Debra K. S. Barker and Connie A. Jacobs (Tucson:

University of Arizona Press, 2022), 109.

9. Jeanetta Calhoun Mish, review of *Streaming, World Literature Today* 89, no. 5 (September–October 2015). See also Matthew Pincus's review in *The Volta Blog*, September 8, 2015, https://thevoltablog.wordpress.com/2015/09/08/review-streaming-by-allison-adelle-hedge-coke/.

10. Allison Adelle Hedge Coke, *Streaming* (Minneapolis: Coffee House, 2014), xii.

11. While I have not quoted from J. Jack Halberstam's work directly in this essay, my thinking about time owes an enormous debt to Halberstam's *In a Queer Time and Place: Transgender Bodies, Subcultural Lives* (New York: New York University Press, 2005). Halberstam's constestation of normativizing strategies of time and geography have informed my own explorations of alternatives to settler-normed impositions of the temporal and the spatial (and their interwoven relationship to each other). Along with Halberstam's, Lee Edelman's work on the ways HIV reshaped such temporal frameworks as longevity has been useful in thinking through how narratives of disappearance may work similarly in relation to Indigenous discourse. This seems especially pertinent for Karenne Wood's poem "The Naming." Lee Edelman, *No Future: Queer Theory and the Death Drive* (Durham, NC: Duke University Press, 2004).

12. Tara Causey, "Stories of Survivance: The Poetry of Karenne Wood," *South Atlantic Review* 77, no.1–2 (2012): 147.

13. Wood, "Prisoners," 73, 77.

14. Karenne Wood, *Weaving the Boundary* (Tucson: University of Arizona Press, 2016), 57, 58.

15. Chadwick Allen, *Trans-Indigenous: Methodologies for Global Native Literary Studies* (Minneapolis: University of Minnesota Press, 2012), xiv.

16. Wood, *Weaving*, 71.

17. Wood, *Weaving*, 58.

18. Rifkin, *Beyond Settler Time*, 5, 7.

Bibliography

Allen, Chadwick. *Trans-Indigenous: Methodologies for Global Native Literary Studies.* Minneapolis: University of Minnesota Press, 2012.

Anderson, Eric Gary. "Carter in Space." *Studies in American Indian Literature* 15, no. 1, In Honor of Carter Revard (Spring 2003): 26–31.

Arnold, Ellen. "Allison Adelle Hedge Coke: Constructing Southern Working-Class Indigeneity." In *PostIndian Aesthetics: Affirming Indigenous Literary Sovereignty*, edited by Debra K. S.

Barker and Connie A. Jacobs, 109–118. Tucson: University of Arizona Press, 2022.

Causey, Tara. "Stories of Survivance: The Poetry of Karenne Wood." *South Atlantic Review* 77, no. 1–2 (2012): 141–152.

Edelman, Lee. *No Future: Queer Theory and the Death Drive*. Durham, NC: Duke University Press, 2004.

Foerster, Jennifer Elise. "Intrigue of the Heart, Tafisha Edwards Interviews Jennifer Elise Foerster." By Tafisha Edwards. *Kweli*, December 22, 2014. https://www.kwelijournal.org/interviews-1/2014/12/26/intrigue-of-the-heart-tafisha-edwards-interviews-jennifer-elise-foerster.

———. *Leaving Tulsa*. Tucson: University of Arizona Press, 2013.

Halberstam, J. Jack. *In a Queer Time and Place: Transgender Bodies, Subcultural Lives*. New York: New York University Press, 2005.

Hedge Coke, Allison Adelle. *Streaming*. Minneapolis: Coffee House, 2014.

———. "Streaming." *World Literature Today*, May 2017. https://www.worldliteraturetoday.org/2017/may/streaming-allison-adelle-hedge-coke.

Massey, Doreen. *The Doreen Massey Reader*. Edited by Brett Christophers, Rebecca Lave, Jamie Peck, and Marion Werner. Newcastle upon Tyne, UK: Agenda Publishing, 2018.

Mish, Jeanetta Calhoun. Review of *Streaming*. *World Literature Today* 89, no. 5 (September–October 2015). https://www.worldliteraturetoday.org/2015/september/streaming-allison-adelle-hedge-coke.

Rader, Dean. "Poems That Contain (and Critique) History: Three First Books." *HuffPost*, December 6, 2017. https://www.huffpost.com/entry/poems-that-contain-histor_b_5830112.

Revard, Carter. *An Eagle Nation*. Tucson: University of Arizona Press, 1993.

Rifkin, Mark. *Beyond Settler Time: Temporal Sovereignty and Indigenous Self-Determination*. Durham: Duke University Press, 2017.

Wood, Karenne. "Prisoners of History: Pocahontas, Mary Jemison, and the Poetics of an American Myth." *Studies in American Indian Literature* 28, no. 1 (Spring 2016): 73–82.

———. *Weaving the Boundary*. Tucson: University of Arizona Press, 2016.

Diné Brevity as Indigenous Theory

Shaina A. Nez

Poetry is an act of human agency and encapsulates what it means to be human. Native and Indigenous poetics have sought to rebuild, reassert, reclaim, and reestablish connections and relationships that return us to our lands, our communities, and ourselves. These connections help bridge our narratives as humane by expressing vulnerability and empathy toward the injustices and reasons for our survival.

In my practice of poetry, I write toward beauty with calm and collective brevity as my worldview. Diné (Navajo) theoretical frameworks *Hózhó* and *Sa'ąh Naagháí Bik'eh Hózhó'ó* (*SNBH*) inform the consciousness of self, relative, ancestor, and community through poetics. I have learned that *Hózhó* means beauty, harmony, and peace in the Diné worldview.[1] *Sa'ąh Naagháí Bik'eh Hózhó'ó* represents the brevity of time from the moment of birth to old age. Diné poetics theorize my worldview as proprioceptive, meaning the senses emerge through our actions. In *SNBH*, there are four processes we, as Diné people, embody: (1) *Nitsahakees* to take time out and think, (2) *Nahat'a* before you do anything plan, (3) *Iina* is to live, and (4) *Siihasin* to reflect on the creative work. *K'é* is another process that allows us to embody love and compassion. We see the world channeled through these concepts. As practicing poets, reimagining form in the diaspora of theory, we are examining our internal senses and worldviews.

Hózhó and *SNBH* unpack these experiences of identity and survival in *Diné bizaad*, meaning the Navajo language, and *Bilagáana bizaad*, meaning the English language.

Brevity means concise and exact use of words in writing or speech. The term also embodies shortness in time. When I reflect on the intentional use of words, I am focusing on brevity across languages. Diné bizaad means the Navajo language, and you will see Diné bizaad and Navajo language used interchangeably within this chapter. The term *brevity* will also be used interchangeably between the intentional usage of words and the concept of time. What I wholeheartedly love about Diné bizaad is the complex, multi-layered, and multi-dimensional aspects of language—when I seem to think I understand a term or phrase—it is a continuing learning process. For instance, when I'm in conversation with my parents, I ask about a single term, such as na'ałkid, which means temperature, time—by the clock, which is uncomplicated.[2] When I ask them both to describe shortness in time, they explain that language spoken in different areas on Dinétah will reveal different descriptions in this language. Shizhé'é (who is originally from Cedar Springs near Teesto, Arizona) will describe time as never-ending, using the words holzhish, and shimá (who is from Lukachukai, Arizona) will describe time as going by quickly.

These comparisons matter because a surviving language widespread across roughly 28,000 miles going in all directions means there was influence by the nature of the location and possibly neighboring tribes. As I consider these two phrases spoken by my parents, I like to use the keywords and begin revisiting tools such as language dictionaries to further explore dimensions of the word "time" in Diné bizaad. When considering another description in conversation, I pronounce t'áá łáhádi, which means once—without repetition—one time.[3] In conversation, I am reminded that t'áá łáhádi means someone is only saying these instructions or commands one time—if you don't do as you are told, then you are closing the willingness to patiently listen, learn, and do (practices of *SNBH*). When I think about brevity in a poem—you are only leaving the reader to listen, learn, and understand once. Meanings in poetry can, of course, be interpreted multiple times, but when you are reading a particular Navajo poem—you are visiting with the Navajo poet—an opportunity to hear and listen, not ask questions such as why. Asking why becomes too invasive; I cannot recall a time that I ever encountered a relative or fellow community member asking such a thing. Perhaps, too, my parents had a way of considering time as nonlinear and my approach was to consider how life practices are given as a measure of time. Two different approaches, but complementary as ever.

When I emerged in the practice of poetry, I was nineteen years old at Diné College, a tribal institution located in Tsaile, Arizona, on the Navajo Nation, attending a creative writing: poetry course. I sat across from from a group of students, watched the sunlight rotate through the window glass, and took out a notebook and pen from my bag. The instructor entered the classroom with a stack of books in hand and placed it on the desk. The chatting immediately ceased and we watched him take out a black Expo and draw a large circle on the whiteboard. He faced us and gave his introduction in Navajo. Hearing the distinct pauses and direct breath pronouncing the slash L (ł), I knew he was a fluent speaker. When he finished, he drew our attention back to the circle on the board posing a question: What should poetry look like on the page?

The image of this black outline of a circle stays with me in my writing practice, whether poetry or prose. I have come to understand the idea of the circle in poetry—it mirrors the shape of *SNBH* life practices. Native American and Indigenous life practices also constitute an Indigenous theory. *SNBH*, for instance, could visually represent a circle as the reflection of time, the brevity I continue to use in my poetry process. The circle starts at the top as a beginning of life; in each quarter of the turn is a point in time on on the journey you are taking—in each stanza or poem composed—I get a little closer to the end of my journey.

In my earliest poem, "They Tell Me" (2010), I am transporting to and from brevity, writing from children's perspective of the trauma withstood during the Boarding School Era.[4] Approaching a tragic experience did not occur to me until I attended a Native American History class discussing this era and came across a black-and-white photograph of three children sitting side-by-side wearing formal shirts and pants. They looked out of place. As I peered at this photograph, the body language—square posture and their eyes petrified—I wondered what was occurring behind the scenes. Who were the children facing as the lens focused on them? What transformations take place when Native American and Indigenous children go through the tactic "Kill the Indian, Save the Man"? Using *SNBH* in the writing process for this chapter, I discuss ahead how *SNBH* shaped my approach to and creation of the poem.

Nitsahakees (to Think)

One could say I privilege imagery to accentuate the form of my poetry—it becomes an orchestration finding the rhythms and a sound play. When crafting an image in a poem, I find myself wondering how these words could be formed without blatantly stating the phrase "Kill the Indian, Save the Man." I'm uncertain if radicalism was framed within my work (though this poem was featured in a Native Activism issue with the *Tribal College Journal*), my hope is that my writings are viewed as observations of tragic experiences as realism. The transformation of each stanza takes place when a reader sees the nature of the poem. When the poem is read aloud, the stanza and language takes form as the air. If the poem translates to the spaces of Diné bizaad—the sounds stays timeless. Sounds from ancestral language are associated with an image, the reader is seeing and experiencing them as a reflection of their relations.

Nahat'a (before You *Do*, Plan)

I've been mentored to think of the page as more than a canvas. What spaces do I want to be intentional with, what shapes can I form, and most importantly are there indirect spaces I'm using? The intentional brevity I'm directing in each stanza first emphasizes the idea of safety. Where will these children feel safe? A child is forcibly removed from their homeland; the term "safe" is often used to justify why boarding schools were established. The transformation was more in terms meant to baptize and ritually purify from sin. From the first stanza, it reads:

> They tell me to come with them, that I will be safe.
> I do, but I am not at all.[5]

"They tell me" is repeated throughout the poem, and following the next line "I do," these lines do not mean to portray any child was open to these promises. In the line, "I do" comes after "but," meaning there's no more to say than what the child assumes.

An unveiling transformation initiates cutting his or her hair, not ensuring the safety as promised. Hair often reflects the wisdom and epistemologies of what the children are taught by parents or elders. Hair has special spiritual and cultural significance, though traditions and styles vary from tribe to tribe. Whether worn long, braided, or bound in a knot, most see hair as a source of strength and power.

> They tell me to cut my hair, so it won't be in my way.
> I do, but where will my wisdom fall?[6]

Names changed from traditional Native and Indigenous languages to English common names, were the ceremonies harmed or affected by this shift? Who are they supposed to be now? Name changing meant agents or overseers could not pronounce it or never cared to begin with about understanding other languages' significance. When baptized, your entire being is supposed to change, name included. The second stanza reads:

> They tell me to change my name because they cannot pronounce it.
> I do, but who am I now?[7]

Diné bizaad and other multiple ancestral languages appear as a deficit—when these pauses and direct breath have been isolated from the embodying existence. English becomes the only form of expression and communication. To speak only English limits Native peoples from their original Indigenous knowledges. In the third stanza, it reads:

> They tell me to never speak my language because it is poison.
> I do, but how will I speak?[8]

The transformation of this child slowly seeps into the eternal memory of *k'é*, *SNBH*, and *Hózhó*. Like many Native American and Indigenous knowledge systems, *k'é* means kinship, but more than that it can also mean love and compassion, *SNBH* refers to the time of birth to old age—the privilege to live over one hundred years old, and *Hózhó* means the balance of all forces that make us Diné. Erasure is revealed in these three stanzas by what is taken from the child, how this child will continue to prosper knowing their ways of being are diminished. In the three stanzas that follow, it reads:

> They tell me to never look to the east and pray.
> I do, but how will my creator hear me?
> They tell me to learn the white man's ways.
> I do, but what about my own ways?
> They tell me to never look back at my culture or way of life again.
> I do, but whose life will I be living now?[9]

Now comes the final tactic of attire to transform the children away from their image. In the majority of boarding school photographs, the clothing is uniform. They don't resemble their place or sense of belonging, hardly recognizing themselves. The stanza reads:

> They tell me to wear their clothes so I will look just like them.
> I do, but I don't recognize the person staring back at me.[10]

These promises by agents meant the children could go home to see their families, however, most never returned. Children attempted to flee from the schools but were brought back for further retribution. In the final stanza, a child endured these demands, hoping they would go back to the lands they belonged to. It reads:

> They tell me to do all these things.
> I do . . .
> So I can return home like they promised.[11]

Iina (as a Device)

Using these Indigenous theories and brevity in poetry, the writing becomes intentional, thought-provoking, and homages to our ancestral languages. What would this poem, "They Tell Me," look like for other Native American and Indigenous languages—visually and by the breaths in spoken language? Here is a translation of the poem, "They Tell Me," in the spaces of Diné Bizaad, if we wanted to see this child's perspective from our homelands in the Southwest:

'ABI'DOO'NIIDĘ́Ę, A NAVAJO-ENGLISH TRANSLATION OF THEY TELL ME

'ábi'doo'niidę́ę	'ábi'doogí 'Ádeeshnííł	t'áadoo t'óó nihił jiní
'ábi'doo'niidę́ę	'atsii' béésh 'ahédiłí baa shił hózhǫ́.	'ádeeshnííł Háísh shini'
'ábi'doo'niidę́ę	kódaolyé łahgo 'áhoodzaa Háísh yinishyé?	Doo ndiista'a'da
'ábi'doo'niidę́ę	doo désh'íí' bich'ijígo ha'a'aah da Háísh sodeezin yáshti'?	'ádeeshnííł
'ábi'doo'niidę́ę	bíhwiidííłááł bilagáana Bik'ehjí	'ádeeshnííł
'ábi'doo'niidę́ę	doo bíhwiidííłááł Diné Bizaad dóó Bik'ehjí da	'ádeeshnííł
'ábi'doo'niidę́ę	háádadiit'ịịhígi désh'íí' łahgo 'áhoodzaa	'ádeeshnííł
'ábi'doo'niidę́ę	'ádeeshnííł dę́ę naashá niséyá 'ádeehadahizhdeesdzíí'[12]	

Siihasin (to Reflect on Indigenous Theory)

The philosophy *SNBH* and *hózhó* mean to achieve a life of beauty and harmony; I take to using the four principles as a process of composing. First, conceptualizing or thinking for yourself: understanding who you are as an existing individual and the awareness of language, culture, and family. *Hózhó*, as defined by Vincent Werito in *Revitalizing and Reclaiming Navajo Thought* (2014), embodies the self, decision, and manner of a Navajo being, stated in the following way:

> While philosophically hózhó could be interpreted as a state of being or a state of existence with harmony and peace, it is really about how the idea or concept influences a person's manner of living and thinking. Put another way, hózhó is more significant when the meaning is conceptualized, actualized, lived, and reflected on at a personal level.[13]

If Diné learns these ways of knowing from a knowledge holder during ceremony, it is not for the sake of knowing, it is to become, practice, and be a part of. The daily life of a Diné individual may pose as waking before dawn, praying, and giving abundance to another day on nihimá nahasdzáán (mother earth). This practice is about beginning the day with purpose, courage, and happiness, and ending the day with reflection—what was accomplished and needs attention the following day.

These ways of knowing to encompass the thought process, *SNBH*, for Diné is rigorously practiced by actively doing. Rex Lee-Jim describes the philosophy as the natural attitude, "*SNBH* is a person's life journey. A person's life is his or her own to live, but a person is connected to family and community. SNBH is spiritually multidimensional and comprehensive. Is it part of the identity of a person and a people?"[14] Diné writers understand *SNBH* as part of their lived experiences used to exercise rhetorical sovereignty (an inherent right to determine their own communicative needs and desires) complementing Diné knowledge shared with the community as well as in scholarly and literary discourse.

In *The Diné Reader: An Anthology of Navajo Literature*, Rex Lee-Jim (2021) uses Diné poetics as well as the essences of Hózhó and *SNBH* in his writing. In the bilingual poem "Saad," and its translation to English, "Language," are as follows:

SAAD

Hodeeyáádą́ą́' honishłǫ́

Adáádą́ą́' honishłǫ́

Ahóyéeł'áágóó honishłǫ́

Saad shí nishłį́

Saad diyinii shí nishłį́

Saad diyinii díí shí nishłį́[15]

(Poem translation to English)

Language

In the beginning I was

Yesterday I was

Today I am

Tomorrow I will be

Forever I will be

Language I am

Sacred language I am

Sacred language this I am[16]

The first stanzas of "Saad" and "Language" feature repetition as song-like, prayer-like, and the powers of language being spoken and coming alive. Language becomes a force to conjure and bring into being; other Native American writers like Leslie Marmon Silko write about this conjuration of language in fiction and nonfiction genres. What remains relevant in Jim's poetry are the four parts of learning and planning, also known as Nitsahakees (Thinking), Nahat'á (Planning), Iiná (Living), and Siihasin (Assurance). These four elements constitute what being Diné encompasses in our daily lives and what knowledge we enact, speak, write, and give abundance to in K'é (family) and communities.

The function of both Diné and Indigenous Knowledge System (IKS) is ethics in discovery and inquiry. Diné knowledge systems and IKS complement the exploration of storytelling in its poetics, pedagogy, and survival.

By exercising breath as an extension of the self, relative, and ancestor, we are in the natural harmony of the elements and land. Breath is air exhaled from our body—our bodies carry intergenerational histories—that turn into voices and speech to communicate from the depths of our core. I referred to the page as a canvas when thinking of space, so what does our breath look like on this particular canvas? In the poetry collection titled *This Land, Our Love*, published by Green Linden Press (issue 14, *Indigenous Ecopoetry*), we explore breath further as an extension of self, relative, and ancestor.

When we use sodeezin (prayer) to greet Diyin Dine'é (Holy people), nihimá nahasdzáán (mother earth), and the four sacred mountains, our voice carries a message. Voice begins its journey in the inner body as breath is exhaled from the lungs, and breath rises into sǫ' (stars). In the poem above, when breath becomes a part of the universe, we can see these variations in the stars as they glimmer across father sky. We know our prayers exist when stars glimmer, the four sacred mountains—Tsisnaasjini' (Blanca Peak) white shell mountain is in the east, Tsoodził (Mount Taylor) turquoise mountain is in the south, Doko'oosliid (San Francisco Peaks) abalone shell mountain is in the west, and Dibé Nitsaa (Hesperus mountain) obsidian mountain is in the north—hear us. We acknowledge these words said for us by our parents and grandparents. As we age, we learn to pray for others mimicking these verbal cues, and when we become a mother, father, aunt, or uncle, the cycle repeats for generational abundance. Our speech expresses thoughts, with a volume and a tone that reveals intention and emotion, linguistic rhythm develops, especially when ending the prayer with hózhó náhásdlíí' (there is beauty again) repeating four times.

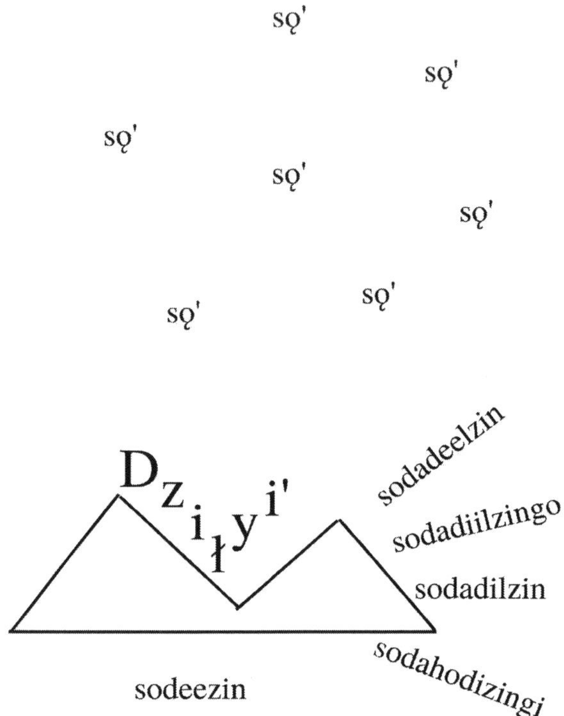

A concrete poem reflecting on prayer, the sacred mountains, and pluralism in Diné bizaad.

"Hweełdí" reflects the historical distress the people endured during the Long Walk. Hwééʼílniiʼ (they were released) is a phrase used as a theme for this poem. Ajéí (heart) are scattered on the ground to represent burials of ancestors dying and their bodies returning to nihimá nahasdzáán (mother earth). Breath in this essence is shuttered—some believe the past should remain in the past; if we call out to the distress, we are bringing these events back to life—however, my intention rests with solitude as I think back to my ancestors. My breath is delicate when speaking about this time and place—I want others to know that this moment in history is pivotal to our breath. The air that passes through our vocal cords, turns to voice, and with the movements of the mouth, can become uttered words of remembrance and acknowledgment of our purpose on this

Hwéé'ílnii'

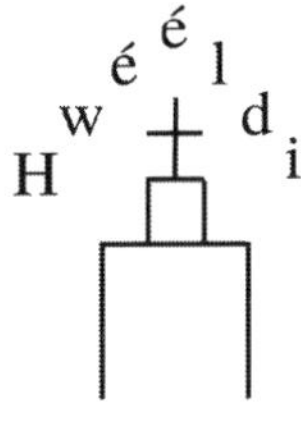

ajéí   ajéí   ajéí

ajéí   ajéí   ajéí

ajéí   ajéí   ajéí

A concrete poem reflecting on The Long Walk of 1864.

earth. The speech itself can influence our breathing rhythm—reciting our ancestral language can affect breathing and, through breathing, it can also alter heart rate and the blood flow in the body and the brain. Our bodies continue to become one with saad (words) and bizaad (language) and, with the air we breathe, we embody these depths of our internal senses and worldviews.

Notes

1. Vincent Werito, "Understanding Hózhó to Achieve Critical Consciousness," in *Diné Perspectives: Revitalizing and Reclaiming Navajo Thought*, ed. Lloyd L. Lee (Tucson: University of Arizona Press, 2014), 25–38.

2. Leon Wall and William Morgan, *Navajo-English Dictionary* (New York: Hippocrene Books, 2016), 113.

3. Wall and Morgan, *Navajo-English Dictionary*, 147.

4. Shaina Nez, "They Tell Me," *Tribal College Journal of American Indian Higher Education* 22, no. 1 (2010): 27.

5. Nez, "They Tell Me," 27.

6. Nez, "They Tell Me," 27.

7. Nez, "They Tell Me," 27.

8. Nez, "They Tell Me," 27.

9. Nez, "They Tell Me," 27.

10. Nez, "They Tell Me," 27.

11. Nez, "They Tell Me," 27.

12. Shaina Nez, "Abi'doo'niidę́ę́, a Navajo-English translation of They Tell Me," trans. Shaina Nez, in the author's possession, 2021.

13. Werito, "Understanding Hózhó to Achieve Critical Consciousness," 29.

14. Rex Lee-Jim, "Introduction," in *Diné Perspectives: Revitalizing and Reclaiming Navajo Thought*, ed. Lloyd L. Lee (Tucson: University of Arizona Press, 2014), 5.

15. Rex Lee-Jim, "Saad," in *The Diné Reader: an Anthology of Navajo Literature*, edited by Esther G. Belin, Jeff Berglund, Connie A. Jacobs, Anthony K. Webster, and Sherwin Bitsui (Tucson: the University of Arizona Press, 2021), 135–136.

16. Lee-Jim, "Saad," 137.

Bibliography

Belin, Esther G., Jeff Berglund, Connie A. Jacobs, Anthony K. Webster, and Sherwin Bitsui, eds. *The Diné Reader: An Anthology of Navajo Literature*. Edited by Esther G. Belin, Jeff Berglund, Connie A. Jacobs, and Anthony K. Webster. Tucson: University of Arizona Press, 2021.

Lee-Jim, Rex. "Introduction." In *Diné Perspectives: Revitalizing and Reclaiming Navajo Thought*, edited by Lloyd L. Lee, 3–13. Tucson: University of Arizona Press, 2014.

———. "Saad." In *The Diné Reader: An Anthology of Navajo Literature*, edited by Esther G. Belin, Jeff Berglund, Connie A. Jacobs, Anthony K. Webster, and Sherwin Bitsui, 135–136. Tucson: University of Arizona Press, 2021.

Nez, Shaina. "'Abi'doo'niidę́ę́, a Navajo-English Translation of They Tell Me." (2021). Translated by Shaina Nez. In the author's possession.

———. "They Tell Me." In "Native Activism." *Tribal College Journal of American Indian Higher Education* 22, no. 1 (2010): 27.

———. "This Land, Our Love." In "Indigenous Ecopoetry." *Under a Warm Green Linden* 14 (2022). https://www.greenlindenpress.com/issue14-shaina-nez.

Wall, L., and W. Morgan. *Navajo-English Dictionary.* New York: Hippocrene Books, 2016.

Werito, Vincent. "Understanding Hózhó to Achieve Critical Consciousness." In *Diné Perspectives: Revitalizing and Reclaiming Navajo Thought*, edited by Lloyd L. Lee, 25–38. Tucson: University of Arizona Press, 2014.

Snowmaking

A Native Poetics of Winter, Mountains, and Bathing

Cj Jackson

Somewhere in the hills between my house and the mountains, I learned to listen to snow. I was eleven, twelve maybe. During the winters, we waited until after the second snowfall to venture outside for sledding, making snowmen, and even bathing. Impatient, though, there was one winter when I was tired of my mom telling me to wait until the snow stuck to one another to go outside. So, I decided to leave without telling anyone. A single dirt road wraps around the fence outside our house and leads south toward the mountain we live next to, a mountain we call sháá'tóhó. The ground was hard, covered in patchy ice spots from snow that had frozen over. Every step I took was a crunch, a sharp release of breath. I slipped a couple of times but didn't stop. Our sledding spot was at the highest point of a creek that only ever filled with water during monsoon season. When my brother and I come out here, we carry those thick plastic sleds from Sam's Club that always end up with scratches on the bottom from rocks hiding in the thinner parts of the snow. As I continued walking, I grew excited. I wanted to feel the bite of cold as I plummeted toward the ground.

It's hard to get lost on the reservation when you've grown up there and dramatic landscape changes are not a common occurrence. You can see for miles in every direction. The mountains don't move, and the roads rarely change. When it snows, though, and the clouds fall onto the earth, and it's impossible to see more than three feet in front of you because the fog is so thick. All noises become muted, too. The sheep stop bleating, the horses stop stomping and neighing. The whole world becomes blank. Quiet. Everything still.

The snow starts picking up again at some point during my walk, and I realize I'm lost. The road I'm following is now completely covered in snow, and the fog wraps around me so tightly that it's hard to see even my hand when I reach out. I know my way back home because my tracks are deep enough that it'll take a few hours before they're covered, too, but for a minute it feels like I've been transported somewhere else. The home I've known all my life suddenly disappears, and I have no name for the plants or rocks or hills I've come to know because there are none. I'm not scared, but a thrilling, dangerous thought pops into my head: I too could disappear into the heavy clouds. Suddenly, I am new to a place I've never encountered before, every familiar landmark blurred into the background behind a warm gray silhouette. This snow, this fog, this winter, is meeting me for the first time, too. I take a deep breath so the sharp air can fill my lungs, and even now, a decade later, I remember the immediate grief that followed. *I can't stay here*, I thought. The snow will dissipate when the sun reaches midday, and I have to go back home before my parents worry. I can't stay here, but this encounter was enough to know that I didn't know my world as well as I thought before. I have much to learn.

When I started my graduate program in Northern Arizona, it didn't surprise me how clueless most people were about the use of sewage effluent to make artificial snow for the Snowbowl ski resort on top of the San Francisco Peaks. My department offered terminal degrees and it funded well, so most of the students came in from out of state. I myself was already familiar with the area, having grown up about an hour and a half's drive east of there on the Navajo reservation. I went piñon picking at the base of the mountain when I was little, came into town every two weeks to pick up groceries and bulk items from Sam's Club, and braved the cold, standing in line for hours to watch high school basketball games in the J. Lawrence Walkup Skydome. I didn't share all these details with the other graduate students, but when we broke for lunch during orientation, I would recommend a couple of burger joints I knew about and that would inevitably lead to a quick explanation about where I'm from and how I knew places to eat.

Some were quick to announce their surprise at having never known the reservation was so close to town. I was happy to share stories about places to visit, even inviting some others on a mini tour around the different landscapes. Some, however, wanted to know about Snowbowl. The first time someone asked me, *So, have you ever been to the ski resort?* I was caught off guard, because everyone in my life up until that point either couldn't afford to go or were vehemently against going. I was so startled that all I said was, *No*, a little aggressively, ending our conversation. But that same question would pop up again for weeks. Someone would say, *I heard there's a ski resort on the mountain. Have you ever been? Would you recommend it?* And each time someone asked me, I gave what I thought was an obvious answer, taking an extra few minutes to explain the history of the resort: that surrounding tribes protested the initial construction and still object to expansion plans because they have ancestral ties to the Peaks; that the snow is made from wastewater and the contamination to environmental wildlife has not been seriously or thoroughly researched; and that the continued dismissal of tribal concerns is an act of desecration.

In my head, though, I am reminded that it's not my place to tell people what they can and can't do. Of course, that doesn't mean I say, *Fuck it*, and not give a shit. It means that I do my best to explain, to listen, to support, and to argue, when needed. But I have to do these things with an understanding that I can really, really care and be overwhelmingly concerned and want the best of something, and still sometimes have someone *not* listen back to me. I can't *make* people see things the way I do. And that doesn't mean I give up, but my mom and dad tell me that there's a point when words aren't even words anymore—just noise. *K'adí*, they say. *That's enough.* Still, knowing the lessons my parents taught me never eased the sharp burning sensation that occurs in my chest when someone is obviously not paying attention to what I'm saying anymore. When the people who asked me about Snowbowl responded with a simple, *Oh, I didn't know that*, I knew no one really heard me. I know that the statistics for the number of people who have intimate knowledge about Native politics and tribal determinisms is low. After the first person asked me about Snowbowl, I knew to expect that most people would know next to nothing about the tribes in Northern Arizona. That wasn't an issue for me. I threw in impromptu history lessons and offered small stories when it seemed appropriate. To me, it wasn't a matter of whether someone knew something beforehand. It was that their knowing didn't match their feelings.

The real issue was the dismissal. Having no one hear me meant that no one heard my anger or the anger of all the tribes who protest the usage of sewage water on the Peaks. It meant that no one cared to listen to me. And that only amounted to more frustration. Why didn't anyone understand the hurt caused by dismissal? Why didn't anyone understand the anger that comes from being reduced to something less important than profit and tourist revenue? My anger was terminal to anyone who stood too close to me, a burn no one wanted to get caught in. What made it worse was the eventual discussion about land rights and ownership. *The San Francisco Peaks aren't part of the reservation, though,* some people said. *Does it matter?* I asked. Not disregarding the obliviousness to dispossession and land theft, why are we—my tribe and the tribes around us—held to an expectation to care more deeply about the world than others? Should that not be the standard for everyone? Part of that frustration was also directed toward myself. I selfishly wanted my anger to be shared by people who didn't share my stakes. Who didn't know the risks I knew. I wanted my home to be more than a tacked-on afterthought. I wanted them to know the offense *and* vindicate it with me. Enough was a threshold I broke many times until I realized my anger was more grief than rage. And maybe that's why no one listened to me. What did they have to lose?

In hindsight, I understood that those feelings of anger and grief emerged from a younger version of myself who learned one day that snow is more wondrous, more enveloping than most people realize. Even at eleven, I knew better than to mess around with something that dangerous. Diné people are known to bathe in snow, placing themselves and their babies in thick white pillows to wash their bodies. They say the process is a cleansing, meant to strip away illness and provide strength for the future. When I asked my parents about this practice, they said I did the same when I was little. They told me I'm supposed to always wait for the *second* snowfall to wash, because the first is supposed to cleanse the ground. You wait for the second snow, because the first is meant for the earth.

The issue is not that I wouldn't bathe in the snow at Snowbowl. The issue is that there is no first snow meant for the earth. Snowmaking begins in November, on bare ground, *before* the first snow of winter even falls. And by the time winter starts, 65 percent of the trails on the mountain are covered with sewage effluent snow.[1] And the issue isn't even that it's artificial snow but that there is no care, no gratitude, no reciprocity, no acknowledgment for the snow and winter seasons that are given to us each year. No respect for the earth to be washed first. Instead, snowmaking dwells on the lack. There's not enough snow, so to give skiers and snowboarders a memorable experience, a snowmaker thickens the thinner parts of the snow trails. To give tourists a consistent season and product, snowmaking guarantees that the winter season runs from late November to early April. At what point does giving become another kind of theft? Snow on the mountains is an optic that gives the impression that global warming is not devastating the change of our seasons. It's easier to ignore environmental catastrophe when the aesthetics of surrounding landscapes occlude the continued effects of colonization and ecological harm, and in this case, why should anyone worry when the Peaks are covered with snow every year?

In the months that followed, I wrestled with the desire to be heard and the want to disappear. I wasn't ashamed of my grief or my anger, but both had morphed into a kind of mourning that was painful to endure. I wondered whether there was an escape. I wondered whether it was possible to make people see things the way I do, the way eleven-year-old me saw something worth listening to in the immersive enfolding of fog and winter. I spent large parts of my childhood waiting for winter to come back. Even as I'm writing this sentence, I'm waiting for my mom to send me pictures of the most recent snow at home. In *Braiding Sweetgrass*, Robin Wall Kimmerer offers one of my favorite questions: On what basis do we select where to invest our allegiance?[2] Winter has always been my favorite season, and it might be shorter now, and the storms might come less often, but I still choose the snow. I choose the trees, the water, the dirt, the mountains. I try—my damn hardest—to choose to invest in the abundance over the lack.

———————————

It never occurred to me to not write poetry. But the last time I had written poetry was back in high school, during freshman year. A friend of mine and I used to trade lines between classes. I would scribble some notes on the corner of my homework, and he would take it and add to what I already started. I stopped because something terrible happened. Looking back now, it's funny to me how something terrible also brought me back.

The poem that emerged from this affair was written over the course of two hours and was only revised once three years later. Most of the elements include references to the reservation. I hadn't realized it yet, but I missed my parents so much that I started to hear the hum of my dad's voice when he sang alongside the peyote songs on his old tape recorder in my literature classes. I missed the footsteps my mom made in the morning when she made coffee and prepared oatmeal for breakfast, telling me in Navajo that I need to hurry because the bus is coming in ten minutes, and she needs to leave or else she'll be late. I missed the smell of dried cedar that my dad would throw into the stove during winter. I missed complaining about having to feed the horses, and pulling the weeds, and having to rummage around for candles when the power went out. I missed the sunsets, when the clouds would turn purple and pink, and I missed the winter, when the clouds would fall so low to the ground that it made a fata morgana of the mountain. My grief wasn't only an accumulation of the dismissals that transpired during conversations about Snowbowl but also the deep realization that I wanted to go home.

So, I started first with those images: cedar, clouds, singing, desert, sunlight. Writing wasn't like talking to people, convincing them to care about how their actions impacted the mountains and the snow. Poetry has no audience. There is no "aboutness" when it comes to a poem, because really, I'm not even sure myself why or what a poem is being written until I've finished. Even then, sometimes "the about" leads to no absolute conclusion. "Aboutness" also often leads me back to lectures from my English professors who insisted that poetry is meant to be examined and analyzed from the text. *The text* tells us what a piece is about. *The text* tells us what's important to notice. If I have a question about *the text*, I conduct research to find an answer that explains what *the text* most likely means. To me, that stance is too rigid and echoes too closely to the distance people take on matters that are built on emotional stakes—like Snowbowl. *I am feeling something*, that is why I write. *I am holding on to too much*, that is also why I write. In poetry resides the place where I can teeter across multiple cable wires and not fear falling. I can have anger and grief and love orbit around me and not become exhausted. But I can also become vexed when something decides to start banging around in my head, refusing to quiet down and rest. I see that something again and again and each time it sounds different.

it's your grief I want to taste

want my lips to graze the cedar skin of your collarbones

how hungry are my hands that sunkiss your cornstalk

how hollow is my white shell without your obsidian

I will pluck you like stars until you are wet and shivering with love

you, mountain I love, I will finger the ridges of you the way the days slide
      across the carpet in dawnlight

like fog at 4:00am when sea-foam is rolling over dark hills into a wider more
      broader desert-scape

I will reach for the yellow on your back and gather you in my palms

I will make you a dayflower and stretch you towards the sun

you, sky shuddering when the singing starts, you have muscled your way
      into my clouds the way honeysuckle

shakes my love

like mountain winds falling upon the great oaks

if you were a body of soil and water, you'd call me home

if you are thirsty for love, then I swear the honeycomb will taste sweeter
      from my hand

& if ceremony becomes the star dust heat death of the universe

then let risk mean that our future is luck and haunting

To me, poetry is a movement, a performance. The images cannot be stationary, because I worry that doing so risks unintentionally, accidentally reproducing colonial aesthetics. Some words are endangered and are held captive by colonial imaginaries that aim to possess and control territories and Native bodies together. Those words have to be creatively sabotaged. Take the word "obsidian," or "cornstalk," or "mountain." A number of tribes have relations to rocks, and plants, and mountains, but I want to know how I myself am seeing and understanding something. How is obsidian not just a rock, but a part of my body? How is cornstalk not just a plant, but a symbol of endurance? As Gloria Bird explains, in becoming attentive to the nuances of language and its ability to "capture" us, we can "eliminate from our vocabulary terms of domination . . . which only serve to keep the power structure in place, unchallenged and unchanged."[3] In a similar manner, when we become attentive to the nuances of the land we write about, the landscapes we imagine, the sounds, the colors, and textures we translate into our work, we succeed at evasion. There are no explicits I will share with you. You only need enough to hear the echo of my parents' laughter, and the vibrato of the next snowstorm's heavy wind. I ask writing to be a form of sovereign investment wherein you only see a glimpse of the pattern of my and my culture's thinking.

When I set out to revise this poem for the first time, I had previously encountered the work Melissa K. Nelson, who calls eco-erotics the "messy and visceral border-crossing entanglement between humans and more than humans."[4] Imagine my surprise when I noticed that initial version was an example of that intentional, accidental, shocking, and mundane "entanglement" Nelson writes about. That wasn't my intention. When I wrote this piece, I only wanted a place to put my grief and my anger. In doing so, I made a place for love, too. It showed me that we are capable of choosing land as the recipient of our investments, as the place we come to know and respect, but the process requires us to pay attention to and act upon the colonial-shaped wounds of land occupation and desecration. In *Poetry Breaks*, Lucille Clifton states: "You come to poetry not out of what you know but out of what you wonder."[5] Poetry, she says, is not solely about answers—it's about questions. The very act of questioning creates the conditions for poetry to be a place of imagination and disobedience, where language simultaneously imagines and defies expectation. I wonder—who else is desperate to see the clouds break during monsoon season? Who else wants to rail against the continued construction of apartments buildings and tourist attractions to ensure the longevity of the pine trees, given the rise of forest fires each year? Who wants to rage and rage and rage? Poetry remains the haven I retreat to when I can't make sense of the mess I feel, the mess I sometimes feel like I made. It's through poetry that I marry the anticipations of excitement and dread when I begin unpacking another issue and another problem for the sake of making livable a new reality. I am both bodied and taken out, but poetry ensures that I never reach the threshold of enough.

Notes

1. "Snowmaking," *Arizona Snowbowl*, December 28, 2022, Snowbowl.ski.
2. Robin Wall Kimmerer, *Braiding Sweetgrass: Indigenous Wisdom, Scientific Knowledge and the Teachings of Plants* (Minneapolis: Milkweed Editions, 2013), 173.
3. Gloria Bird and Joy Harjo, *Reinventing the Enemy's Language: Contemporary Native*

Women's Writing of North America (New York: W.W. Norton & Co., 1997), 19–31.

4. Melissa K. Nelson, "Getting Dirty: The Eco-Eroticism of Women in Indigenous Oral Literatures," in *Critically Sovereign: Indigenous Gender, Sexuality, and Feminist Studies*, ed. Joanne Barker (Durham: Duke University Press, 2017), 232.

5. Lucille Clifton, "Poetry Breaks: Lucille Clifton on What Poetry Is," Academy of American Poets, March 30, 2017, https://poets.org/.

Bibliography

Bird, Gloria, and Joy Harjo. *Reinventing the Enemy's Language: Contemporary Native Women's Writing of North America*. New York: W.W. Norton & Co., 1997.

Clifton, Lucille. "Poetry Breaks: Lucille Clifton on What Poetry Is." Academy of American Poets, March 30, 2017, https://poets.org/.

Kimmerer, Robin Wall. *Braiding Sweetgrass: Indigenous Wisdom, Scientific Knowledge and the Teachings of Plants*. Minneapolis: Milkweed Editions, 2013.

Nelson, Melissa K. "Getting Dirty: The Eco-Eroticism of Women in Indigenous Oral Literatures." In *Critically Sovereign: Indigenous Gender, Sexuality, and Feminist Studies*, edited by Joanne Barker, 229–260. Durham: Duke University Press, 2017.

"Snowmaking." *Arizona Snowbowl*, December 28, 2022. Snowbowl.ski.

The Resonance of Poetry

Molly McGlennen

When we were water
we dove and scouted
like loons, swallowed
pebbles by night . . .
When we were water
we turned into ourselves
claimed by heart circles
that have never washed away.
—Molly McGlennen, "Bearings IV," in *Our Bearings: Poems*

One of the clearest memories I have from my childhood is sitting under the kitchen table at my grandmother's house. This memory could be from any day or year from my childhood; my family and I visited my maternal grandparents' house on a very regular basis. I was one of twenty grandkids, my mom was one of eight children, my grandmother, one of fourteen. We were a network of extended family living in and around Minneapolis, Minnesota.

Unlike many of my cousins who would run outdoors as soon as they could, I often preferred to hide away beneath the table and listen to the adults talk and laugh—and maybe fight—into the evening. I thought I was secretly listening, but I clearly see now that they knew I was there, sometimes giving me a little nudge with their foot and then laughing. No one seemed to mind. It may have been my first way of recording the world. In and with my own body. Listening to story.

Basil Johnston notes that when an Ojibwe child is in her cradleboard, "it is after four to six thousand hours of listening—to the birds, the wind, the insects—the child utters [her first] word."[1] I cannot help but think that as a child growing up I was encouraged to absorb the environment around me in this manner—encouraged that listening necessarily preempted speaking or any embodied expression. The world abundant with sound. The world constantly teaching.

While I cannot recall verbatim the conversations they had, I have held tightly to small pieces of stories, often the ones swollen with pressure—of losing and finding work; of union disputes; of bar fights; but also jokes, teasing, and laughter. Stories I was much too young to comprehend. Yet, what remains indelible is the way these often-contentious, always emotion-filled storytellings continually brought my extended family together over the generations. If I was logging hours of listening, I was almost certainly configuring a way to score these sounds—even without my knowing it, somehow beyond myself. Sounds were not always linguistically constituted either. There were reverberations from bodies all around—bodies of land, of water, of animals, or the wind. Even bodies of memories and dreams.

> Some of life's first lessons
> are learned on the water:
> Quiet keeps
> the fish close.
> *Plant your feet*
> *evenly. Observe*
> *everything.*[2]

My mom's brothers and sisters were and are big people. Her five brothers ranged from 6'4" to 6'8." One of my mom's sisters is 6'3." Six of the eight worked construction, some for their entire lives, some only seasonally. A point of family pride is their work helping to raise the Minneapolis city skyline. So when they came together at my grandma's house, talking around the table could easily end up at the basketball hoop outside—where everyone gathered. A pickup game would emerge, with us little cousins launching up shots at the rim between runs. This is probably where I saw my first hook shot, well before I would see Julius Irving, my favorite player, on TV.

When things were quieted down, perhaps around a bonfire in the yard, I remember being especially captivated by the words floating all around me. Mostly of missed opportunities, of things lost, of what might or should have been for my family—but also that teasing, that laughter. The nearly impossible task of capturing the incandescence of language in my hand. What I was capable of, like dribbling the basketball or finding kindling for the fire, was a different type of gathering, knowing what my body could and could not do. I reflect on why poetry—out of all the genres of writing—has compelled me the most. Perhaps poetry accesses that ability to gather, a means to converge each loosened fragment, no matter how inscrutable, as close as possible to one's heart. And it can become a mechanism to release new patterns of expression, the way a spark breaks off from the flames, transformed and crackling toward the horizon—a gesture of poetry's potential.

In observing what I call "the shape" of poetry in my book *Creative Alliances*, I write about the presence of spirals in Indigenous women's poetry, which in turn illustrates how "Native people consciously look back at traditions, teachings, and experience in order to make decisions to move forward."[3] Evincing this coiling, poetry carries the potential to take up pieces from a past to incorporate into a present, which in turn calibrates a more balanced vision for and path toward a future. Engaging in the poetic process could be the way we tune our bodies to the vibration of sounds produced generations ago.

> Breath guides
> the trail in.
>
> Fuse foot and pine needle.
>
> Ground as keel
> or compass.
>   Ancient foot traffic.
>
> This earth body could be:
>   calendar
>   forecast
>   index.
>
>
> Markers ahead   squint eyes.
> See ancestor dispatch.

> Spot Lady's Slipper
> (could be moccasin flower)
> amongst Tamarack.
>> Another earth memo—
>> wood for snowshoes.
>
> Slender shape of White Spruce cones
> open. Season about to turn.
>
> Identify Basswood.
>> Remember cradleboards
>> or saw-toothed leaves to run
>> fingers along.
>
> Point to clearing. Call back
> forest language as we look for traces
> of cupmarks, tools, messages.
>> Signposts of tenure
> or family records.[4]

One of the first classes of students at Carlisle Indian School included Oneida tribal member Dennison Wheelock. A distinguished musician and composer, Wheelock traveled internationally as a soloist and with the Carlisle Indian Band. He, too, was among the group of founders of the Society of American Indians, the first national Native rights organization run by Native people who sought meaningful reform during the Progressive Era. A social advocate, Wheelock was a successful lawyer representing Native and non-Native clients, and represented Native nations before the U.S. Court of Claims and the U.S. Supreme Court. He also, by chance, served as my great-grandmother's and her brother's (my great-great-uncle) attorney in the late 1920s when they sought official enrollment in the Minnesota Chippewa Tribe. Wheelock died only a year after he took on their case, around the time the famed Meriam Report was submitted, which revealed extensive "tribal deficiencies" of Native lives and livelihoods.

I imagine the tables around which that generation of my family gathered, raucously or carrying great grief, figuring out their Native citizenship in an era that was particularly hostile to American Indians, when my grandma, nearing nine years old and completing what would be her final year of school in fourth grade, would take up—as her siblings did—as a laborer to support the extended family. I imagine the courage they must have summoned as they sought enrollment during a time the federal government, not surprisingly, worked relentlessly and systematically to *detribalize* Natives.

This part of Ojibwe history, and specifically how it shaped my family as Ojibwe descendants in Minneapolis, has been a poetic touchstone for my creative practice. When I imagine a present-day connection to these historical gatherings, I engage a type of poetics beyond an analysis or reportage—beyond "recording." On a certain level, the poetics is a refusal to the type of record- keeping performed by the state, of citizenship-making or denying, of the codification and consolidation of Native bodies through the Nelson Act, and through the dubious salve of House Resolutions that offered government placation for all that was stolen—lands, languages, and lives.

Choices made under duress prove nevertheless to be sophisticated and dynamic when revealed in our stories. Audra Simpson might call something like this "a politics of refusal," whereby Native peoples, fully "mindful of the range of possibilities for political life, for identification and identity within and against recognition," reveal something much more than a rejection of state definitions: "There was something that seemed to reveal itself at the point of refusal—a stance, a principle, a historical narrative, and an enjoyment in the reveal."[5] I want to submit here, too, that a poetics is also at work, the consciousness of knowing specifically how and why we express ourselves the way we do and in relationship with whom—and the potential joy and pride felt through that proclamation. Rather than Native peoples' choices seen as ironic or tragic, or even a particular era of Native history as predestined, Native peoples' own ways of expressing resistance reveal a poetics of possibility—a refusal to be extinguished. Indigenous people infusing poetics with praxis on their own terms. When I write, I create resonance with these very specific historical practices.

All these years later, I do not know why or how Dennison Wheelock was chosen or assigned to my family. General Pratt's prized student, Wheelock was anathema to Native people, historian Laurence Hauptman writes. While Wheelock worked on behalf of Native people, he was also known to "trick Indians out of their land patents after tribal lands were allotted."[6] We have only a receipt from him, payment of ten dollars made by my family for his services for their "Enrollment in the Minnesota Chippewa Tribe." The receipt lies in a stack of documents and photos that are kept in a manila envelope that I inherited from my mom and her cousin, enrollment never realized in our immediate family. Poetry acknowledges and cares for these complicated inheritances, when western archival practices would serve to bury them. Poetry also illuminates the complicated context from which we forge our lives and our relations and heritages—foiling the capture by and closure within state records. While those documents may indicate that we have disappeared to some, my extended family's lives and practices never indicated any such absence.

> Like the hands who held their once-body whole
> Like the hands who chose to break below the surface
> Before those boulders-made-pebbles came crashing ashore.[7]

Poetics, in general, theorize not only the structure and form of poetry but also the ways in which we talk about and understand it as literature. In the context of the history of English verse, the study of poetry has mainly attended to the composition of meters and pattern of syllables. Of course, musicality and rhythm are the properties of verse, and are the guideposts for poets' creative process. For me, however, rhythms are produced even without language—a meter attentive to other reverberations, origins, and histories. When I create a poem, I am accessing those earliest vibrations produced by people, yes, but also by the lands and waters that define the people. The practices, rituals, stories, and language that define the people. In their whole and broken form; in their places of gathering and places of disbandment; in the connective tissue that secures ancestors to progeny, creator to descendants.

Like a tracking system, this mode of poetics urges me on to figure out where the jagged edges of meaning meet. If the poem is a place of discovery, then poetry—in its most efficient state—implies and incites mobility. It seems to me that therein lies the origins of sounds, messages, visions, beyond oneself; it is rarely uttered that it is enough to "only be" in your body as it is, as it moves, with all its messiness, fault lines, and wild potential. Where does poetry start? The question opens up poetry's role in making sense of all that we carry with us, all that makes up our original vibration.

And yet, poetry is not personal narrative. It is not nonfiction (nor is it fiction). In *A Poetry Handbook*, Mary Oliver asserts, "Poems begin in experience, but poems are not in fact experience, nor even a necessarily exact reportage of an experience. They are imaginative constructs, and they do not exist to tell about the poet or the poet's actual experience—they exist in order to be poems."[8] In fact, we poets often look to poetry itself to grant us the language to recognize it, define it, understand it as the genre it is. Poems exist in order to be poems.

There is nothing particularly Indigenous about the desire to write a poem or even creating a means by which to write one. There is, however, something undeniably Indigenous about how the genre is exercised and for what purposes—the creative gestures marked by participation in the creation of the poem itself. So much Native American poetry evinces the way that the genre can be taken up as an instrument to communicate with the very vessels into and for which we are born—our bodies and spirit, our nations, our lands and waters, our ancestors, our children and grandchildren, our knowledge. Into and out of these imperfect and wondrous bodies no matter their forms. That is, the conduit for making good relations.

Engaging our creative spirit alters our attention to time and space, and heightens our awareness to our body's movements and to rhythms that spark all around us. It grants accessways to places we did not know exist, that we could not conceive of. If memory is a body of water, then poetry is the act of casting the net out, again and again, patiently, quietly, drawing in exactly what we might expect there *and* some things we have never seen before. Marilou Awiakta explains how, for her, this model of gathering originates in "primal space, where everything is connected" and thought develops in "the round" rather than linearly.[9] I would add that knowledge as developed and perceived through poetry opens and widens from the inside, the way a ripple moves on the water when you dip your toe into the lake. The way a story grows deeper relevance as your grandmother's voice echoes in your remembrances of her. The way poetry provides a means to locate ourselves in relationship to a network of people and places and memories. The way poetry is an act of dedication, a line to speak to one another.[10]

Under that kitchen table, I listened and gathered everything I could carry. When I place myself there, all these decades later, I am synched with the vibrations of my making, which is necessarily connected to a network of beings. As one would tune a piano, one enters the act of creating poetry. I begin by tuning my instrument by ear to the octaves above and below—to forebears and progeny, to my homescape, to my inheritances of story. Once tuned, I look for the language and its rhythms along the trails left like mnemonic pegs.

Engaging poetry is always a petition for sentience, for understanding the signs. And through these methods of engagement, we continue to intentionally tap into the extended networks of our designs.

> There through the lines of birch, like
>
> parchment, each one lifts off. Rises above you.
>
> You hear yourself from the past.
>
> You hear yourself.[11]

Notes

1. Basil Johnston, *Ojibwemowin: Ojibwe Oral Tradition*, episode 5, "Waasa Inaabidaa: We Look in All Directions," directed by Lorraine Norrgard, narrated by Winona LaDuke, PBS Eight, WDSE-TV, Duluth, MN, 2002.

2. Molly McGlennen, "Snake River V," in *Our Bearings: Poems* (Tucson: University of Arizona Press, 2020), 44.

3. Molly McGlennen, *Creative Alliances: The Transnational Designs of Indigenous Women's Poetry* (Norman: University of Oklahoma Press, 2014), 32.

4. Molly McGlennen, "Bonfire II," in *Our Bearings*, 59–60.

5. Audra Simpson, *Mohawk Interruptus: Political Life Across the Borders of Settler States* (Durham: Duke University Press, 2014), 107.

6. Laurence M. Hauptman, "From Carlisle to Carnegie Hall: The Musical Career of Dennison Wheelock," in *The Oneida Indians in the Age of Allotment, 1860–1920*, ed. Laurence Hauptman and L. Gordon McLester III (Norman: University of Oklahoma Press, 2006), 132.

7. Molly McGlennen, "Remains II," in *Our Bearings*, 70.

8. Mary Oliver, *A Poetry Handbook* (New York: Harcourt Brace & Company, 1994), 109–110.

9. Marilou Awiakta, "Daydreaming Primal Space: Cherokee Aesthetics as Habits of Being," in *Speak to Me Words: Essays on Contemporary American Indian Poetry*, ed. Dean Rader and Janice Gould (Tucson: University of Arizona Press, 2003), 57.

10. Molly McGlennen, *Fried Fish and Flour Biscuits* (London: Salt Publishing, 2010), 1.

11. Molly McGlennen, "Development I," in *Our Bearings*, 26.

Memory Strings

Formative Moments in My Life with Poetry

Inés Hernández-Ávila

the dreaming woman
finds her path lit by song worlds
rich with dance and sound

> *sometimes dreams frighten*
> *the spirit flies to war sites*
> *the heart cannot breathe*

sometimes a father
tells the story of eagle
dreaming a rescue

> *dreamer mother shares*
> *her secrets with her daughter*
> *laughter becomes her*

Ayatom timíip qéemu, "memory string," and the creating of one is a Niimiipuu women's contemplative practice that marks moments or beings that live in our hearts. The memory string can signal love, grief, hope, honoring, celebrating, and more. Each section of this essay is represented by beads of different colors, with brass beads to signal transitions, and a tiny bell inserted as well, to softly remind me who I am. (I thank Angel Sobotta for this teaching.) I have used five "plus signs" to signal each section. For me, the sign is a balanced cross, and for the Niimiipuu, five is a sacred number.

+++++

I'lp'ílp: I will begin with red beads, to mark my birth, my roots. I have always loved language. My Niimiipuu mom made sure I fell in love with reading, with story, with words. She only went up to seventh grade in school, but she and her sisters were really good writers who carried on an amazing letter-writing correspondence (letters full of story, painful moments, joyful moments, hilarious moments, letters interspersed with Niimiipuutimtki) throughout their adult lives (especially when my mom moved to Galveston, Texas, to marry my dad). My first cousin, thus my sister, Connie and I have remarked on our moms' abilities as writers—someone must have cared enough about them to teach them, but we also knew, as Connie has said, "they were just smart." My dad helped me more with science and math—these were his strengths, along with his discipline, his art (he could quickly do an intricate sketch of anything you asked of him), and his creativity.

From childhood, I was a nerd, reading under the covers with a flashlight at night when I was supposed to be sleeping—my mom would catch me and make me stop. And I would, for a moment, until she left the room, and then I would try to figure out a way to keep reading. I remember vividly my mom taking me to the public library every week, and I would check out seven books (the limit at the time). Every week. Beginning in elementary school. I remember one summer reading as much mythology as I could from all over the world. Another summer I read all of Steinbeck. Somewhere along the way, probably in fifth or sixth grade, I wrote my first poem, a pretty terrible poem I realized even then, but I have to laugh at one of the lines (the only one I remember), "These 24 hours in a day are not enough for me." Ouch. Bad line. But the sentiment is funny, probably having to do with not having enough time for reading.

In a serendipitous moment, between the time I wrote the previous paragraph, and a little later that day, I opened Facebook just for a glance and discovered a comment from Mona Susan Power: "I wish readers were given a magical clock where we could push a button to be granted 24 extra hours in any given day purely for reading. It wouldn't add time to the calendar, or bring on added fatigue. We'd just live half our lives . . . reading."[1] I guess I was already feeling like that as a child. One of my Mexicana friends in high school would say to me, "Ayy, Inés, cómo te gustan los libros!"[2] When I was in my twenties, thirties, I had some relationships with men who were jealous of my attention to books (clearly a warning sign to beware).

Tenderly, I place a brass bead.

+++++

X̣éx̣us: Here I will have green beads, to signal movement and hope. I grew up in poetry as a social justice activist in the 1970s in Texas, where I was born and lived until I was thirty-two. This formation connected me to the power of poetry for social transformation, for its ability to make "heart-to-heart" connections.[3] I was a community organizer with the Chicanx Movement, where everyone understood that I was both Mexican American and Nez Perce. I took part in the national Floricanto Festivals in Austin (1974), San Antonio (1975), and Albuquerque (1976), where for the first time we read with other Native writers. "Floricanto" as a concept means "flower-and-song," a translation of "in xochitl in cuicatl," the term in Nahuatl.[4] This concept was a central element of the pedagogy in the schools of higher learning for the ancient Nahuatl people. Those of us studying this tradition realized that over five hundred years ago, the Nahuatl people of central Mexico understood poetry (and the arts) as the path to truth, through the dialogue in one's heart with the Supreme Being, or with the Mystery, and they made this concept central to their pedagogy.

How did this understanding begin to play out for me as a poet? I remember during the Austin and San Antonio Floricantos, every day we held community readings where anyone would have us, schools, universities, community centers, senior citizens centers, parks, such was our desire to share our work, for free. The Floricanto Festivals were beautifully democratic. Everyone had to get there on their own. No one had their way paid. No one received an honorarium. No hierarchies were permitted. We were all equals. The site committee made sure folks had places to stay and food to eat. This is my memory of poetry as a collective act for community.

One evening at Metz Elementary school in East Austin, as I was sitting in the audience listening to others read, I suddenly took up pen and paper and began writing furiously. My fingers had trouble keeping up with what was coming forth—a poem, "Para Teresa," which is a signature poem for me. It is about being confronted, in sixth grade, by five pachucas in the girls' bathroom, challenging me for being a "teacher's pet." Pachucas/os/es were the early rebels in the Mexicanx/Chicanx community—the ones who were placed in "slow learner" classes because of the structural racism of the school. (I actually admired them, because I sensed a defiant dignity in the way they dressed, held their heads up high, and walked tall. I would not have known how to say this as a child. I just knew they seemed "cool.") For a reason unknown to me, from first grade I was tracked into the "smart classes," where I was the only person of color. In responding to Teresa's accusation, I wrote:

> *I did nothing for the teachers.*
> I studied for my parents and grandparents
> who cut our honor roll lists
> whenever their nietos' names appeared
> for my shy mother who mastered her terror
> to demand her place in mother's clubs
> for my carpenter father who helped me patiently
> with my math.
> For my abuelos que me regalaron lápices
> en la Navidad
> and for myself.
> Porque reconocí en aquel entonces
> una verdad tremenda
> que me hizo a mí un rebelde
> aunque tú no te habías dado cuenta.

The overall message of this poem is that I am letting Teresa know that we were both rebels, each with our own ways. I let her know that I respect her and would call her sister if she would give me permission. In that auditorium, listening to all the poets with all my being, my heart was moved to write, and to walk up to the stage for the open mic readings. I read, and I revealed something of my face-and-heart. Somehow this poem struck a chord in the Movement. Somehow my story connected to many similar stories. I was asked to read the poem countless times, at marches, rallies, keynote addresses. People wanted to hear it and were grateful to hear it, over and over. The poem has received standing ovations. It has a life of its own. It was then that I came to be recognized and honored as a poet. It was then that I knew I had come of age. The poem also reveals what would become a practice for me, the code-switching between English and Spanish—it's the way Tejanas/os/ es talk—we move back and forth without giving it a thought. Once, long ago, though, I told a dear Chicano historian friend who is like a brother to me, "Yes,

I know two colonizer's languages, but at what price?" My heart will always ache for not having learned Niimiipuutimtki while I was growing up. But moving between the two languages has always been something that is part of me. It comes out perhaps *because* I'm from Texas, as in this poem, "Momentos."

The cold rain
penetrates my bones
today
I feel winter again
and want to
hole up
in my room

Memories of
different times
arouse my
dormant hand

Gotas pesadas de lluvia
caen y me llaman
la atención

Acabo de ver el tecolote
La curandera le hace
una limpia a la mujer

I wonder where
woodpecker
has gone
his diligence
me estiraba

Es que la tierra está llorando
porque no puedo estar
sin tí

Gently, I place a brass bead.

+++++

Maqsmáqs: Yellow beads, in gratitude for the light that helped me see and feel so many literary worlds. My three degrees are in English, mainly because there were no Native Studies programs back then, and yes, I have an abiding love for literature, so English it was (I was also a Spanish major as an undergrad, where I found two especially helpful mentors). I lived with a split consciousness of sorts back then, negotiating the institution of mainstream academia, where I was one of three people of color in my graduate program (and I rarely saw the other two), and being a full-blown community activist, state-wide political organizer, and cultural worker (poet, singer, traditional dancer, member of two different theater troupes). I was impacted by the works of so many English and American poets, some immediately recognizable, and some perhaps not so remembered. I was struck by a short poem by Stephen Crane, where he says, "A man said to the universe/"Sir, I exist!/"However," replied the universe,/"The fact has not created in me/A sense of obligation."[5] I wrote my own version, "The man said,/ Who are you?/Where are you from?/I have not given you permission to exist./ And the woman replied,/I am who I am/I am from here/I am because I say so."[6] I felt for Crane—he died so young at twenty-eight, in many ways bereft, which is the intimation of his poem. I thought, "What would I do in such a situation?" I decided to preempt the universe, and "the man"—"the heteropatriarchal capitalist/racist system," to announce my insistence on my right to live.

In a nod to T. S. Eliot's line from "The Wasteland,"[7] "HURRY UP PLEASE IT'S TIME," one of my very early poems has to do with the regimentation of time from a western perspective:

> And the hurry-up, please,
> it's time machine
> wants to regulate the heart
> of everyone
> and everything.

> But I will take my time
> to make my time count
> Clocks do not intimidate me
> nor do arbitrary calendars
> presumptuous rulers
> of nothing but themselves.

The insistence on *dead lines* in the west, the unrelenting ways that this society regulates our lives, even from childhood, in elementary school, where we begin to learn to live by the clock, like all good workers in a capitalistic society. I was already feeling the frustration of being confined and constrained, especially because I was living in a community that was another world entirely. Loving literature is one thing. Being in a staid, conforming English graduate program where the one professor who had discovered "ethnic" literature literally claimed it as "his" area, where one female professor told me to my face that she and her family members in South Texas were "good to their Mexicans," where a white male graduate student told me as I was walking into seminar, chuckling, "You'd better hurry, spic, if you're late, they could deport you!" (I fixed that immediately by telling the professor, "It's me or him, if he stays in the seminar, I'm leaving." The professor, at least, had the student drop the course.)

Just imagine. The contrast. Returning to our independent study group in the community, we discovered the concept of education/learning in the Nahuatl belief-system, "in ixtli in yollotl," cara-y-corazón, face-and-heart, as one word. The ideal pedagogy of the wise teacher is to encourage the emergence of the face-and-heart of each student, to provide light for them to do this, to see their reflection clearly in a mirror, not distorted. (Light is central. For the Niimiipuu, we are supposed to be light givers.) This is a nurturing of autonomy, and for the ancient Nahua, a central methodology is through poetry. One of the names for the Supreme Being in that belief-system is Moyocoyani, the one who invents himself/herself/themself.[8] Taken all together, it is exhilarating to me that this Indigenous belief-system recognized what I would call a sacred relationship between poetry, individual autonomy, the creative energy of the universe, and the distinct originality of each person—theory, pedagogy, methodology, all interrelated in such a nuanced way. I trust this to be one of the understandings we might hold in common. I suggest that these kinds of discoveries should compel us to work more on our own original languages. As some of the contributors to this volume show us, doing this work is revelatory and liberatory for all of us.

In Austin, Texas, in the 1970s, I was a member of an activist collective of writers, musicians, artists, theater people—we called ourselves CASA, Chicanes Artistas Sirviendo a Aztlán, Chicanx Artists Serving Aztlán, and yes, I know the word "Aztlán" is incredibly problematic, but it is what we used back then. CASA also means "home." Inspired as we were by the Nahuatl teachings we were studying in group, we decided to offer workshops on poetry and art to young people, grades K–12, wherever teachers would allow us into their classrooms. We of course credited the ancient Nahuatl philosophy for the way we framed and structured our workshops, especially letting the students know that we were honoring the artist in each one of them. We were so successful that teachers began asking for workshops to continue what we had started, and we organized annual citywide Floricanto Festivals for youth, showcasing their artwork and their poetry. We did all of this for free, until a friend suggested to us that we could get funds from the Austin City Arts Council, which we did. We were surprised to get funding, that was never even on our minds. We were just so grateful to have access to the youngsters. This is what I love about the power of poetry, the power of the word, of words—to encourage people to live a poetic artistic life, a life, at its best, wonderfully autonomous, creative, original. These ancient concepts move me deeply. I took them to heart and they became part of my own poetic practice and pedagogy. They continue to serve me when I teach poetry, and when I integrate creative expression into any course that I teach.

This next brass bead I place humbly.

+++++

This sequence of beads is the color sky blue, haykaatwáako?s, for my roots. I am of the generation of our early poets. I was present and paying attention when all the social movements began manifesting in national and international arenas. I was hungrily looking for writers like me. I remember when I first read Américo Paredes's *With His Pistol in His Hand*, about the Texas-Mexican folk hero Gregorio Cortez defending his people, I was stunned to see Paredes write "we Mexicans" in the narrative.[9] It was the first time I had read a person of color writing *from* his community, and by doing so, insisting on the dignity of that community. At about the same time, I was reading N. Scott Momaday's *House Made of Dawn*, and his essay "Man Made of Words," and Paulo Freire's *Pedagogy of the Oppressed*, and Miguel León-Portilla's *Aztec Thought and Culture*, and *Akwesasne Notes*, and the early anthologies of Native and Chicanx literature. As a person who is Niimiipuu/Nez Perce, enrolled on the Colville Reservation, and Texas-Mexican (and Mexican Indigenous from the area of San Luís Potosí), I found these texts pivotal. Through them, I discovered that I was possible, that my complete person was possible, that being mixed blood was not something wrong, but instead a gift from my parents to me, that my paternal grandparents teaching me Spanish from childhood was the tool that would allow me to work with Indigenous writers throughout much of Latin America. That my love of literature would take me by the hand and lead me to poetry.

Because I was a cultural worker, activist poet, and performer in those heightened years of all the social movements making themselves known, the collective of which I was a member, besides focusing on Chicanx issues, and working in solidarity with Native, Black civil rights, women's, farmworker, prisoner, and immigrants' rights movements in the United States, we turned our attention to Latin America, to Mexico, Guatemala, Chile, Cuba, El Salvador, Nicaragua, Peru. We felt responsible to keep up with the struggles in the rest of the hemisphere. We knew we were all connected, and we were inspired by the way the poets in those struggles were articulating heartfelt messages. Otto René Castillo (1934–1967), the Guatemalan poet and guerrilla fighter, who was tortured and burned alive, had two collections of poetry. The one I'm most familiar with is *Vamonos Patria a Caminar* [Come, country, let's walk]—in the poem by the same name he adds, "Yo voy contigo" ["I will go with you."]. The collection is powerful, evincing *coraje* (the term in Spanish means both rage and courage), and at the same time tenderness. In the poem "Apolitical Intellectuals," he says, "One day/the apolitical/intellectuals/of my country/will be interrogated/by the simplest/of our people./They will be asked/what they did/when their nation died out/slowly,/like a sweet fire/small and alone."[10] Here is when I began to confirm the ability of poetry to frame, to theorize, to envision, in this case, for an entire country. In the case of Guatemala, and Chile, we knew that the U.S. government had a major role in the overthrow of two democratically elected presidents, in Guatemala, Jacobo Arbenz, in 1954, and Salvador Allende, in 1973 (on the first 9/11). When I think of those early poets like Castillo, Roque Dalton (El Salvador), Pablo Neruda, Victor Jara, Violeta Parra (Chile), Atahualpa Yupanqui (Argentina), I also think of John Trudell, Simon Ortiz, Wendy Rose, Chrystos, and so many more of our Native poets in the United States.

I am grateful that I knew to leave Texas in 1982 to come to California, because without realizing it, the move would put me closely in touch with countless Native peoples and wonderful elders throughout the state. I immediately became involved with DQ University, the tribal college in Davis (which is no longer functioning as a college, unfortunately, but that is another story).[11] I was present when DQU sponsored a tribunal to put Ronald Reagan on trial for crimes against humanity in 1982. People came from all over the world, including the young Rigoberta Menchú, and amid all the political discussions there was poetry. In fact, it was the first time I heard John Trudell read. The poetry that emerge(d/s) from social struggle is a poetry that not only raises consciousness, but also lifts the hearts and spirits of the peoples who are struggling, and serves as a vehicle for international solidarity between diverse communities. Native poets know this. I am in touch with Indigenous poets from throughout the Americas, and I have been fortunate to have built relationships with Mayan writers and artists in Chiapas for over twenty years. They are part of my formation.

The Colombian Indigenous poet Hugo Jamioy, in an interview during the 2023 International Festival of Poetry in Medellin, says that in his language there is no word for poetry. Instead, he speaks of Camëntŝá, the language of seven thousand Indigenous peoples of Colombia. When he is asked what his favorite word is in his language, he responds, "Jabuainan," which means "to plant the Word in the Heart," "sembrar la palabra en el corazón." When asked how that is done, he says, "By being firm. Without forgetting the teachings of our fathers, mothers, grandparents and wise ones, who, from before they were born, they created a sowing with their words and the music of the environment. This generates a spiritual energy that the very language recognizes. And with that same energy, the word is gifted."[12] Again, this concept of the flowering word that emanates from the heart is familiar among so many poets south of the United States. While we might not use the same words, we do have poets like Simon Ortiz who early on reminded us of our sacred relationship with language. In the Niimiipuu belief-system, we know that the heart always leads.

I place this next brass bead asking for good health to keep writing.

+++++

Cíicyele: Purple beads for this Niimiipuu grammie, to signal exhilarating extended kinships, not only with humans but with all the more-than-humans. As to what the future will bring me in retirement, there are artistic practices I am yearning to take up again—poetry, of course, although I don't think I've ever really left it (it has been a loving, faithful companion), the visual arts, music. I know that I will continue working on my language. I am a member of Luk'upsíimey/The North Star Collective, a Niimiipuu/Nez Perce creative writers' group. We meet (as much as we can—sometimes our schedules prevent us from all being present) every Friday, for two hours, to do language work, to give each other writing prompts, after which we share what we have written with each other, and to plan our work as a collective. I thank Beth Piatote for insisting that I join the group. I was feeling culturally isolated in Davis, California, living away from both sides of my family, and wanting to learn Niimiipuutimtki. In all honesty, my relationships with Indigenous writers from the South, especially those from Chiapas, inspired me, and reinforced in me the need to turn to Niimiipuutimtki because of how our belief-system is embedded in our language. Beth kept urging me to connect, and I finally did, in 2018, when I accepted her invitation to perform as an Auntie in the chorus of Aunties, along with Angel Sobotta, for her play *Antikoni*. Phil Cash Cash also performed as Kreon in the play.

The Luk'upsíimey members include the founders, Phil Cash Cash and Beth Piatote; Angel Sobotta, Julian Ankney, Kellen Trenal, Sarah Hennessey, and me. We have done two writers' retreats at the Nez Perce Homelands in Wallowa, Oregon, we've done literary readings/performances together, we've published together, we've presented at conferences (in varying combinations), and more, so much more, often thanks to Beth's extraordinary envisioning, organizing, and fundraising skills. My most recent initiated project with Luk'upsíimey was to take a delegation of four of us (along with two translators) to San Cristobal de las Casas, Chiapas, in August 2022, to meet with Mayan poets and scholars engaged in literature and language revitalization. This delegation is historic, as the first such meeting between Native writers from the United States with Mayan writers from Chiapas. This kind of work is part of my dream, this is who I am as a poet, cultural worker, Indigenous rights activist. I love for us to see each other, listen to each other, learn from each other, extending our kinship networks as far as we can take them.

In Chiapas, we presented the writers with a humble chapbook of our work, poems selected and translated into Spanish specifically for them. Our chapbook was titled *wiic'íiqin hitoláaycix / "words going upriver" / palabras yendo rio arriba: Poesía de [Poetry from] Luk'upsiimey: The North Star Collective—Luk'upsíimey: La Colectiva Estrella del Norte.* We began each of our sections with a language acknowledgment. Here is mine:

> ʔíin ʔehéetewise núunim niimiipuutímtki. Sáykiptatas íinim waquiswit. Loxcwí·sa.ʾcíq·peme tĭm·es. Wé·tesnim tĭm·es nuuniim wé·tes, nuuniim tímine, nuuniim waquiswit.

> *I love our Nez Perce language. It is medicine for my spirit. I am excited. Our dictionary is a map to our land, to our hearts, to our spirits.*

> *Amo a nuestra lengua Niimiipuu. Es medicina para mi espíritu. Me llena de alegria. Nuestro diccionario es un mapa para nuestras tierras, nuestros corazones, y nuestros espíritus.*

At our closing dinner, we participated in a wonderful reading with our Mayan colleagues.

My work with my language is slow, but like the Zapatistas say, "Lento, pero avanzo"—"I'm slow, but I move forward!" In "Song for My Grandmother, iinim qá·caʔ, Alice Moyesa," I attempted a trilingual poem—here are two excerpts:

> Grandma, qá·caʔ, píke of my pike—mother of my mother
> Abuela, qá·caʔ, píke de mi pike—madre de mi madre
> Hiskalálayca
> An eagle is soaring around for you
> Un águila está rondando en el cielo para ti.

> . . .

Qá·caʔ Grandma, Alice Moyesa—abuela

maná·ʔetke qá·caʔ wé·t ʔi·ke w

Oh! Grandmother, are you also going to dance?   ¡O! Abuela, ¿vas a bailar también?

I see you smiling—te veo sonriendo

I am weaving our language with my heart   Tejo nuestro idioma con mi corazón.

What I have found in working with Haruo Aoki's incredible 1304-page *Nez Perce Dictionary* is that I feel understood.[13] I feel the dictionary as an amulet. I receive healings. I feel the words my tongue yearns to pronounce correctly, with the music that happens when our language is spoken fluently. I will most likely continue this work in my next life, but I will do as much as I can with the time I have left in this one. When I'm working with Niimiipuutimtki, I feel the "earth's vibrational memory" (a term from Dharug scholar, Jo Anne Rey)[14] of our homelands. I feel Wallowa Lake. I feel my Grandpa Tom and my Grandma Alice in Nespelem. I feel Hinmatonwyalatkit. I feel my ancestors speaking to me. In the late 1990s, in preparing for an Indigenous writers' convocation in Venezuela, I phoned my Uncle Frank Andrews, at the time one of the remaining elders fluent in our language (he has since passed away). I asked him if he would teach me a song to share, and he did. I asked him if he had any advice for me for the trip. He astonished me by saying, "Be bold." I think his spirit has been accompanying me everywhere I go, and he likes what he is seeing. I have come full circle. I started in Galveston, Texas, I'm an isleña, an island person, because of my dad. But I'm also a mountain person, from my mom. I am deeply grateful to be the daughter of my parents, because together, they gave me vision, they literally taught me to see and to be true to myself, as a human being, an activist, a thinker, an artist, and a poet.

I place this brass bead singing.

+++++

Yoosyóos: Blue beads to almost complete this string. Blue, like a Moroccan blue, a deep, vibrant blue, I have a relationship with this blue, this blue is in my world, in my words. For me, poetry is a language of the heart, with spirit working memory, with memory reminding us of the land, with the body and our poems filled with story, for the healing of our personal and collective histories. This language of the heart can come in the form of reverie, of fight-back, as Simon Ortiz says, or song. However it comes, in whatever language(s) it comes, poetry is a space of freedom.

+++++

Here is where I place the tiny bell, kaló kaló, as the gentle reminder to myself to remember, and in this memory string, to signal that I am done. Qe'ciyéw yew, thank you for reading.

Notes

The poem at the start of this chapter appears in my essay, "In Each Trace of Footstep: The Constant Song of SpiritMemory (for my Mom, Janice Hernandez)," in *Eating Fire, Tasting Blood: Breaking the Great Silence of the American Indian Holocaust*, ed. MariJo Moore (New York: Thunder's Mouth Press, 2006), 255.

1. Mona Susan Power, Facebook, June 23, 2023.
2. "Wow, Inés, how you love books!"
3. Lawrence W. Gross, *Anishinaabe Ways of Knowing and Being* (Burlington, VT: Ashgate Publishing, 2014), 64.
4. Miguel León-Portilla, *Aztec Thought and Culture: A Study of the Ancient Nahuatl Mind*, trans. Jack Emory Davis (Norman: University of Oklahoma Press, 1990), 75–79.
5. Stephen Crane, "A Man Said to the Universe," Poetry Foundation, https://www.poetryfoundation.org/poems/44049/a-man-said-to-the-universe.
6. My poem was written originally in Spanish: "Soy quien soy/Soy de aquí/Soy porque yo digo."
7. T.S. Eliot, "The Wasteland," Poetry Foundation, https://www.poetryfoundation.org/poems/47311/the-waste-land.
8. León-Portilla, *Aztec Thought and Culture*, 10–16, 95.
9. Américo Paredes, *With His Pistol in His Hand: A Border Ballad and Its Hero* (Austin: University of Texas Press, 1958).

10. Otto René Castillo, "Apolitical Intellectuals," *Socialist Platform*, June 26, 2008, http://socialistplatform.blogspot.com/2008/06/three-poems-by-otto-rene-castillo.html.

11. The acronym "DQ" represents the names of Deganawideh, the Haudenosaunee Peacemaker, and Quetzalcoatl, the Mesoamerican Plumed Serpent, also known as the god of wisdom. The Haudenosaunee requested that the founders of DQU publicly use only the initial for the Peacemaker's name.

12. Joseph Casañas Angulo, "Hugo Jamioy: 'La palabra "poesía" no existe en nuestro idioma,'" *El Espectador*, May 5, 2023, https://www.elespectador.com/entretenimiento/gente/hugo-jamioy-la-palabra-poesia-no-existe-en-nuestro-idioma/?utm_source=interno&fbclid=IwAR0A2RhAhENzzWUrdbloRybY9AjFYYJvF56_sfzz7xkjlenZ5tnFJN7HrUQ.

13. Haruo Aoki, *Nez Perce Dictionary* (Berkeley: University of California Press, 1994).

14. Jo Anne Rey, "Changing Places: Weaving City Learnings into Country Futures," in *Indigenous Future and Learnings Taking Place*, ed. Ligia (Licho) López López and Gioconda Coello (New York: Routledge, 2021), 17. Rey cites Elder Bilawara Lee, who notes, "From the beginning of time, every event and every creative process that happened on Mother Earth, effectively left behind a seed. This seed is seen as a memory that infused the earth after the event, just as a flower leaves behind a cloned copy of itself in the form of a discarded seed" (17). This passage also presents the Elder's distinction between Dreamtime and Dreaming.

The Sound of a Butterfly Opening and Closing Its Wings

Musings on Nez Perce Sound Poetics

Michael Wasson

Years ago, I was a boy in my homeland. Around that area, *hinkilípe,'* near the place of jaw bones, the sky was constant, gorgeously present, harsh, a wash of crags and gnarled pines. Veins of rivers throbbed their songs of travel. Winters came and stayed through February, *'alatam'áal*, the time of fires, *'ilelú'qse*, to warm a self, even *'áala hi'lwéhtse*, to warm beside the fire, but even more *múx múx*, the ignition of fire as it sounds. I hear a long *múux* somewhere behind my irises, the *táq táq*, the crackle of flames, in a room of my childhood while a voice chooses not to speak.

This seasonal shift into crueler stretches of cold from November through February would fall to my open, ecstatic mouth. Snow became water on my tongue. When that bead of a Plateau winter, already water in the throat, passed through my chest, into the belly of my boyish body, *c'ís* smeared along my inner flesh, a thumb smudging a dark wall. *c'ís* is an imprint of survival, both linguistically and in the history of a *nimíipuum* body. It is the sound of a single drop of water. Somewhere my grandfather is saying listen. Look, yes, but listen. Somewhere, before sunrise, my grandfather and uncle would keep us hungry to "heighten our senses." This hunger to hear is a poetics that my life is trying to locate.

How many years go by without the sound of the dead making its way into the world? I ask myself how I can touch a leaf, thump my palm against a bench, carry hunger in my belly, or watch a morning robin pluck at the earth without hearing what elders, teachers, and linguists archived of us. In this archive of our bodies are the sounds our ghosts crave to teach us in earnest. The boy in me is knocking my ribcage with an aspen branch just to make a noise. What is that? Listen to it. *ʾóx̣ox̣ox̣*. I ask myself, when I am curious about a poem that wants me to write it: When does *yóx̣*, there, split from its y, its palatal glide near the front ridge in the mouth, and clatter into these *ʾox̣* sounds? In a story, I am hearing bones rattling against each other. There. Over there. That otherworldly assortment of racket, here, in a body I was given. However, bones remaining mean that the ghosts still around are asking about me.

As a young college student in my freshman year, I began noting the sounds of our land and of what we would call the animal people. These are what Haruo Aoki terms phonosymbolic words, utterances that establish a relationship between the phonetic sound and the meaning it conveys.[1] As such back then, these became a point of departure toward a realm both haunted by the dead and kept alive because, as I read and studied stories, I would hear these beautiful fragments of onomatopoeia as my elders and teachers discussed the language in question, the beauty of remembering how their own parents and grandparents would express meaning. Cries of animals would name themselves. Frogs in summer would sound like people gossiping. All these little peeks into my language meant that the ghosts of my body shared a worldview: The land and its animal people speak their world to life. I was enamored, in love with this developing knowledge.

There was a minor hint to this land-language-body relationship that my oldest elder-teacher mentioned. "This is the land of the butterflies, yes," he said of our current town, from the end of the table. He lightly pressed his fingertips together, slowly opening his hand, closing it, the soft, worn-down sandpaper of his skin there in front of me: *weʾé weʾé*.

This is my favorite poem.

we'é
we'e

In his hands, I imagined a butterfly at the end of a drying branch extending from wet driftwood. A white butterfly pinned to its life, opening to warm its thorax and abdomen. Centuries ago, perhaps, these butterflies came to name the land where they would live. Someone or a group of people would discover this bright little insect, like an early flower in a field before more blooms begin to take over, and instead of what we commonly call *téeptep*, which phonosymbolically expresses the soft, fricative, and flap-like movement of butterflies as well and clips the rhythmic vowel repetitions with the bilabial touch of lips, that human who discovered a lone butterfly stood there, and instead said:

we'é
we'é

Now, in this century, there are in comparison to centuries before so few butterflies in the central town of the Nez Perce Reservation, Lapwai, Idaho. However, pronouncing *we'é* begins to return the blood in them, a life born of our throats lurching the voice forward, the belly pausing briefly for the glottal stop, and accenting its final vowel, repeating its own sudden, deliberate flesh out. My grandfather always says to listen. Every day is a promise in which I am trying my best to stay alive to hear everything I can. When my oldest elder keeps his hand aloft, steady enough to call it sad, I write it in my notes as such and check Haruo Aoki's *Nez Perce Dictionary* to see if it was archived: "*we'é we'é*. The sound of a butterfly opening and closing its wings. Slowly."[2]

I sit with my jotted scribble. I remember what is no longer as prevalent around here, in the land of so many of my people. My elder's hand, the sunlight seared into it, the dust illuminated behind him near the window of the Language Center, along B Street and Parade Avenue, rests on the table.

We *nimíipuu* are taught about the land and the stories that shape our world as an oral map. I hear these teachings often. For instance, we are told to remember the stories of the moon, the insects, *'iceyéeye* or Coyote, the loneliness in the hills, the hurt and humor of our orated tradition. My grandfather tells me a story of all the animals who failed to make a meeting called by *'iceyéeye*, and we see their beastly backs along the large, meadowlike hillside, where boulders rest. Petrified. When I imagine those animals that we could never meet in our human world, I wonder how the few butterflies would flitter, land on each, and I could hear each small poem open and close.

When I was still a high schooler, my friend's grandfather took long trips to see all the landmarks of our accustomed land and to remember their place names according to what his elders taught him. It was taxing on his body, I could see. Each landmark he encountered was named after sounds, for stories, animals, places where tasks were meant to be done, places that involved the work of our bodies and the haven of flora. Every time he returned to the small trailer that my friend lived in with his family, he was in this space between a history in his DNA and his grandchildren sleeping soundly in their rooms. This land he returned to in the evening was where we can be reminded of early summer, a flux between *téepťep* and *we'é we'é*.

The map of our mouths and imaginations brings us into a survival of ourselves and takes us back to where we are safe. My friend's grandfather, doing his work only by his body, talking to himself about the sunny mountain ranges that fragmented our storied creation, but he could see how it all put him together. That night, when everyone was sleeping, I was still in my midteens at that time, I heard him crying in the living room. I imagined the whole room bloom over, and him remembering how the land of the dead is a place of soft light. In this memory of him, the sound of light, *líw líw*, floods my head. My last recollection of him was this, him crying toward a land of light, this brightness blasting each citizen of our little sovereign Nez Perce nation, seeing our entire land again renewed, in his twilight years.

This memory landed in me when I learned that my strictest language teacher had passed. Away from my homeland, for almost a decade at this point, I still repeated these little words, almost to keep the *nimíipuu* of me alive yet privately in the dark of midnights. I was told how my one-on-one mentor teacher, who would ask me demandingly, "If you don't pronounce correctly, how will we know who you are in the next world?" Repeating over and over, the vocabulary we were instructed not merely to memorize but to learn by heart lay there on printed paper. But she scolded, "Don't just look at the word. Listen. *téepwey*," she said, with the appropriate amount of frication, the proper placement of the tongue, the beautiful emergence of air forking from the mouth, just the way she learned it in her childhood. I listened. I promised to her, deep in my head, I was going to say it just like her. I finally got it, *"ɫéepwey."* She accepted, *"ca'á ca'á, 'ácqa—yó'qo ta'c*! Now you can hear the butterflies in the word, no?"

A poem, already in my late twenties, that wants me, reveals it. This poem's own poem, a way to bring me back to my people:

> 6. America declares these dreams I have every night to be re—dreamed &
>   pressed into names

> 5. Upended petals of *qém'es*
> abandoned like torn butterfly wings—*we'é we'é* I pray

> 4. I pray that nobody ever
>   hears us[3]

I know every dream I have is contextualized as American. The bones that hold me up in my body are American. Each word uttered is the language of my exile. But two moments happen, as I know each dream is fashioned in its Americanness and the tongue of westward expansion. The flower petals surface in the poem, blued enough to be camas, holding their bulbous bellies that we traditionally gather in late spring and early summer. No longer are the dreams of survival simply what the country dictates. They are the butterflies of my people's land, the entire Plateau has a way to come forward to life, opening valleys and meadows in my young mind. Torn, lying like early fallen leaves in the autumn of our earliest memories. As soon as the poem pauses, the poem has an occasion for resurgence. A teaching that tells me to live with it. Sit with it.

We'é we'é, I pray. The poem tells me to stop. As I was told to do accordingly during my family's prayers, stop and listen. Sit still. Settle down. Slow your breath. Imagine, boy, where these prayers are going. The line breaks in space, and like the poem of a simple butterfly opening and closing its wings, I repeat my action: I pray. But I don't pray to be heard. Do I? This paradox of announcing to never be heard is, of course, a call to be heard. I pray. The line fractures and is swallowed in the white landscape of the page. I pray that you are listening to me, to my land, its expanse of memories, to my elder's taut and tender hand, to every field and meadow that is erased of its once-abundant butterflies dotting my people's imagination.

Imagination is where I am headed, toward wonder. But I need to stop often to remember the history around a word or its sound contextualized within an utterance. The language we are given is the only apparatus we continually hold to make sense of and corral the world. What of us, the *nimíipuu* still left on the face of the earth? What of the young children in schools learning to speak and read our heritage tongue as our elders pass on to other worlds to wait for us? Fittingly, according to Layli Long Soldier, in her poem "38," in which we are to respect an utterance as a haven of accountability, "Everything is in the language we use."[4] In form and the myriad function of a poem's motion to bring us into worlds of awe and restored prayer, the poem I remember most is the single repetition of breath and tender beauty that merges a history of my land's ecological condition with my current American existence, where my colonizer's language can no longer occupy everything.

Years ago, I was a boy in my homeland. The concept of *wíiwyeteq'is* is taught to us in how we learn to organize and respect occasions in our lives. It gives ceremony to knowledge we are made to hold. We make relationships and create spaces of respect for each other. For me, it has meant the language of our survival. More simply, this knowledge means to inhabit a present growth-mindset, or more literally, to grow as an elder.[5] Every sound remembered, we place onto the page, each element of this language and the world or bodies from which language arrives, I persistently argue in respect to a praxis and poetics of being, as my elders did, to listen. Remain in awe.

Now, many years later, here is the persisting image that wants to sit with me, as I continue to breathe in this *nimíipuum* body my family and homeland, the place of jawbones and the land of butterflies, has given me to make a life of myself. There is a body near a river only we know in our homeland, the Lochsa River. A yellow butterfly flutters staggeringly, lands on what appears to be a young cadaver, without a sound. It is near sundown, and the valley is alive, but it is waiting for something. As I approach to identify whose body this is, the butterfly begins to vanish, slowly, of course. The final, brief fragment of this circumstance ripples, *we'é we'é*. The sound and its meaning are there, beautiful in my eyes and mouth, opening and closing. Despite a country's long-standing history of sanctioned erasure, I hear it, at last, before it disappears.

Notes

1. Haruo Aoki, "Symbolism in Nez Perce," in *Sound Symbolism*, ed. Leanne Hinton, Johanna Nichols, and John J. Ohala (New York: Cambridge University Press, 1995), 15–16.
2. Haruo Aoki, *Nez Perce Dictionary* (Berkeley: University of California Press, 1994), 1270.
3. Michael Wasson, "Countdown as Slow Kisses" Poem-a-Day, Academy of American Poets, https://poets.org/poem/countdown-slow-kisses.
4. Layli Long Soldier, *Whereas* (Minneapolis: Graywolf Press, 2017), 51.
5. Joyce M. McFarland, Emma M. McMain, Angel Sobotta, Josiah Blackeagle Pinkham, and Zoe Higheagle Strong, "Nez Perce College and Career Readiness: Wíiwyeteq'is 'Growing into an Elder,'" *Journal of Indigenous Research* 8 (2020): 3–4, https://digitalcommons.usu.edu/cgi/viewcontent.cgi?article=1122&context=kicjir.

Bibliography

Aoki, Haruo. "Symbolism in Nez Perce." In *Sound Symbolism*, edited by Leanne Hinton, Johanna Nichols, and John J. Ohala, 15–22. New York: Cambridge University Press, 1995.

Long Soldier, Layli. *Whereas*. Minneapolis: Graywolf Press, 2017.

McFarland, Joyce M., Emma M. McMain, Angel Sobotta, Josiah Blackeagle Pinkham, and Zoe Higheagle Strong. "Nez Perce College and Career Readiness: Wíiwyeteq'is 'Growing into an Elder.'" *Journal of Indigenous Research* 8 (2020): 1–8. https://digitalcommons.usu.edu/cgi/viewcontent.cgi?article=1122&context=kicjir.

Wasson, Michael. "Countdown as Slow Kisses." Poem-a-Day, Academy of American Poets. https://poets.org/poem/countdown-slow-kisses.

Index

Contributors' Biographies

Esther Belin is the author of two poetry books, *From the Belly of My Beauty* (1999) and *Of Cartography* (2017), and co-editor of *The Diné Reader: An Anthology of Navajo Literature*. Belin's visual art combines a variety of disciplines and works to reframe the mythical primitivism often associated with Indigenous cultures. She is a citizen of the Navajo Nation and lives on the Colorado side of the four corners. Belin is a member of Saad Bee Hózhǫ́ǫ́: Diné Writers' Collective, and teaches in the Native American and Indigenous studies department at Fort Lewis College and in the low-residency MFA program at the Institute of American Indian Arts.

Kimberly Blaeser, past Wisconsin Poet Laureate and founding director of In-Na-Po (Indigenous Nations Poets), is a writer, photographer, and scholar. She is the author of six poetry collections, including *Ancient Light, Copper Yearning*, and the bilingual Résister en dansant/Ikwe-niimi: Dancing Resistance. Blaeser edited *Traces in Blood, Bone, and Stone: Contemporary Ojibwe Poetry* and wrote the monograph *Gerald Vizenor: Writing in the Oral Tradition*. Her photographs, picto-poems, and ekphrastic pieces have appeared in exhibits such as *Visualizing Sovereignty* and *No More Stolen Sisters*. An Anishinaabe activist and environmentalist, she is an enrolled member of White Earth Nation and grew up on the reservation. The 2024 Mackey Chair in Creative Writing at Beloit College and a Vassar College Tatlock Fellow, Blaeser is a professor emerita at University of Wisconsin–Milwaukee and a MFA faculty member for Institute of American Indian Arts in Santa Fe. Her accolades include a Lifetime Achievement Award from Native Writers' Circle of the Americas. Blaeser splits her time between her home in rural Wisconsin and a water-access cabin near the Boundary Waters Canoe Area Wilderness in Minnesota.

Carolyn M. Dunn is an award-winning poet and playwright whose works have been staged across Turtle Island. A Louisiana Creole (African, Tunica/Choctaw/Biloxi, Ishak, Acadian, French and Freedmen descent), her recent books include *Echolocation: Poems, Stories and Songs from Indian Country: L.A.* (2013); *The Stains of Burden and Dumb Luck* (2017); *Decentered Playwriting: Alternative Techniques for the Stage* (2024); *Three Plays by Carolyn Dunn* (edited by Sarah d'Angelo). Carolyn is an associate professor of theater and dance at California State University Los Angeles and founder/managing editor/publisher of That Painted Horse Press (TPHP). She is currently working with the Atakapa-Ishak Nation of Southwest Louisiana on their revitalization and recognition efforts and with the Tunica-Biloxi tribe's Language, Culture, and Revitalization program on their children's book series for TPHP. Her plays *The Frybread Queen*, *Ghost Dance*, and *Soledad* have been developed and staged at Native Voices at the Autry in Los Angeles. Her current projects include the pow-wow comedy play *Chasing Tailfeathers* and the film adaptation of her play *The Bone Picker*.

Inés Hernández-Ávila (Niimiipuu/Nez Perce and Tejana) is professor emerita of Native American studies from University of California, Davis. She is enrolled with the Colville Confederated Tribes. A Ford Fellow, she is one of the six founders of the Native American and Indigenous Studies Association. She is a scholar-activist, poet, essayist, visual artist, translator, and a member of Luk'upsíimey/The North Star Collective, a group of Niimiipuu creative writers and language workers. She is collaborating with the Library of Congress's Hispanic Division, to include more Indigenous writers from Latin America in their *Palabra* archive. She has developed relationships with Indigenous writers from throughout Mexico (with emphasis on Mayan writers in Chiapas), Guatemala, and Mapuche writers in Chile. Her painting, "Coyote, Looking Deeply," is the cover art for *Native American Rhetoric*, edited by Lawrence Gross.

Kuʻualoha hoʻomanawanui is a Kanaka ʻŌiwi writer, artist, scholar, and kiaʻi aloha ʻāina from Wailua Homesteads, Puna, Kauaʻi. She is a professor of Hawaiian literature at the University of Hawaiʻi-Mānoa, where she specializes in Indigenous Hawaiian and Pasifika literatures. She is chief editor of ʻŌiwi: A Native Hawaiian Journal and director of Ka Ipu o Lono, a Native Hawaiian digital humanities resource of Hawaiian literature. Her first book, *Voices of Fire: Reweaving the Lei of Pele and Hiʻiaka Literature* (2014), won honorable mention in best new Indigenous scholarship from the Modern Language Association in 2017. She is a co-editor with Cristina Bacchilega and Joyce Pualani Warren of the anthology *An Ocean of Wonder: The Fantastic in the Pacific* (2024). Her poetry, short fiction, nonfiction, and scholarship have been published both in Hawaiʻi and abroad. She is also an active member of the all-volunteer Hawaiʻi Wild Bird Rescue group.

Cj Jackson is a Diné writer and scholar from the Navajo Nation in Arizona. Their work primarily focuses on queer Indigenous poetics and the cultural and political reclamation of relational ethics in the wake of historical dispossession and environmental catastrophe. Jackson is an assistant professor in the Department of Native American Studies at the University of California, Davis. Other publications by them appear in *Chapter House Journal*, *Hayden's Ferry Review*, *Yellow Medicine Review*, and more.

Layli Long Soldier is an Oglala Lakota poet, writer, and artist. She's served as a contributing editor to *Drunken Boat*. She was awarded the Lannan Literary Award for poetry in 2015 along with a National Artist Fellowship from the Native Arts and Cultures Foundation. Her first poetry chapbook was *Chromosomory* (2010). Her first book, *Whereas* (2017), was awarded the National Book Critics Circle Award, the PEN/Jean Stein Book Award, and was a finalist for the 2017 National Book Award for Poetry and the 2018 Griffin Poetry Prize.

Casandra López is a California Indian (Tongva/Luiseño/Cahuilla) and Chicana writer who has received support from CantoMundo, Bread Loaf, and Tin House.

She's the author of the poetry collection *Brother Bullet* and has been selected for residencies with Storyknife, Hedgebrook, and Headlands Center for the Arts. Her memoir-in-progress, *A Few Notes on Grief*, was granted a 2019 James W. Ray Venture Project Award. She teaches at University of California San Diego.

Janet McAdams's new and selected poems, *Buffalo in Six Directions / Búfalo en seis direcciones*, was recently published in bilingual editions in Mexico and Argentina. Her other poetry collections include *Feral*, the chapbook *Seven Boxes for the Country After*, and *The Island of Lost Luggage*, which won both the Diane Decorah First Book Award from the Native Writers Circle of the Americas and an American Book Award. Her critical writing on contemporary Indigenous poetry has appeared in the *Kenyon Review*, the *Women's Review of Books*, the *Cambridge Companion to Modern American Poetry*, and other journals and edited collections. A writer of mixed Scottish and Muscogee (Alabama Creek) ancestry, she is the founding editor of *Salt Publishing's Earthworks Series of Indigenous Poetry* and an emerita professor of Kenyon College, where she held the Robert P. Hubbard Chair in Poetry.

Molly McGlennen was born and raised in Minneapolis, Minnesota, and is of Anishinaabe and European descent. She earned a PhD in Native American studies from University of California, Davis and an MFA in creative writing from Mills College. She is a professor of English and Native American studies as well as the Anne McNiff Tatlock '61 Chair in Multidisciplinary Studies at Vassar College. Her creative writing and scholarship have been published widely. McGlennen is the author of two collections of poetry: *Fried Fish and Flour Biscuits* and *Our Bearings*. Her poems have appeared in *Poetry, Academy of American Poets' Poets. org (Poem-a-Day)*, *Red Ink, Great Lakes Review, Yellow Medicine Review*, and *Sentence*. McGlennen also authored a critical monograph, *Creative Alliances: The Transnational Designs of Indigenous Women's Poetry*, which earned the Beatrice Medicine Award for outstanding scholarship in American Indian literature.

Shaina A. Nez is Táchii'nii born for Áshįįhi. She serves Diné College as a senior lecturer in creative writing and English. She is a doctoral candidate in justice studies with the School of Social Transformation and Inquiry at Arizona State University. She earned her MFA degree in creative writing from the Institute of

American Indian Arts in Santa Fe, New Mexico. Her work has appeared in "A Gathering of Native Voices" (*Massachusetts Review*); "Nonwhite and Women: 131 Micro-Essays on Being in the World," winner of the 2023 Silver IPPY award in the category of adult multicultural nonfiction; and *Issue 14: Indigenous Eco-poetry*. She is the founder of Diné Artisans Authors Capacity Building Institute (DAACBI), a fellowship supporting the development of thriving Diné artisans and authors with professional preparation in the Northwest region of New Mexico. DAACBI is proudly funded by the New Mexico Economic Development Department the new Creative Industries Division.

Craig Santos Perez is an Indigenous Chamoru from the Pacific Island of Guam. He is the co-editor of eight anthologies and the author of six books of poetry and the academic monograph *Navigating Chamoru Poetry: Indigeneity, Aesthetics, and Decolonization*. He has received the National Book Award, the American Book Award, the PEN Center USA/Poetry Society of America Literary Prize, as well as fellowships from the National Endowment for the Humanities, the Ford Foundation, the Mellon Foundation, the Lannan Foundation, and the American Council of Learned Societies. In 2022, he received the Association of Writers and Writing Programs' George Garrett Award for Outstanding Community Service in Literature for his contributions to and advocacy for Pacific Islander literature.

Beth Piatote is a writer of fiction, plays, poetry, essays, and scholarship and an Indigenous language revitalization activist. Her books include the scholarly monograph *Domestic Subjects: Gender, Citizenship, and Law in Native American Literature* (2013) and the mixed-genre collection *The Beadworkers: Stories* (2019), which was longlisted for the PEN/Bingham Prize and the Aspen Words Literary Prize. Her scholarly and creative works appear in many journals and anthologies, including *Kenyon Review, POETRY, World Literature Today, American Quarterly*, and *PMLA*. She is an associate professor of English and comparative literature at the University of California, Berkeley, and the founder of the Indigenous Poetics Lab. She is Nez Perce, enrolled with the Confederated Tribes of the Colville Reservation.

Rain Prud'homme-Cranford is a FATtastically-queer daughter/sister/auntie/cousin/partner and adopted mom/auntie as well as a (dis)Abled Louisiana

Creole poet-scholar-teacher-musician-artist whose work oft dialogues Louisiana Creole, Gulf Indigenous, and/or circum–Gulf Creole cultures and landbases alongside issues of gender, environmental justice, body/fat, and disability/chronic illness. An associate professor of English at University of Calgary and associate professor at University of Louisiana, she is the executive editor-publisher and "Book Doula" for That Painted Horse Press (TPHP). Rain is currently at work with the Atakapa-Ishak Nation of Southwest Louisiana on their revitalization and recognition efforts and the Tunica-Biloxi tribe's Language, Culture, and Revitalization program on their children's book with TPHP. Her books include *Miscegenation Round Dance: Poèmes Historiques* (2021) and *Louisiana Creole Peoplehood: Afro-Indigeneity and Community* (2022). Her current project includes a series of art works titled *Terra Pinguis* exploring bodies of size in harmony with their ecologies.

Jake Skeets is Black Streak Wood, born for Water's Edge. He is Diné from Vanderwagen, New Mexico. He is the author of the poetry collection *Eyes Bottle Dark with a Mouthful of Flowers*, winner of the National Poetry Series and the American Book Award. He holds an MFA in poetry from the Institute of American Indian Arts. He won the 2018 Discovery/*Boston Review* Poetry Contest and has been nominated for a Pushcart Prize. He is a member of Saad Bee Hózhǫ́: A Diné Writers' Collective and currently teaches at Diné College in Tsaile, Arizona.

Michael Wasson is the author of *Swallowed Light* (2022), the French/English special edition *Self-Portrait with Smeared Centuries* (2018) translated by Béatrice Machet, and the chapbook *This American Ghost* (2017). He is a 2019 Ruth Lilly & Dorothy Sargent Rosenberg Poetry Fellow and a 2018 Native Arts & Cultures Foundation National Artist Fellow in Literature. His poems and prose appear in *American Poets, Beloit Poetry Journal, Harvard Review, Kenyon Review, The Nation, New York Times, Poetry, Poetry Northwest*, and the anthologies *Best New Poets 2017, Essential Queer Voices of U.S. Poetry, Shapes of Native Nonfiction: Collected Essays by Contemporary Writers*, and *When the Light of the World Was Subdued, Our Songs Came Through: A Norton Anthology of Native Nations Poetry*. He is nimíipuu from the Nez Perce Reservation in Idaho, and he currently lives in Tokyo, Japan, where he lectures at J. F. Oberlin University and Soka University.

Natahnee Winder is an assistant professor in the Department of Indigenous Studies and the School of Public Policy at Simon Fraser University. She is an enrolled citizen of the Duckwater Shoshone Tribe and comes from an intertribal lineage of Navajo, Southern Ute, Pyramid Lake Paiute, and Black heritages. She holds two bachelor of arts degrees in sociology with a concentration in social welfare and Native American studies with an emphasis on nation building and leadership from the University of New Mexico. Natahnee was the 2015–2016 Henry Roe Cloud Fellow at Yale University. She completed her PhD in sociology at the University of Western Ontario. Her dissertation was a comparative analysis of the residential school history of Canada and the United States based on the perspectives of Indigenous university students using photovoice.

Tanaya Winder is an author, singer/songwriter, poet, and motivational speaker who comes from an intertribal lineage of Southern Ute, Pyramid Lake Paiute, Navajo, and Black heritages. She is an enrolled citizen of the Duckwater Shoshone Nation. She is a 2016 National Center for American Indian Enterprise Development "40 Under 40" emerging American Indian leader. Winder cofounded *As/Us: A Space for Women of the World*, a literary magazine publishing works by BIPOC women. She holds a BA in English from Stanford University and an MFA in creative writing from the University of New Mexico. Winder's performances and talks blend storytelling, singing, and spoken word to teach about different expressions of love and "heartwork." Her poetry collections include *Words Like Love* and *Why Storms Are Named After People and Bullets Remain Nameless*. Her specialties include youth and women empowerment, healing trauma through art, creative writing workshops, and mental wellness advocacy.

Aazheyaadizi: Worldview, Language, and the Logics of Decolonization, Mark D. Freeland | 978-1-61186-380-2

As Sacred to Us: Simon Pokagon's Birch Bark Stories in Their Contexts, edited by Blaire Morseau | 978-1-61186-462-5

Bawaajimo: A Dialect of Dreams in Anishinaabe Language and Literature, Margaret Noodin | 978-1-61186-105-1

Centering Anishinaabeg Studies: Understanding the World through Stories, edited by Jill Doerfler, Niigaanwewidam James Sinclair, and Heidi Kiiwetinepinesiik Stark | 978-1-61186-067-2

Curator of Ephemera at the New Museum for Archaic Media, Heid E. Erdrich | 978-1-61186-246-1

Document of Expectations, Devon Abbott Mihesuah | 978-1-61186-011-5

Dragonfly Dance, Denise K. Lajimodiere | 978-0-87013-982-6

Encountering the Sovereign Other: Indigenous Science Fiction, Miriam C. Brown Spiers | 978-1-61186-405-2

Facing the Future: The Indian Child Welfare Act at 30, edited by Matthew L. M. Fletcher, Wenona T. Singel, and Kathryn E. Fort | 978-0-87013-860-7

Famine Pots: The Choctaw–Irish Gift Exchange, 1847–Present, edited by LeAnne Howe and Padraig Kirwan | 978-1-61186-369-7

Follow the Blackbirds, Gwen Nell Westerman | 978-1-61186-092-4

Gambling on Authenticity: Gaming, the Noble Savage, and the Not-So-New Indian, edited by Becca Gercken and Julie Pelletier | 978-1-61186-256-0

Indian Country: Telling a Story in a Digital Age, Victoria L. LaPoe and Benjamin Rex LaPoe II | 978-1-61186-226-3

The Indian Who Bombed Berlin and Other Stories, Ralph Salisbury | 978-0-87013-847-8

Indigenizing Philosophy through the Land: A Trickster Methodology for Decolonizing Environmental Ethics and Indigenous Futures, Brian Burkhart | 978-1-61186-330-7

Indigenous Journeys, Transatlantic Perspectives: Relational Worlds in Contemporary Native American Literature, Anna M. Brígido-Corachán | 978-1-61186-469-4

Indigenous Poetics, edited by Inés Hernández-Ávila and Molly McGlennen | 978-1-61186-526-4

Louise Erdrich's Justice Trilogy: Cultural and Critical Contexts, edited by Connie A. Jacobs and Nancy J. Peterson | 978-1-61186-403-8

Masculindians: Conversations about Indigenous Manhood, edited by Sam McKegney | 978-1-61186-129-7

Mediating Indianness, edited by Cathy Covell Waegner | 978-1-61186-151-8

The Murder of Joe White: Ojibwe Leadership and Colonialism in Wisconsin, Erik M. Redix | 978-1-61186-145-7

National Monuments, Heid E. Erdrich | 978-0-87013-848-5

Ogimawkwe Mitigwaki (Queen of the Woods), Simon Pokagon | 978-0-87013-987-1

Ottawa Stories from the Springs: Anishinaabe dibaadjimowinan wodi gaa binjibaamigak wodi mookodjiwong e zhinikaadek, translated and edited by Howard Webkamigad | 978-1-61186-137-2

Picturing Worlds: Visuality and Visual Sovereignty in Contemporary Anishinaabe Literature, David Stirrup | 978-1-61186-352-9

Plain of Jars and Other Stories, Geary Hobson | 978-0-87013-998-7

Sacred Wilderness, Susan Power | 978-1-61186-111-2

Seeing Red—Hollywood's Pixeled Skins: American Indians and Film, edited by LeAnne Howe, Harvey Markowitz, and Denise K. Cummings | 978-1-61186-081-8

Self-Determined Stories: The Indigenous Reinvention of Young Adult Literature, Mandy Suhr-Sylsma | 978-1-61186-298-0

Shedding Skins: Four Sioux Poets, edited by Adrian C. Louis | 978-0-87013-823-2

Sounding Thunder: The Stories of Francis Pegahmagabow, Brian D. McInnes | 978-1-61186-225-6

Stick Houses: Stories, Matthew L. M. Fletcher | 978-1-61186-522-6

Stories for a Lost Child, Carter Meland | 978-1-61186-244-7

Stories through Theories/Theories through Stories: North American Indian Writing, Storytelling, and Critique, edited by Gordon D. Henry Jr., Nieves Pascual Soler, and Silvia Martinez-Falquina | 978-0-87013-841-6

That Guy Wolf Dancing, Elizabeth Cook-Lynn | 978-1-61186-138-9

Those Who Belong: Identity, Family, Blood, and Citizenship among the White Earth Anishinaabeg, Jill Doerfler | 978-1-61186-169-3

Visualities: Perspectives on Contemporary American Indian Film and Art, edited by Denise K. Cummings | 978-0-87013-999-4

Visualities 2: More Perspectives on Contemporary American Indian Film and Art, edited by Denise K. Cummings | 978-1-61186-319-2

Writing Home: Indigenous Narratives of Resistance, Michael D. Wilson | 978-0-87013-818-8